WORLD BOOK

DISCOVERY
ENCYCLOPEDIA

6
I J K L

World Book, Inc.
www.worldbook.com

World Book, Inc.
180 North LaSalle Street, Suite 900
Chicago, Illinois 60601
USA

For information about other World Book publications,
visit our website at **www.worldbook.com**
or call **1-800-WORLDBK (967-5325).**

For information about sales to schools and libraries,
call **1-800-975-3250 (United States)**
or **1-800-837-5365 (Canada).**

**The Library of Congress has cataloged a previous edition of
this title as follows:**

World Book discovery encyclopedia.
    p. cm.
  Includes index.
  Summary: "A 13-volume, illustrated, A-Z general reference
encyclopedia for students in the primary grades, providing
guide words, pronunciations, and other traditional reference
features as well as an atlas of world maps, special features, and
a cumulative index"--Provided by publisher.
  ISBN 978-0-7166-7415-3
  1. Children's encyclopedias and dictionaries. I. World Book, Inc.
AG5.W836 2009
031--dc22

         2008035576

This revised edition: ISBN 978-0-7166-7421-4

Printed in the United States of America by CG Book Printers,
North Mankato, Minnesota
1st printing September 2021

Ii

is the ninth letter of the alphabet for the English language.

 I i ℒ i

Handwritten letters vary from person to person. *Manuscript* (printed) letters (above left) have simple curves and straight lines. Cursive letters (above right) have flowing lines.

The small letter i developed about A.D. 300 from Roman writing. Monks who copied manuscripts during the 800's made the letter smaller. By about 1500, the letter had the shape that is used today.

A.D. 300   800   Today

Special ways of expressing the letter I

Sign Language Alphabet   Braille   International Flag Code

Development of the letter I

The ancient Egyptians	The Semites	The Phoenicians	The Greeks	The Romans
about 3000 B.C., drew this symbol of a hand.	about 1500 B.C., simplified the Egyptian symbol.	about 1000 B.C., changed the letter. They named it *yod,* their word for *hand.*	about 600 B.C., made the letter a single line. They called it *iota.*	gave the letter I its present form about A.D. 114.

Ice

Ice is frozen water. In nature, ice forms on lakes and rivers. It also forms on wet streets and sidewalks when the weather is cold. Snow, sleet, frost, and hail are other kinds of natural ice. Glaciers (*GLAY shuhrz*) are huge sheets of ice that cover large areas of land.

People use ice for many reasons. Millions of people use ice to chill drinks. The food industry ships and stores meat, fish, vegetables, and fruit in ice. The low temperature of ice slows the growth of germs that spoil food. People also treat burns or cuts with ice. Ice also helps stop bleeding and swelling.

Ice forms when the temperature of water falls to 32 °F (0 °C). This temperature is called the freezing point

How ice is formed

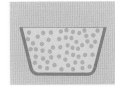

At room temperature, water molecules move about freely.

As water gets colder, the molecules move closer together.

When water freezes, the molecules move apart and form stiff crystals. The water becomes ice.

of water. Ice begins to melt when its surroundings become warmer than 32 °F.

People have used ice for thousands of years. Before ice machines were developed, people shipped ice from cold places to warm places. During the early 1800's, fast-moving ships carried ice from the northern United States to South America, India, and other warm places.

In 1851, John Gorrie, a surgeon from Florida, built the first commercial ice-making machine in the United States. He used the ice to cool his patients' rooms.

Other articles to read: **Frost; Glacier; Hail; Iceberg; Refrigerator**

Woolly rhinoceroses roamed the land during the last ice age.

Ice Age

An ice age is a time in Earth's history when huge sheets of ice covered large areas of land. An ice age usually lasts about 100,000 years. The most recent ice age ended about 11,500 years ago. Most scientists believe there will be another ice age in the future.

The last ice age took place during a period of time called the Pleistocene Epoch (*PLY stuh SEEN EHP uhk*). This epoch took place from about 2 million years ago to about 11,500 years ago.

During this last ice age, large ice sheets called glaciers (*GLAY shuhrz*) formed in North America, Europe, and Asia. These sheets of ice slid slowly across the land. Prehistoric people and animals moved ahead of the ice to find food and places to live.

Some prehistoric people called Neandertals (*nee AN duhr TAWLZ*) lived in what is now Europe during the last ice age. Many lived in caves to escape the harsh cold.

Huge mammoths and woolly rhinoceroses also roamed the frozen land. Their thick, shaggy coats helped them stay warm.

When the ice melted, the environment of many prehistoric people changed. This change greatly affected their way of life. In some places, people began to learn how to raise food. They became the first farmers.

Other articles to read: **Glacier**

Ice cream

Ice cream is a popular frozen food. It is made mostly of milk, sugar, and flavorings. Ice cream comes in many flavors. The most popular flavor in the United States is vanilla.

People in many parts of the world eat ice cream. Most of the ice cream we eat today is made in ice cream factories.

In an ice cream factory, milk and sugar are blended in a huge vat. Then the mixture is pasteurized (*PAS chuh ryzd*) to kill harmful germs. Next, it is homogenized (*huh MAWJ un nyzd*) to make the ice cream smooth. The mixture is then cooled. After flavorings and colorings are added, the mixture is put in a freezer. Fanlike blades in the freezer whip air bubbles into the ice cream. Without the air bubbles, ice cream would be as hard as ice cubes.

Ice cream is eaten in many parts of the world.

Most ice cream is made in factories.

Then the ice cream is packaged. It is placed in a hardening room for at least 12 hours. Now it is ready to be shipped to stores.

Some people enjoy making their own ice cream. Homemade ice cream is not as smooth as the ice cream sold in stores. That's because it has been stirred by less powerful blades.

Jacob Fussell, an American milk dealer, started the first ice cream plant in Baltimore, Maryland, in 1851. Ice cream cones were first served at the 1904 World's Fair in St. Louis, Missouri. Ice cream bars appeared in 1921.

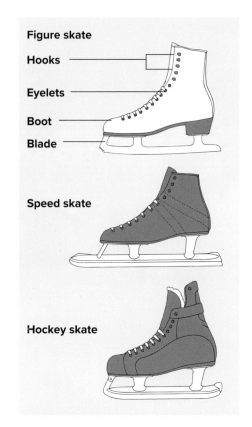

Types of ice skates

Ice skating

Ice skating is a fun activity in which people glide over smooth ice on skates. The skates used in ice skating are boots with metal blades attached to the bottom. Many people enjoy skating outdoors on frozen ponds and rivers. Others like skating on indoor rinks where the ice is smoother. Also, on rinks, there is no danger of falling through thin ice. Ice skating is good exercise too.

Kinds of ice skating

There are two main ice-skating sports—figure skating and speed skating. Figure skaters perform leaps, spins, and other graceful movements. They usually skate to music. There are competitions for single skaters, for pairs (a man and a woman), and for ice dancing. The movements used in ice dancing are like the steps used in ballroom dancing.

In speed skating, the skaters race around a frozen track. They cover distances of 500 to 10,000 meters. Speed skaters swing their arms for a smooth, flowing motion. In races longer than 1,500 meters, they save energy by swinging only one arm.

In pack skating, a number of speed skaters take part in a series of races. The winners go on to the final races. Different races are held for children of different ages.

Many people enjoy watching figure skating and ice skating competitions. Champion figure skaters and trick skaters also thrill crowds at colorful ice shows. In addition, people enjoy playing or watching ice hockey, a fast sport in which players wear ice skates.

Skates

Figure-skating boots have higher tops than the boots worn by speed skaters. A figure-skate blade has two edges. Skaters skate on one edge at a time. The bottom of the blade curves slightly inward, so only a small part of it touches the ice at one time. This makes it easier to perform tricky movements. The front of the blade has several teeth, or jagged parts, that grip the ice during jumps and spins.

A speed-skate blade is straight, flat, and thin. These blades help the skater to start quickly and travel fast. Some skaters reach a speed of 35 miles (56 kilometers) per hour.

A hockey-skate blade is curved at each end. These curves enable the player to make turns and other moves more easily.

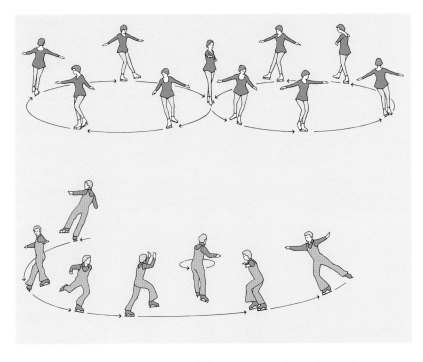

Figure skaters learn to perform such graceful movements as the figure 8 (top) and the axel jump (bottom).

Speed skaters race around a frozen track.

History of ice skating

People have skated on ice for at least 2,000 years. Remains of ice skates dating from 50 B.C. have been found in Roman ruins in London. The earliest skates were made of animal bones, which people strapped onto boots. People used these skates to get around in winter. In time, they began to enjoy races too.

Skate blades made of iron were used in the Netherlands about 1250. All-steel blades were first made in the 1850's, and skating became popular. About 1870, an American ballet dancer named Jackson Haines started modern figure skating. Today, figure skating and speed skating are events in the Olympic Games.

Other articles to read: **Hockey, Ice; Olympic Games**

Iceberg

An iceberg is a huge piece of ice that floats in the sea. Some icebergs are many miles long. They are always bigger than they look. Most of the iceberg is under water.

Icebergs in the North Atlantic Ocean come from Greenland. They break off the ice sheet that covers Greenland and fall into the sea. Icebergs also come from the Antarctic icecap. Some of these icebergs are many times larger than those found in the North Atlantic. When an iceberg starts to break away, it makes noises that can be heard for miles. It sounds like loud explosions and rolling thunder. When it drops into the sea, it causes huge waves.

Icebergs can be dangerous to ships. The famous ship *Titanic* struck an iceberg and sank in 1912. About 1,500 people died.

Other articles to read: **Glacier**

Iceberg

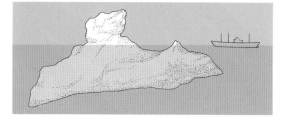

The top of an iceberg melts, leaving the bottom underwater. The hidden ice is dangerous to ships.

Iceland is an island country in the North Atlantic Ocean, close to the Arctic Circle. Iceland is warmer than most places so far north because the Gulf Stream flows around it. The Gulf Stream is an ocean current that carries warm water from the south into parts of the North Atlantic.

Iceland is sometimes called the *Land of Ice and Fire.* Glaciers (*GLAY shuhrz*), or huge rivers of ice that flow very slowly, move past hot springs and volcanoes. Sometimes volcanoes erupt under the sea. A famous hot spring called Geysir spouts water about 195 feet (59 meters) into the air. Icelanders use water from hot springs to heat their buildings.

Most Icelanders live in villages and small towns near the coast. About half the people live in or around Reykjavik, the capital and largest city. Icelanders do not have family names. They have a first name, such as Erik or Inga. Their second name is made up of their father's first name followed by either *son* (for boys) or *dóttir* (for girls). If Erik and Inga's father's name was Jón, their names would be Erik Jónsson and Inga Jónsdóttir.

It is hard to grow crops on most of this windswept island. Small farms raise sheep, cattle, and small Icelandic horses. The sea is rich in fish, however. Many people catch fish or work in fish-freezing plants. Manufactured products include aluminum, cement, chemicals, and machinery.

People from Scandinavia and Viking settlements in Britain settled in Iceland from about A.D. 870. They set up a meeting of leaders called the Althing, the world's oldest parliament. Iceland was ruled by Denmark from 1380 to 1944, when the people voted for independence. Today, the Althing is made up of elected lawmakers.

Other articles to read:

Vikings

Canada
Arctic Ocean
Greenland
(Denmark)
Finland
Arctic Circle
Sweden
ICELAND
Norway
United Denmark
Kingdom
North
Atlantic
Ocean
Ireland
E U R O P E
France

Iceland and its neighbors

Iceland in brief

- **Capital:** Reykjavik.

- **Area:** 39,769 mi^2 (103,000 km^2). *Greatest distances*—east-west, 300 mi (483 km); north-south, 190 mi (306 km). *Coastline*—1,243 mi (2,000 km).

- **Population:** *Current estimate*—372,000; *2020 official government estimate*—364,134.

- **Official language:** Icelandic.

- **Chief products:** *Agriculture*— cattle, hay, sheep. *Fishing*— capelin, cod, haddock, herring, redfish, saithe. *Manufacturing*— aluminum, cement, chemicals, electrical equipment, food products, machinery.

- **Money:** *Basic unit*—Icelandic krona.

- **Form of government:** Republic.

- **Climate:** Mild summers and cool winters in the coastal lowlands; colder inland.

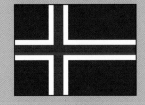

Flag

Idaho

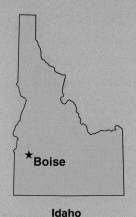

Idaho

Idaho is a state in the Rocky Mountain region of the United States. Washington and Oregon border Idaho on the west. Montana and Wyoming lie to the east. Canada lies to the north. Nevada and Utah are south.

The capital and largest city of Idaho is Boise (*BOY zee*). It lies in the southwestern part of the state at the foot of the Boise Front Mountains. The Boise River flows through the city. Pocatello, another important city, lies in the middle of a farming area. It serves as a trading and shipping center for crops and livestock. Other large cities in the state include Idaho Falls, Meridian, and Nampa.

Land. Idaho is a land of awesome scenic wonders. It has snow-covered mountains, powerful river rapids, quiet lakes, steep canyons, and ice caves. The waters of the Snake River rush through Hells Canyon. Hells Canyon is even deeper than the Grand Canyon. Coeur d'Alene Lake is one of the most beautiful mountain lakes in the world. Shoshone Falls, on the Snake River, is higher than Niagara Falls.

Idaho

State flag

State seal

Sawtooth Mountains in Idaho

The Rocky Mountains cover northern and central Idaho. Borah Peak, in the center of the state, is the highest mountain. Flatter land and many valleys lie among the mountains, where farmers raise wheat and peas. There are also peaceful lakes and colorful meadows. Herds of sheep graze on the mountain slopes during the summer.

The Columbia Plateau (*pla TOH*) sweeps across the lower part of the state. A plateau is an area of high, flat land. Part of the plateau is a large plain with farmland for crops and livestock.

Resources and products. Farming is important in Idaho. The biggest crop is potatoes. Idaho farmers also grow wheat, hay, barley, and sugar beets. Many farmers raise cattle and run dairy farms.

In recent years, a number of small industries have moved to Idaho. Many factories now make computer parts, food products, machinery, and chemicals. Lumber and wood products are important, too.

Silver is mined in the mountains. Other important minerals include crushed stone, lead, and phosphate rock.

Important dates in Idaho

Prehistory	Native American peoples that lived in the Idaho region before Europeans arrived included the Nez Perce and Shoshone.
1805	U.S. explorers Meriwether Lewis and William Clark passed through the Idaho region on their way to the Pacific Coast.
1809	David Thompson built the first fur-trading post in Idaho.
1860	Franklin, Idaho's first permanent settlement, was founded. Gold was discovered on Orofino Creek.
1863	The U.S. government established the Idaho Territory.
1874	Utah Northern Railroad entered Idaho Territory at Franklin.
1877	U.S. troops defeated the Nez Perce Native American group in October in the Nez Perce War.
1890	Idaho became the 43rd U.S. state on July 3.
1951	For the first time in history, scientists used nuclear energy to create electricity. This feat was accomplished at the National Reactor Testing Station near Idaho Falls.
1955	Arco became the first community in the world to receive all of its power from nuclear energy. The National Reactor Testing Station supplied the town's power for one hour on July 17.
1972	Ninety-one miners died in a fire at the Sunshine silver mine in Shoshone County.
1990	Idaho celebrated its centennial (100th anniversary) as a state.

Idaho in brief

- **State capital:** Boise, Idaho's capital since 1865. Lewiston served as capital from 1863 to 1865.
- **Area:** 83,569 mi² (216,443 km²), including 926 mi² (2,398 km²) of inland water.
- **Population:** 1,839,106.
- **Statehood:** July 3, 1890, the 43rd state.
- **State abbreviations:** Ida. (traditional); ID (postal).
- **State motto:** *Esto Perpetua* (Let it be perpetual).
- **State song:** "Here We Have Idaho." Words by McKinley Helm and Albert J. Tompkins; music by Sallie Hume-Douglas.
- **Largest cities in Idaho:** Boise (205,671); Nampa (81,557); Meridian (75,092); Idaho Falls (56,813); Pocatello (54,255); Caldwell (46,237).
- **Governor:** 4-year term.
- **State senators:** 35; 2-year terms.
- **State representatives:** 70; 2-year terms.

**State bird
Mountain bluebird**

**State flower
Syringa**

Iguana

The iguana (*ih GWAH nuh*) is a type of lizard. Most iguanas live in deserts or other dry areas, but some live in wet, tropical places. All iguanas are active during the day and sleep at night.

Iguanas eat fruit, flowers, and leaves. Most other lizards eat insects. Plants are hard for other lizards to digest. An iguana can digest plants because tiny living things called *bacteria* live in its gut. The bacteria help an iguana to digest plants.

Female iguanas lay eggs. They may travel up to 2 miles (3.2 kilometers) to find the right place to make a nest. Some iguanas live to be 30 years old.

There are several different types of iguanas. The green iguana may grow to be 6 feet (1.8 meters) long. The marine iguana and the land iguana live on the Galapagos Islands, off the coast of Ecuador. The marine iguana is the only lizard that lives in the sea.

Green iguana

Illegal immigration

Illegal immigration is the act of moving to a country without permission from that country's government. People who immigrate illegally are known as illegal, unauthorized, or *undocumented* immigrants or *aliens* (noncitizens). They live in a country without the proper immigration documents. Such documents include *visas* (permits to enter or stay for a set period). If discovered, illegal immigrants could be *deported* (sent back to their original country).

People immigrate unlawfully for different reasons. Many are seeking better economic opportunities. Others are escaping conflict, natural disasters, mistreatment, or poverty. Such people are called *refugees*. Not all illegal immigrants enter a country unlawfully. For example, some are students, temporary workers, or visitors who enter the country legally. But they stay after their visas expire. The nations most affected by illegal immigration are those with a high standard of living. They include the United States, Canada, and the countries of Western Europe.

Other articles to read: **Immigration**

Illinois

Illinois is a state in the Midwestern region of the United States. Iowa and Missouri lie to the west of Illinois. Indiana and Kentucky lie to the east and south. Wisconsin is north of Illinois. The northeast tip of Illinois borders Lake Michigan.

Illinois is also called the *Land of Lincoln*. Abraham Lincoln, the 16th president of the United States, spent most of his life in Illinois.

Springfield, the capital of Illinois, lies in the middle of the state in a busy farming region. Abraham Lincoln's home still stands near the center of Springfield.

Chicago is the largest city in Illinois. It is a huge city along the shores of Lake Michigan. Millions of people live there. Chicago has interesting places to visit, such as museums and zoos. Its lakefront has beaches and colorful harbors.

Land. Most of Illinois is a gently rolling plain. Millions of years ago, glaciers—huge sheets of ice—moved very slowly across this land. The glaciers flattened the land and made small hills. Later, the region was covered with prairie grass. As the grass died out and rotted away, it made the soil very rich for farming.

Northwestern Illinois had no glaciers, so it has bigger hills and valleys. The Mississippi River forms the western border.

Resources and products. Illinois is an important farming state. Ever since pioneer days, corn has been the state's most important crop. Soybeans are second. Hay, wheat, rye, and oats are grown, too.

Illinois

Illinois

State flag

State seal

State Capitol in Springfield

Illinois, continued

Illinois in brief

- **State capital:** Springfield, the capital of Illinois since 1839. Earlier capitals were Kaskaskia (1818–1820) and Vandalia (1820–1839).
- **Area:** 56,354 mi² (145,956 km²), including 836 mi² (2,165 km²) of inland water but excluding 1,562 mi² (4,045 km²) of Great Lakes water.
- **Population:** 12,812,508.
- **Statehood:** Dec. 3, 1818, the 21st state.
- **State abbreviations:** Ill. (traditional); IL (postal).
- **State motto:** State Sovereignty, National Union.
- **State song:** "Illinois." Words by Charles H. Chamberlin; sung to the tune of "Baby Mine" by Archibald Johnston.
- **Largest cities in Illinois:** Chicago (2,695,598); Aurora (197,899); Rockford (152,871); Joliet (147,433); Naperville (141,853); Springfield (116,250).
- **Governor:** 4-year term.
- **State senators:** 59; 2- or 4-year terms.
- **State representatives:** 118; 2-year terms.

State bird
Cardinal

State flower
Native violet

Farmers also grow apples, cabbage, beans, peaches, and pumpkins.

Livestock production is a big business in Illinois, and there are many hog farms. Farmers also raise cattle and chickens.

Illinois is an important coal-producing state. About two-thirds of Illinois sits on top of a huge coal bed.

The Chicago area is the one of the largest manufacturing regions in the United States. But factories all around the state make such products as prepared foods, machinery, chemicals, metal products, printed materials, and computer products.

Other articles to read: **Black Hawk; Chicago; Grant, Ulysses S.; Lincoln, Abraham; Marquette, Jacques; Mississippi River; Mound builders; Reagan, Ronald Wilson; Wright, Frank Lloyd**

Important dates in Illinois

Prehistory	Native American peoples known as mound builders lived in the Illinois region hundreds of years before Europeans arrived. They built huge mounds to bury their dead and to support temples. Monk's Mound, near Cahokia, is the largest such mound in the United States.
1673	Louis Jolliet of Canada and Jacques Marquette of France explored parts of what is now Illinois.
1699	French priests founded a settlement in Cahokia, the oldest town in Illinois.
1717	The Illinois region became part of the French colony of Louisiana.
1763	Great Britain took over what is now Illinois from France.
1783	The Illinois region became part of the United States under the treaty ending the American Revolution.
1818	Illinois became the 21st state on December 3.
1832	Illinois settlers defeated the Sauk and Fox Native American groups in the Black Hawk War.
1861	Springfield lawyer Abraham Lincoln became the 16th president of the United States. He led the country through the Civil War (1861-1865).
1871	The Chicago Fire destroyed much of the city.
1893	The World's Columbian Exposition was held in Chicago.
1920's	Illinois built many hard-surfaced roads for cars and trucks.
1942	Scientists at the University of Chicago controlled an atomic chain reaction for the first time. This important event led to the development of the atomic bomb and of nuclear energy.
1971	A new constitution went into effect.
1993	Floods caused heavy damage in Illinois.
2009	Barack Obama of Illinois took office as the first African American president of the United States.

Imagination

Imagination is the picturing of something in the mind. For example, it's a hot day. You daydream that you are swimming in a cool stream, or eating an ice cream cone. Neither the stream nor the ice cream cone are really there, of course. They are in your imagination.

When you imagine something, you think of it so clearly that you can sometimes make a picture of it in your mind. Imagination allows people to remember things they have seen and done before, and also to make up things they have never seen and never done.

A person who writes a story, paints a picture, or composes music is using his or her imagination. An inventor uses imagination to make something new from what is already known.

Other articles to read: **Dream**

Children use their imaginations to paint pictures.

Immigration

Immigration means coming to another country to live. People who do this are immigrants in their new country. The act of leaving one's country is called *emigration.*

Throughout history, millions of people have become immigrants. They have made a fresh start in lands where everything was new to them. Often, they have faced danger and hardship. The greatest immigration worldwide took place from the early 1800's to the 1930's. In that period, about 60 million people moved to a new land. Most of these people came from Europe. More than half went to the United States.

Immigration to the American Colonies began in the 1600's. These were the Thirteen Colonies that later became the United States. The largest number of immigrants arrived between the 1880's and the early

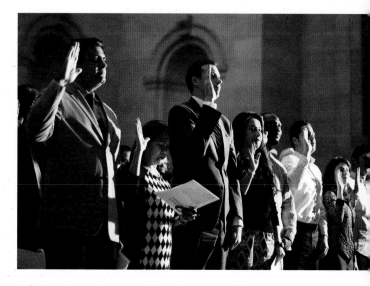

Immigrants take an oath to become citizens of their new country.

1920's. Most of these people came from Europe. Today, many immigrants move to the United States from Mexico, China and other parts of Asia, and the Caribbean.

Other countries around the world have received large numbers of immigrants at certain times. For example, Jewish immigrants poured into the new nation of Israel soon after it was founded in 1948.

Some people have to flee from their home country because of war or *persecution* (cruel treatment). Sometimes they have to leave to get enough to eat. These people are called *refugees*. But the main reason for immigration has been economic opportunity—the chance to have a better job or better land for farming.

Other articles to read: **Illegal immigration.**

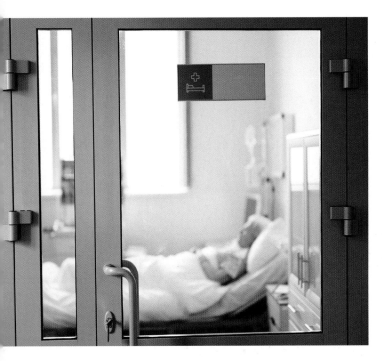

If a person's immune system isn't working properly, special care must be taken to protect against disease.

Immune system

The immune system protects the body from sickness. It often fights off some illnesses before people know they are sick. Even when people feel ill, their immune system is working hard to stop the illness before it causes much harm. Sometimes doctors give people medicine that helps the immune system fight an illness.

Many parts of the body work together in the immune system. Some of the most important parts are white blood cells. White blood cells are round and colorless. They are so tiny that they can be seen only with a microscope.

White blood cells are one of the body's strongest weapons against things that cause illness. These things include *bacteria* and *viruses*. Bacteria and viruses are tiny "invaders," seen only with a microscope, that enter the body. They can cause colds, sore throats, upset stomachs, and many other such illnesses. Some white blood cells surround bacteria and digest them. Other white blood cells produce substances that kill bacteria and viruses or make them harmless. These substances are called antibodies.

Sometimes the immune system makes mistakes. It tries to protect the body from substances that do not cause illness. These substances may be things like pollen, which is the harmless dust that comes from plants, dust, mold, and feathers. When the immune system acts as though these things are harmful, it causes an *allergy*. A person with an allergy to a certain substance may sneeze or get itchy because of it.

Other articles to read: **AIDS; Allergy; Bacteria; Disease; Immunization; Inoculation; Virus**

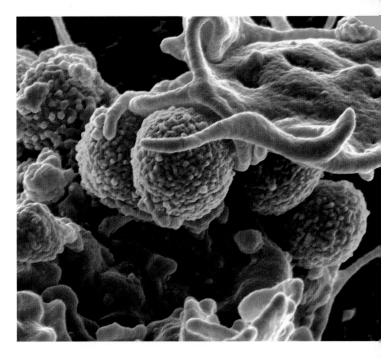

White blood cells surround bacteria cells (green), as seen under a microscope

Immunization

Immunization (*IHM yuh nyz ay shuhn*) is a way of protecting the body against a disease. The body can fight many diseases by producing substances called antibodies. One type of immunization causes the body to make antibodies against a disease without actually causing the disease. This type of immunization is called vaccination (*vak sihn NAY shuhn*). Another type of immunization uses a *serum,* which has antibodies already in it.

A British doctor named Edward Jenner made the first vaccine (*vak SEEN*) in 1796. He used it to prevent a disease called smallpox. Today, we have vaccines to prevent measles, mumps, whooping cough, and many other diseases. Most vaccines are given as shots. But some are swallowed.

Other articles to read: **Disease; Immune system; Inoculation; Pasteur, Louis; Salk, Jonas Edward**

An infant is immunized with polio vaccine to protect against disease.

Rouen Cathedral, Full Sunlight **by Claude Monet**

Impressionism

Impressionism (*ihm PRESH uh nihz uhm*) is a style of art. Impressionism became popular in France in the late 1800's. The French impressionists often worked outdoors and painted quickly. The impressionists studied the science of color and light. They wanted to catch the way light changed the look of an object. The artist Claude Monet, for example, painted a haystack at different times of the day. Each painting was different because the sunlight hit the haystack in a different way.

Impressionists also created music, writings, and sculpture, using sounds, words, and shapes to make people think of certain images or ideas.

Other articles to read: **Cassatt, Mary; Degas, Edgar; Monet, Claude; Renoir, Pierre Auguste; Van Gogh, Vincent**

Gold objects like these figures of a man and a llama were used by families of Inca nobles.

Inca

The Inca (*IHNG kuh*) were a native South American people. They ruled one of the largest and richest empires in North and South America. The Inca took over the lands of their neighbors and governed well. They built roads, bridges, and stone temples. They learned how to water desert land and cut huge flat steps into hillsides to grow crops. Their empire lasted from about 1438 to the 1530's. Spanish soldiers, who came in 1532, fought the Inca and destroyed their empire.

Daily life

Most Inca were farmers. They grew corn, cotton, and potatoes. They also grew and ate a root called oca and a grain called quinoa. The Inca made clothing from wool and cotton. Men wore tunics, with a cloak for cold weather. Women wore long dresses and shawls. Rich people wore fine clothing and jewelry.

Most people lived in mud and stone houses with straw roofs. Nobles, or rich and important people, lived in large palaces and had fine pottery and gold objects. The palaces were built of huge stones fitted together without cement.

The Inca had no writing and no money system. Instead, they traded and exchanged products. They sent messages by runners. They also used fires and smoke signals. The Inca used knotted strings to keep records. They had no wheels, so most people walked. Nobles were carried in a litter, a wooden frame with a couch. Servants carried the litter on their shoulders. Llamas carried all the heavy loads.

Inca beliefs

Religion was important to the Inca. Their chief god was Viracocha. The emperor also prayed to the sun god Inti. Inca people never made a decision without trying to find out the will of the gods.

Rise and fall of the Inca

The Inca homeland was around Cusco in what is now southern Peru. Around the year 1200, the Inca began to spread out and rule over their neighbors.

The Inca empire began about 1438 when the ruler Pachacuti made Cusco the center of government. The Inca empire grew to

Inca Temple of the Sun

include parts of what are now Colombia, Ecuador, Peru, Bolivia, Chile, and Argentina.

Pachacuti's grandson, Huayna Capac, died about 1527. Two of his sons, Huáscar and Atahualpa, fought one another over control of the empire. In 1532, Atahualpa won. But that same year a Spanish force of 167 men led by Francisco Pizarro marched into Peru. The Spaniards defeated the Inca and captured Atahualpa. They demanded a room filled with gold and a room filled twice with silver for his freedom. The Inca gave them this treasure, but the Spaniards killed Atahualpa anyway.

Huáscar was already dead. He had been killed on Atahualpa's orders. So now the Inca had no leader. The Inca could not stop the Spaniards from taking over their empire. The Spaniards tried to wipe out all the Inca customs, but they failed. Today, some *Indigenous* (native) peoples in Peru and some other countries still live much as the Inca did. They speak Quechua, the Inca language. They weave cloth in the Inca style, and they practice Inca healing ceremonies.

Other articles to read: **Peru**

Independence Day fireworks

Independence Day

Independence Day in the United States of America is celebrated on July 4 each year to celebrate the country's birthday. On July 4, 1776, the Declaration of Independence was adopted by a group of American leaders called the Continental Congress. Independence Day has been celebrated on July 4 ever since. In 1941, the U.S. Congress made July 4 a national holiday.

In the early days, fireworks and gunfire were part of Independence Day celebrations. However, many people were hurt or killed in accidents, so many cities and states made the sale of fireworks against the law in the 1900's. People today mark Independence Day with parades and programs, games and plays, athletic contests, and picnics. Some cities hire people trained to put on a fireworks display. Americans everywhere join in the national celebration.

Other articles to read: **Declaration of Independence**

India is a large country in southern Asia. It has more people than any other country in the world except China.

India is bordered by Pakistan and the Arabian Sea in the west. China, Nepal, and Bhutan lie on the north. To the east are Bangladesh, Myanmar, and the Bay of Bengal. The Indian Ocean lies to the south.

The capital of India is New Delhi in northern India. New Delhi was built in the early 1900's. It is a modern city with skyscrapers and wide, tree-lined streets. The city has many gardens, parks, and fountains too.

Mumbai, which used to be called Bombay, is India's largest city. It is also the country's chief western seaport. Mumbai lies on an island off western India. Bridges link the city with the mainland of India.

Land. The northern half of India is made up of the Himalaya region and the Northern Plains.

The Himalaya region stretches across northeast India. The Himalaya are the highest mountains in the world. Snow covers the tallest peaks the year around. Tigers, deer, and rhinoceroses roam the lower slopes.

Flag

India is one of the most crowded countries in the world. Streets in cities such as Kolkata are very busy.

Family dinner in India

South of the Himalaya region lie the Northern Plains. This is a low, flat area with wide valleys made by the Brahmaputra, Indus, and Ganges rivers. India's richest farmland is found in these river valleys. The Thar Desert lies in the western part of the Northern Plains.

The Ganges River is India's greatest river. It starts high in the Himalaya and flows into the Bay of Bengal.

The southern half of India is a peninsula that juts into the Indian Ocean. A peninsula is land that has water on three sides. The Deccan Plateau (*pla TOH*) forms most of India's southern peninsula. Mountains called the Eastern Ghats rise along the east coast. The Western Ghats stretch along the west coast. Elephants, monkeys, and other wildlife roam in the forests of the mountains.

People. India has many different groups of people. The two largest are the Dravidians (*drah VIH dee uhnz*) and the Indo-Aryans (*ihn doh AHR yuhnz*). Most Dravidians live in the south. Most Indo-Aryans live in the north. Smaller groups live in the country's forest and hill areas.

More than 1,000 languages are spoken in India. Almost half the people speak Hindi, one of India's national languages. Most of India's people live in villages and farm the nearby fields. These farmers often live in small houses made of dried mud and straw.

In recent years, many country people have moved to the cities to look for work. As a result, the cities are now overcrowded. There aren't enough homes, water, or electric power for all the people. Many people live on the streets or in one-room shacks.

Religion is important to the Indian people. Most are Hindus, but there are some Muslims, Buddhists, Christians, Jains, and Sikhs.

Resources and products. Most people in India are farmers. They grow crops mainly to feed their families. Rice is the biggest crop, but they grow wheat, corn, and many other crops, too.

India is the world's leading producer of many plant products. These include cauliflower, mangoes, sesame seeds, and tea.

India has more cattle than any other country. In most of India, farmers use cattle to plow the land. Dairy farming is also important. Farmers sell milk from their water buffaloes and use animal skins to make leather goods.

India is one of the world's top producers of iron and steel. Indian factories use the iron and steel to make airplanes, cars, bicycles, and other products. India has many cotton mills, too.

Many Indians make handcrafted items at home or in small factories. These include carpets, brass objects, jewelry, leather goods, and wood carvings.

India is rich in iron ore, coal, and petroleum. The country has smaller deposits of many other minerals. It also has deposits of diamonds, emeralds, gold, and silver.

History. India is an ancient land. About 4,500 years ago, a group of people in the Indus River Valley built cities. They had ways of writing, counting, measuring, and weighing things. About 3,700 years ago, the Indus Valley people died out, but no one knows why.

About 3,500 years ago, Aryan people from central Asia settled in northern India. When they arrived, they found a people called the Dravidians. The warlike Aryans took over the Dravidians' land and pushed some of them south. The Aryans built villages and developed the Hindu religion.

For hundreds of years, India was controlled by a series of dynasties (*DY nuh steez*), or ruling families. One of these dynasties

India and its neighbors

India in brief

- **Capital:** New Delhi.
- **Area:** 1,222,548 mi² (3,166,384 km²). *Greatest distances*—north-south, about 2,000 mi (3,200 km); east-west, about 1,700 mi (2,740 km). *Coastline*—4,252 mi (6,843 km), including 815 mi (1,312 km) of coastline of island territories.
- **Population:** *Current estimate*—1,355,491,000. *2020 official government estimate*—1,326,155,000.
- **Principal official language:** Hindi. *Other languages with official status:* English ("associate national language"), Sanskrit, and 16 regional languages.
- **Chief products:** *Agriculture*—bananas, cabbages, coconuts, corn, cotton, jute, mangoes, milk, millet, onions, oranges, pepper, potatoes, *pulses* (peas, beans, and lentils), rice, sesame seeds, sorghum, sugar cane, tea, wheat. *Manufacturing and processing*—bicycles, brassware, cement, chemicals, computers, clothing and textiles, fertilizer, food products, iron and steel, leather goods, machinery, medicines, motor vehicles, petroleum products, rugs. *Mining*—coal, iron ore, limestone, natural gas, petroleum.
- **Money:** *Basic unit*—Indian rupee. One hundred paise equal one rupee.
- **Form of government:** Federal republic.
- **Climate:** Northern and central India have mild, cool temperatures from October to February. In the northwest and north-central regions, temperatures occasionally drop below freezing. Southern India lacks a true cool season, but the period from October to February is not as hot as the rest of the year. The entire country, except the mountains, is hot from March to June. From June to September, rains brought by seasonal winds called *monsoons* bring relief from extreme dry heat. The northeast and west coast receive heavy rainfall.

23

was founded by Babur, a Muslim, in 1526. When this dynasty ruled India, it was known as the Mughal Empire. In 1498, Vasco de Gama, a Portuguese explorer, reached India. The Portuguese took over areas on the western coast.

During the 1600's, the British became very powerful in India. In the 1700's and 1800's they expanded their control over most of India. In 1857, the Indian people rebelled against the British. But the British quickly stopped the rebellion.

In the late 1800's and early 1900's, more Indians began speaking out against British rule. By 1920, Mohandas K. Gandhi was a leader in the struggle for the independence of India. During this time, there was much fighting between India's Hindus and Muslims. The Muslims wanted their own country, and they wanted to call it Pakistan. In 1947, Indian and British leaders divided India into two independent nations—India and Pakistan.

Other articles to read: **Buddhism; Gandhi, Indira; Gandhi, Mohandas Karamchand; Ganges River; Himalaya; Hinduism; Islam; Kolkata; Muslims; Nehru, Jawaharlal; New Delhi; Sikhism; Tagore, Rabindranath; Taj Mahal**

Many people in India belong to the Hindu religion. They believe the Ganges River is sacred and bathe in its waters.

Indian, American

American Indians were the first people to live in the Americas. They were living there for thousands of years before Europeans arrived. Today, many Indians call themselves Native Americans. In Canada, they are called First Nations, Aboriginal, *Indigenous,* or native peoples.

The earliest people to inhabit the Americas probably came from Asia at least 15,000 years ago. At that time, there was a land area instead of water between Asia and North America. The people followed the animals they hunted across this land from Asia to what is now Alaska. The distance was about 50 miles (80 kilometers). Today, the land that connected the continents is covered by water. It is called the Bering Strait.

Over time, people spread all across the Americas. When Christopher Columbus arrived in 1492, native people were living from the Arctic in the north all the way to the tip of South America. Columbus thought he had reached the Indies, which then included India, China, the East Indies, and Japan. So he called the people he met "Indians."

Native American life before the Europeans

Native Americans formed hundreds of groups, or tribes, across North and South America. Each tribe or nation had their own way of life and their own language.

Some groups, such as the Aztec and the Maya of Central America, built large cities. The native peoples of eastern North America and other Native American groups lived in small villages. Native peoples who lived at the tip of South America moved from place to place looking for food.

Native American families spent most of their time finding food, clothing, and a place to live. The families joined together in bands. Several bands in the same area formed tribes. Other groups had a more complex organization. The Iroquois became famous as the *Five Nations,* or *Iroquois League.* This was the most complex North American Indian organization.

The food Native Americans ate depended on where they lived. Some hunted or fished for most of their food. Others got most of their food from gathering wild seeds, nuts, and

A Cherokee woman does traditional beadwork.

The Mohawk hunted animals in the forest and grew crops for food.

The cliff dwellers lived in communal houses made of stone.

roots. The Plains Indians of the central United States ate mostly buffalo meat and other game. The Pueblo of the Southwest, the Middle American Indians who lived in Central America, and the Indians of the Andes were farmers. These people grew beans, corn, and squash.

Many Native Americans made their clothes from animal skins and fur. Some groups of the Northwest Coast of North America made cloth from tree bark and plants called reeds. The Pueblo, Aztec, Inca, Maya, and some Caribbean groups wove cotton cloth.

Native Americans built many kinds of homes. Some groups, such as the Haida of the Northwest Coast and the Iroquois of the Northeast, built houses big enough for several families.

The Pawnee dug large pits in the ground and covered them with layers of grassy earth called sod. They were called earth lodges. The Plains Indians built cone-shaped tipis of buffalo skins. The Native Americans of the Northeast made dome-shaped wigwams covered with leaves or bark.

Native Americans did not have horses or cattle before the Europeans came. They often traveled by water. Many Native Americans made narrow boats, called canoes, of tree bark. They were light and easy to carry. They also made light boats from reeds. Most people carried their own loads. The Plains Indians used dogs (before horses) to pull their loads, too.

The arrival of the Europeans

Many European explorers and settlers came to the Americas in the 1500's and 1600's. Their arrival ended the Native American way of life forever.

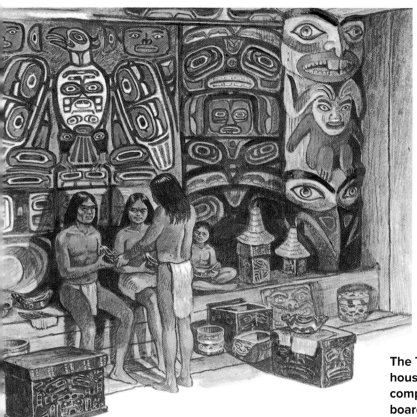

The Tlingit in the Northwest built houses of wood. In the chief's compartment, the cedarwood boards were painted with designs.

Explorers, fur traders, and settlers spread across the New World. Missionaries, who wanted to teach the Native Americans about Christianity, also came to the New World. At first, most of the Native Americans did not mind the newcomers. They taught the settlers many things. European explorers followed Native American trails to find water and deposits of copper, gold, and other minerals. The Native Americans showed the settlers how to travel by canoe. They also taught the newcomers how to grow foods they had never seen before. These new crops included avocados, corn, peanuts, peppers, pineapples, potatoes, squash, and tomatoes.

The Europeans brought many things to the Native Americans. These included metal tools, guns, and liquor. They also brought cattle and horses.

Native Americans and the arriving Europeans had very different ways of life. Some Europeans tried to understand the Native Americans' ways. But others cheated the Native Americans and stole their land. When the Native Americans fought back, thousands of them were killed. Even more died from diseases the settlers brought from Europe. These diseases included measles and smallpox.

Land was a big problem between the Native Americans and the white settlers. The settlers wanted the land for farming, for grazing their cattle, and for mining. They believed they should own the land. But the Native Americans did not believe that anyone could own land. Instead, Native Americans saw themselves as caretakers of the land. So when the Native Americans signed over

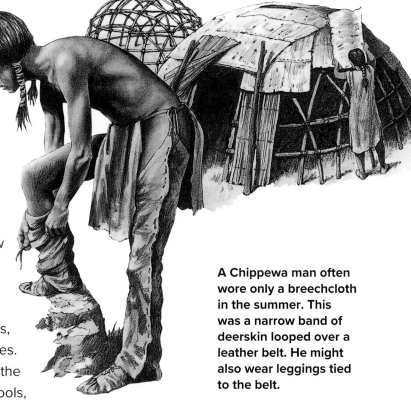

A Chippewa man often wore only a breechcloth in the summer. This was a narrow band of deerskin looped over a leather belt. He might also wear leggings tied to the belt.

With horses, the Plains Indians could travel faster, carry heavier loads, and hunt and fight with greater skill.

Modern powwows feature Native American music and dancing. These gatherings bring tribes together to celebrate their heritage.

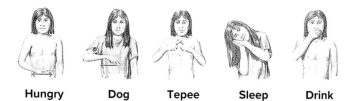

| Hungry | Dog | Tepee | Sleep | Drink |

Sign language helped different tribes of the Plains talk together. Here are some sign language "words."

land to the white settlers, they thought that they could still hunt and farm the land too. But the settlers thought that the land belonged only to them. As a result, bitter fights broke out between the Native Americans and the settlers.

As the years went by, more settlers moved westward across North America. The Native Americans were forced off land that had been their home for centuries. Most Native Americans were made to move onto reservations. These reservations were large areas of land set aside by the U.S. government for the Native Americans.

Native Americans today

Most native peoples in North America still do not completely follow the ways of white people. In some areas of Central and South America, several tribes have kept their language and their way of life. But most tribes have a new way of life that is a mixture of Native American and European customs.

Many Native Americans in the United States work hard to keep control of their land and their rights to fish and hunt. They would also like to handle Native Americans matters without the government getting involved. And they try to protect their land and waters from pollution.

Other articles to read: **Aztec; Black Hawk; Brant, Joseph; Crazy Horse; First Nations; French and Indian wars; Inca; Indian wars; Inuit; Joseph, Chief; Mound builders; Osceola; Pocahontas; Pontiac; Quanah; Sacagawea; Sand painting; Sequoyah; Sitting Bull; Tecumseh; Thorpe, Jim; Toltec; Totem; Wigwam; Winnemucca, Sarah**

Indian Ocean

The Indian Ocean is the third largest ocean in the world. It is almost totally surrounded by land—Africa, Asia, Australia, and Antarctica. Because of its smaller size and its position among large bodies of land, the Indian Ocean's tides are not as great as the tides of the Atlantic and Pacific oceans. Tides are the rise and fall of the ocean waters. The pull of the sun and the moon causes the tides.

Currents also move the ocean waters. Currents are like rivers in the ocean. The wind causes the currents in the Indian Ocean to move in a certain direction. Those in the northern part of the ocean move west in winter and east in summer. Those in the southern part of the ocean move in a circle.

Ships passing through the Suez Canal and Red Sea link Europe and eastern Asia by way of the Indian Ocean. There are huge oil fields underneath the Indian Ocean. People use this oil for running machines and other purposes.

Other articles to read: **Suez Canal**

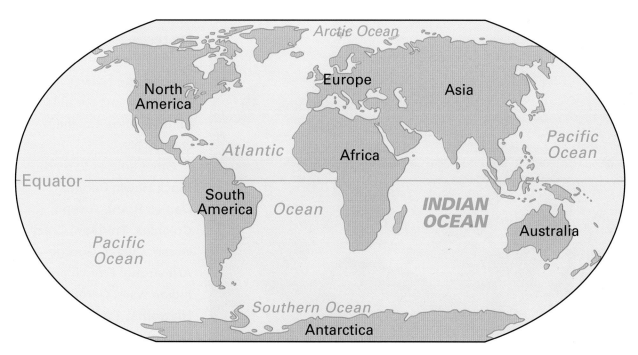

Indian Ocean

Indian wars

The Indian wars were the battles between Native Americans and white people for the lands that became the United States.

English settlers started their first small colonies along the Atlantic coast of the United States in the early 1600's. At first, the colonists and Native Americans got along well together. But soon more and more colonists began moving onto Native American lands. Disagreements grew into wars. The Indian wars lasted until the 1890's.

Most Indian wars started with a fight between a Native American group and the white people who lived nearby. Sometimes an *Indigenous* (native) person or a settler would be killed during the fight. This would start an Indian war. Sometimes other Native American tribes joined the fighting.

Native American peoples and white colonists got into wars mainly because they did not understand each other's way of life. The Native Americans hunted wild animals for food and clothing. The colonists were farmers, and they cut forests down to make farmland. Without the forests, the wild animals had nowhere to live. So the Native Americans either had to move on to new hunting grounds or stay and fight.

As time went on, more colonists came to settle the land. They had big families, and they wanted more land. They outnumbered the Native Americans and pushed them westward. In the end, the Native Americans lost the battle for their lands and their ways of life.

Other articles to read: **Black Hawk; Boone, Daniel; Brant, Joseph; Colonies, Thirteen; Crazy Horse; Custer, George Armstrong; French and Indian wars; Geronimo; Hiawatha; Joseph, Chief; Osceola; Pontiac; Sitting Bull; Smith, John; Tecumseh**

American soldiers captured and killed the Sioux leader Sitting Bull during the Indian Wars.

Indiana

Indiana is a state in the Midwestern region of the United States. It lies between Illinois and Ohio. Michigan borders Indiana on the north, and Kentucky lies to the south. Lake Michigan lies at the northwestern tip of the state.

Indiana is called the *Hoosier State*. But no one knows for sure where the word *hoosier* came from.

Indianapolis, the capital and largest city of Indiana, lies in the middle of the state. It is sometimes called the *Crossroads of America*. Indianapolis is a major center for manufacturing and shipping. Indianapolis is also famous for automobile racing. The most important races are the Indianapolis 500 and the Allstate 400 at the Brickyard.

Land. Much of Indiana is a low plain with rolling hills and shallow valleys. Millions of years ago, glaciers—giant sheets of ice—moved very slowly across this land. The glaciers flattened the land and made small hills. Later, the area was covered with prairie grass. As the grass died out and rotted away, it made the soil rich for farming.

The south part of Indiana never had any glaciers, however. Instead, it has a series of steep hills called *knobs*. Some underground streams have made deep caves in the earth. Indiana also has miles of sand dunes in the north, along the shores of Lake Michigan.

Indiana

Indiana

State flag

State seal

Cataract Falls in Indiana

31

Indiana, continued

The Wabash River and its branches are Indiana's most important rivers. Indiana also has many lakes and waterfalls.

Resources and products. Indiana is a major farming state. Farmers grow corn, soybeans, hay, and wheat. They also grow vegetables, such as cucumbers, snap beans, sweet corn, and tomatoes.

Livestock production is important, too. Indiana farmers raise cattle, hogs, and turkeys.

Indiana is a leading manufacturing state. Factories make car parts and trucks. They also make steel, aluminum, chemicals, and machinery. Indiana's mines produce coal, crushed stone, petroleum, sand, and gravel.

Other articles to read: **Automobile racing; Harrison, William Henry; La Salle, Sieur de; Mound builders; Tecumseh**

Indiana in brief

- **State capitol:** Indianapolis, the capital of Indiana since 1825. Earlier capitals were Vincennes (1800–1813) and Corydon (1813–1824).
- **Area:** 36,184 mi² (93,716 km²), including 361 mi² (935 km²) of inland water but excluding 233 mi² (604 km²) of Great Lakes water.
- **Population:** 6,785,528.
- **Statehood:** Dec. 11, 1816, the 19th state.
- **State abbreviations:** Ind. (traditional); IN (postal).
- **State motto:** *The Crossroads of America.*
- **State song:** "On the Banks of the Wabash, Far Away." Words and music by Paul Dresser.
- **Largest cities in Indiana:** Indianapolis (820,455); Fort Wayne (253,691); Evansville (117,429); South Bend (101,168); Hammond (80,830); Bloomington (80,405).
- **Governor:** 4-year term.
- **State senators:** 50; 4-year terms.
- **State representatives:** 100; 2-year terms.

State bird Cardinal

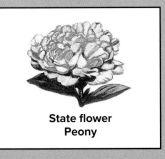

State flower Peony

Important dates in Indiana

Prehistory	The first people to live in what is now Indiana were probably Native Americans known as mound builders. They buried their dead in large mounds, many of which can be seen today.
1679	French explorer Robert Cavelier, Sieur de La Salle, traveled into the Indiana region.
1732?	The French founded Vincennes, Indiana's first permanent settlement.
1763	France gave up the Indiana region to Great Britain after the French and Indian War.
1779	During the American Revolution, Virginia soldier George Rogers Clark and his troops captured Vincennes from the British. This victory gave the Americans control over the Indiana region.
1800	The U.S. government set up the Indiana Territory.
1811	General William Henry Harrison's troops defeated an army of several Native American groups in the Battle of Tippecanoe.
1816	Indiana became the 19th U.S. state on December 11.
1894	Elwood Haynes designed one of the first successful gasoline-powered automobiles in Kokomo.
1911	The first Indianapolis 500 automobile race was held.
1956	Engineers completed the Northern Indiana Toll Road, a large highway.
1980's and 1990's	Indianapolis carried out building programs called redevelopment projects. New offices, hotels, and other buildings were built in older sections of the city.

Indonesia is a country in Southeast Asia. It is made up of more than 17,500 islands. These islands stretch thousands of miles across the Pacific and Indian oceans between the rest of Asia and Australia. All the islands lie near the equator (*ih KWAY tuhr*). The equator is an imaginary line around the middle of Earth halfway between the North and South poles.

Jakarta is the capital and largest city of Indonesia. It lies on the island of Java.

The islands. The islands of Indonesia are divided into three groups: the Greater Sunda Islands, the Lesser Sunda Islands, and the Moluccas. The western half of the island of New Guinea is also a province of Indonesia.

Most Indonesians live on one of the Greater Sunda Islands. These islands include Borneo, Sulawesi, Java, and Sumatra.

Borneo is the third largest island in the world. A small part of it belongs to Brunei and Malaysia. A much larger part, called Kalimantan, belongs to Indonesia. Kalimantan has thick tropical rain forests and mountains.

Flag

Rice fields in Bali

Legong dancers in Ubud, Indonesia

Sulawesi, the most mountainous island of Indonesia, has many volcanoes. Java has more people than any of the other islands. In Sumatra, mountains cover part of the island, while farms, swamps, and thick rain forests cover other parts.

The Lesser Sunda Islands stretch from Bali to Timor. These islands have many mountains. The western islands of this region have more tropical rain forests than do the drier eastern islands.

The Moluccas lie between Sulawesi and New Guinea. Halmaher is the largest island of this group. Hundreds of coral reefs and islands lie between the larger islands.

People. About 300 different groups of people live in Indonesia. The Javanese and Sundanese are the largest groups. The people of Indonesia speak more than 250 languages. Bahasa Indonesia is the official language. Most Indonesians follow the religion of Islam.

Many Indonesians live in small farm villages. Their main food is rice. They serve it with meat, fish, and vegetables. Village women often wear colorful skirts called sarongs. The men wear pants or sarongs.

Some farm families still live in traditional Indonesian houses that stand on stilts, or wooden poles, about 6 feet (1.8 meters) high. Some Indonesian people build long houses. About 100 people live in each long house.

Some Indonesians, especially in Java, have only one name. For example, the name of the country's first president was Sukarno.

Resources and products. Farming is the chief industry of Indonesia. Coffee, palm oil, rubber, sugar cane, tea, and tobacco are grown on big plantations. Rice, the most important food crop, is grown mostly on small farms.

Indonesia has large deposits of petroleum, natural gas, and tin. It is one of the chief producers of petroleum in the world. Petroleum and natural gas are used for heating homes, running machines, and other purposes.

Indonesia has a growing fishing industry. Large fleets catch anchovies, mackerel, sardines, scad, and tuna. Indonesia's forests produce valuable hardwoods, such as ebony and teak. Manufacturing is growing in Indonesia, too.

History. As early as 4,500 years ago, ancient Indonesians made tools of iron and bronze, wore cloth, and sailed the seas as traders. Later, small kingdoms developed on the islands, especially on Java and Sumatra.

In the 1200's, the Indonesian islands were part of a large trading route between Arabia and China. Portuguese, English, and Dutch traders arrived in the 1500's. They fought for control of the islands. By the late 1700's, the Dutch controlled most of the trading. The region became known as the Dutch East Indies or the Netherlands Indies.

In the early 1900's, the Indonesians began to speak out for independence. Sukarno was the leader of the independence movement. During World War II (1939–1945), Japanese forces took over Indonesia. After the war, Indonesian nationalists declared independence in 1945. The Dutch tried to regain control of the country, and there was much fighting. The Netherlands officially recognized Indonesia's independence in 1949. Sukarno became the nation's first president. Both Indonesia and the Netherlands claimed western New Guinea. In 1962, the United Nations negotiated an agreement between them. The United Nations turned control of western New Guinea over to Indonesia in 1963.

Other articles to read: **Jakarta; New Guinea**

Indonesia and its neighbors

Indonesia in brief

- **Capital:** Jakarta.

- **Area:** 737,815 mi² (1,910,931 km²). *Greatest distances*—east-west, about 3,200 mi (5,150 km); north-south, about 1,200 mi (1,930 km). *Coastline*—22,888 mi (36,835 km).

- **Population:** *Current estimate*—274,248,000. *2019 official government estimate*—268,100,000.

- **Official language:** Bahasa Indonesia.

- **Chief products:** *Agriculture*—bananas, cassava, cocoa, coffee, corn, hogs, palm oil, poultry and eggs, rice, rubber, sugar, sweet potatoes, tea, tobacco. *Fishing*—anchovies, mackerel, sardines, scad, tuna. *Forest industry*—plywood, teak, timber. *Manufacturing*—cement, chemicals, clothing, food products, motor vehicles, processed rubber products, textiles, tobacco products, wood products. *Mining*—aluminum, bauxite, coal, copper, gold, natural gas, nickel, petroleum, silver, tin.

- **Money:** *Basic unit*—Indonesian rupiah.

- **Form of government:** Republic.

- **Climate:** Indonesia has a tropical climate, with hot, humid weather and heavy rainfall most of the year. The average temperature is 80 °F (27 °C).

Ruins of the Indus Valley civilization have been uncovered at Mohenjo-Daro, Pakistan.

Indus Valley civilization

The Indus Valley civilization was one of the world's first great civilizations. It began about 4,500 years ago in the Indus and Hakra river plains of what are now Pakistan and northwestern India. About 2500 B.C., farming and herding communities that traded with each other grew to share a common culture. In time, the civilization covered what is now most of Pakistan and parts of Afghanistan and northern India. The Indus people developed a system of weights and measures. They also developed a writing system, but scholars are not able to read it.

The Indus Valley civilization centered around the cities of Mohenjo-Daro and Harappa. The two cities probably had more than 35,000 inhabitants each by about 2500 B.C. The Indus people planned their cities carefully. Buildings were made of brick and raised on mud-brick platforms to protect them from flooding. Most homes had water supplied from a nearby well. In cities, houses were connected to a drainage system. City people traded with farmers and miners for such goods as cotton, lumber, grain, and livestock. The Indus people traded with other civilizations in the region.

The Indus people produced a variety of objects, including tools, ornaments, and utensils. They used such materials as bronze, ivory, silver, gold, and stoneware. Indus sculptors made clay and limestone figurines of animals and people, probably for use in religious rituals.

The Indus civilization broke up into smaller communities by 1700 B.C. The breakup was partly caused by the Hakra River drying up and the course of the Indus River changing. The river changes affected Indus life, and many people left the cities. However, some aspects of Indus life continued in the smaller communities.

Other articles to read: **India; Pakistan**

Industrial Revolution

The Industrial Revolution was both a time period and a series of changes that took place in the way people lived and worked. These changes happened in the 1700's and early 1800's. During this time, people began to use certain kinds of machines to do work. These machines were powered by fuels such as steam or coal. Before the Industrial Revolution, people had done work by hand or with simple machines.

Factories during the Industrial Revolution

The Industrial Revolution began in Great Britain during the 1700's. It spread to other parts of Europe and to North America beginning in the early 1800's.

Before the Industrial Revolution, most people worked at home on farms or in small village workshops. The workers supplied most of the power for making things. Water wheels made power too.

In the 1700's, people began wanting more products to buy. Traders began looking for ways to make things cheaply. At about the same time, the steam engine was invented. Spinning machines for making cloth were invented too. New ways to make iron were also found.

These new machines, and the workers to use them, were brought together for the first time in factories. Factories began to produce large amounts of goods for less money. The world soon changed from one that was made up of farms and villages where people worked at home to one where most people lived in cities and worked in factories.

Other articles to read: **Coal; Factory; Invention; Railroad**

Infant. See Baby.

Inflammation

Inflammation is how the body responds to injury or infection. Inflammation causes redness, swelling, heat, and pain. Inflammation brings white blood cells, which are part of the body's disease-fighting immune system, to the location of injury or infection. Inflammation, together with the immune system, begins healing.

When inflammation occurs uncontrolled, or when it is not needed, it can damage healthy tissue. Rheumatoid arthritis and certain other diseases are caused by uncontrolled inflammation. Inflammation also occurs when the blood supply to part of the body is interrupted and later restored. This happens in heart attack or stroke. This kind of inflammation can lead to further damage. Scientists believe that inflammation also plays a role in other diseases, including cancer.

Treatments for inflammation work to relieve the symptoms, such as fever, pain, and swelling. Aspirin and certain other drugs reduce inflammation.

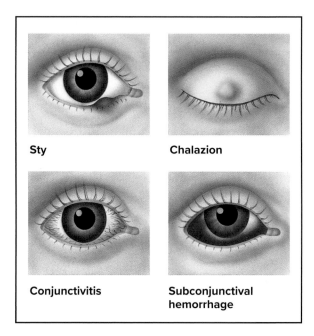

| Sty | Chalazion |
| Conjunctivitis | Subconjunctival hemorrhage |

Various kinds of eye inflammation

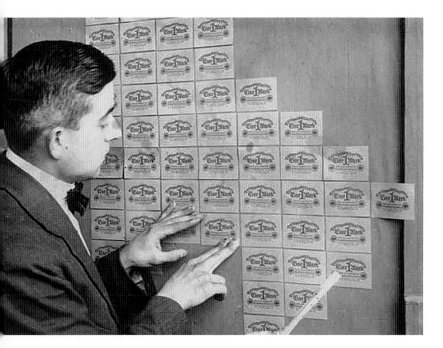

Inflation in Germany in the 1920's was so bad that money was almost worthless. Banknotes had lost so much value that they were used as wallpaper, because they were much cheaper than actual wallpaper.

Inflation

Inflation is a continuous increase in prices. If the cost of such things as food, houses, clothes, travel, and movies keeps going up, then there is inflation. In a time of inflation, prices go up and the value of money goes down. The value of money depends on what the money can buy. For example, suppose that a student could buy five pencils for a dollar last year. But this year the student can buy only four pencils for a dollar. The value of the dollar this year is less than it was last year. So the value of money has gone down.

Here is another example of inflation: Suppose a worker's pay goes up by $10 during a time when there is no inflation. The worker can then spend $10 more for things he or she wants, such as new shoes. But when there is inflation, prices go up. The worker cannot buy as many shoes as before.

Inflation can happen when people want things that they cannot find in the stores. People will then pay higher prices to get what they want. Inflation can also happen when workers get paid more money. Some businesses may raise prices in order to pay their workers more money.

Inflation affects people's lives. Some people may have to borrow money in order to pay for things that cost a lot. Some may start a garden to grow their own food in order to save money. The government sometimes helps control prices or workers' pay.

Influenza

Influenza (*ihn floo EHN zuh*) is a disease. It is often called flu (*floo*). People catch flu from other people. It is caused by a virus (*VY ruhs*), or germ. People with flu have chills, fever, and headaches. Their bodies ache, and they feel weak. Flu usually lasts about a week.

People with flu breathe the virus out into the air. Other people catch flu by breathing in the virus. It gets into the nose, throat, and lungs and may spread within the body.

People can get vaccinations (*VAK sih NAY shuhnz*), or shots, that protect them against flu. Many people get flu shots at the beginning of winter. More people catch flu in winter, maybe because they spend more time indoors together.

Other articles to read: **Immunization; Inoculation**

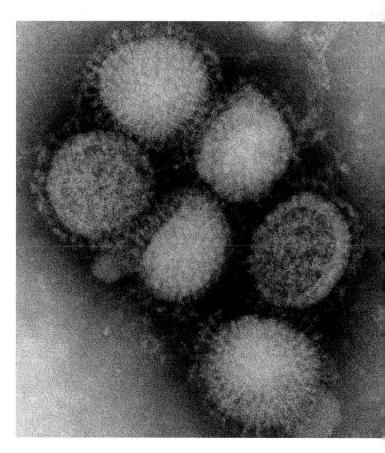

Influenza viruses

This infrared photograph shows the areas where heat is escaping from a house.

Infrared rays

Infrared (*ihn fruh REHD*) rays are an invisible form of energy. They are also called *heat rays* or *thermal radiation.* A warm object *emits* (gives off) infrared rays because of its heat.

As an object's temperature increases, it emits more infrared rays. If the temperature becomes very high, the object will emit rays of visible light as well as infrared rays.

The British astronomer Sir William Herschel discovered infrared rays in 1800. He split sunlight using a *prism.* A prism is an object that spreads white light into a *spectrum,* or rainbow, of colors. Using a thermometer, Herschel measured the temperature at various parts of the spectrum. He noticed that the temperature was high even beyond the red end of the spectrum, where there was no visible light. He realized this heat came from invisible rays.

Other articles to read: **Heat; Prism**

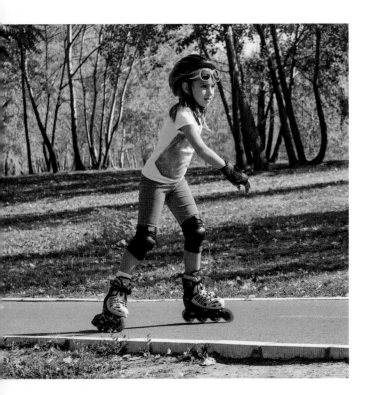

In-line skating

In-line skating

In-line skating is a type of roller skating in which people glide along on wheeled boots called in-line skates. However, the wheels of the skates are placed in a different way from roller skates. In-line skates have four or five wheels set one behind the other. Roller skates have two pairs of wheels set side by side. In-line skating is a fun and active sport.

In-line skates have a high boot that covers the ankle. The boot may be made of leather, plastic, or nylon. It is fastened with buckles, laces, or straps. The wheels and a brake are attached to the bottom of the boot. The brake is usually a rubber pad behind the wheels at the heel of the skate. The skater can stop by lifting the toe of the skate so that the brake pad touches the ground.

In-line skating became popular in the mid-1980's. Many people enjoy in-line skating on city sidewalks and along pathways in parks. In-line skating is good exercise too. It keeps the skater's heart and lungs healthy. It also builds up the leg muscles. Some in-line skaters enter contests to show off their skills.

In-line skating is a fast sport. It is easy to pick up speed, and many in-line skaters have been hurt in falls. So it is important to always wear a helmet when in-line skating. It's also a good idea to wear pads on your knees and elbows, and wrist guards.

Other articles to read: **Roller skating; Skateboarding**

Inoculation

Inoculations (*ih NAHK yuh LAY shuhns*) are shots or jabs. People sometimes get inoculations to protect themselves from a certain disease. The material in the shot helps people's bodies fight against the disease.

Many inoculations contain dead germs, or live germs that are too weak to cause disease. Others contain poisons that are treated so that they do not make a person sick.

Inoculations were first used in ancient China, India, and other places. In 1796, an English doctor called Edward Jenner began using inoculations. He protected people against a dangerous disease called smallpox.

Other articles to read: **Disease; Immunization**

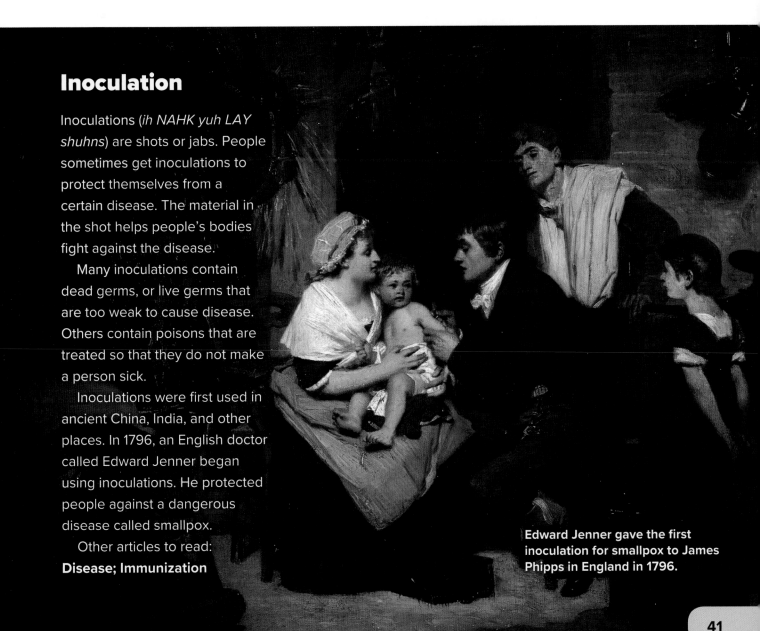

Edward Jenner gave the first inoculation for smallpox to James Phipps in England in 1796.

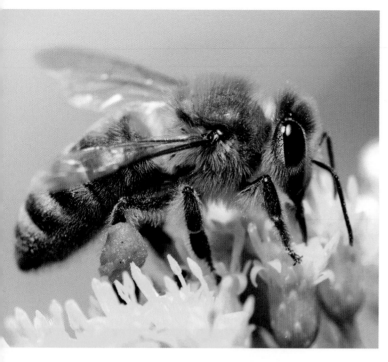

Bees carry pollen from one plant to another.

Some insects, like this moth, are beautifully colored.

Insect

Insects are small animals with six legs. Bees, ants, wasps, butterflies, cockroaches, and ladybugs are insects. So are mosquitoes, grasshoppers, and fleas.

There are about a million kinds of insects, and they live everywhere. Insects can be found in tropical jungles and in the arctic cold. They live high in the mountains and in low, dry deserts.

Many people think that spiders are insects, but they aren't. Spiders have eight legs, but insects have six legs. A spider's body has two main parts, but an insect's body has three main parts. Also, most insects have wings and antennae (*an TEHN ee*), or long, thin feelers. Spiders have no antennae.

The world of insects

Most insects are less than a quarter inch (6.4 millimeters) long. The smallest ones are fairy flies and some kinds of beetles. These insects are so tiny that they could fit through the eye of the smallest needle.

Some insects are much bigger. The Goliath beetle is more than 4 inches (10 centimeters) long. The Atlas moth can spread its wings about 10 inches (25 centimeters).

Insects come in every color of the rainbow. Some butterflies and moths have bright, colorful marks on their wings. Sometimes, the color of an insect helps it blend in with its surroundings. Beetles that live in the ground are black or brown. Some kinds of moths have the same color as tree bark.

Why insects are so successful

Almost every kind of animal must struggle to survive, or stay alive. Insects are good at surviving. Insects have been able to change so that they can live in the worst conditions. Some can live in very hot water. Some have been frozen solid—and still lived. Many insects can eat almost anything. Some will even eat cloth, cork, face powder, and paste.

Insects have also survived because they are small. They can hide from enemies in the tiniest places, and they do not need much to eat.

Most insects have wings, and they fly. This makes it easier for them to search for food and to get away from their enemies. Most insects lay many eggs, too. So they make many more of their own kind.

Why insects are important

Many insects help people. These insects are called beneficial (*behn uh FIHSH uhl*) insects. Bees, wasps, butterflies, and moths are beneficial insects. They pollinate plants, which means that they carry pollen from one plant to another. Plants use pollen to make seeds, which make more plants. Insects pollinate such fruits as oranges, apples, and plums. They also pollinate such vegetables as peas, onions, carrots, and cabbages.

The fairy fly is one of the tiniest insects. You need a magnifying glass to see it in real life.

Insects are food for birds, fish, frogs, lizards, skunks, and many other animals. Some people eat insects. In South Africa, people roast termites and eat them like popcorn.

Some insects give us valuable products. Bees make honey and beeswax. Silk is made by silkworms.

Many insects help keep parks and gardens clean. They do this by eating animal wastes. They also eat dead animals and plants.

Harmful insects

Of all the insects in the world, only a few are harmful to people. They do a lot of damage, though. Harmful insects damage plants and destroy crops. They can also

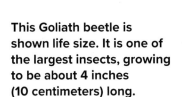

This Goliath beetle is shown life size. It is one of the largest insects, growing to be about 4 inches (10 centimeters) long.

The adult firefly and the larva (baby insect) look very different.

The eastern subterranean termite lives underground.

The assassin bug has a nasty bite.

The giant water bug grows to the size shown here.

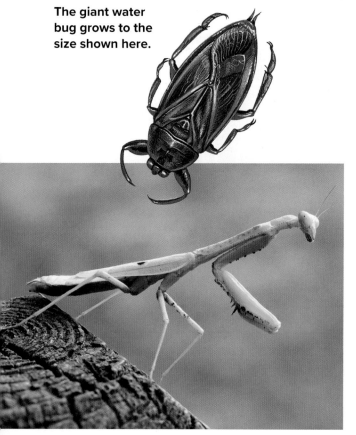

The Carolina mantid can damage plants and destroy crops.

cause damage in the home. Clothes moths and carpet beetles ruin clothing and rugs. Termites attack the wood in buildings. Some insects can spread disease when they bite. Certain kinds of mosquitoes spread malaria and other dangerous diseases.

There are many ways to get rid of harmful insects. People swat flies and pick beetles off plants. Areas with lots of water are drained to keep mosquitoes away. Government workers try to keep harmful insects from coming into the country on airplanes and ships. Farmers use special farming methods that can prevent or stop insect damage. For example, they may plant or harvest crops when insects are few, or when the insects are not laying eggs.

Sometimes, scientists bring predatory (*PREHD uh tuhr ee*) insects to problem areas. Predatory insects eat harmful insects. For example, ladybugs are predatory insects. They eat some of the insects that ruin crops. People often use chemicals to kill harmful insects, too.

The bodies of insects

An insect's body has three main parts. These parts are the head, the thorax (or middle section), and the abdomen. All insects also have a tough shell on the outside of their bodies. It is called the exoskeleton. The exoskeleton is like a suit of armor. It protects

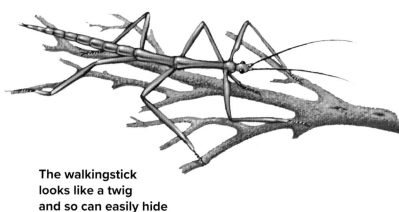

The walkingstick looks like a twig and so can easily hide from its enemies.

the insect's organs, or inside body parts.

The insect's head includes the mouthparts, eyes, and antennae. The mouthparts are used for feeding. Most adult insects have two huge eyes. But they cannot move or focus their eyes. They can only see things that are close to them. They have no eyelids, so their eyes are always open.

Almost all insects have two antennae between their eyes. They use their antennae to smell and to feel. They use smell to locate food and to find their way around. They also use smell to find a mate and a place to lay their eggs.

The thorax is the middle section of an insect's body. The insect's legs are attached to its thorax. All insects have three pairs of legs. The wings are attached to the thorax, too.

The insect's abdomen is used for digesting food. The parts used for mating are also in the abdomen. So are the parts for getting rid of waste and extra water.

Most insects do not have ears. Instead, they have tiny hairs on their antennae or other parts of their body. These hairs shake when sound waves hit them. Crickets and long-horned grasshoppers have their "ears" on their front legs. Ants and male mosquitoes hear through their antennae.

Other articles to read: **Ant; Bee; Beetle; Bug; Butterfly; Caterpillar; Centipede; Cicada; Cockroach; Cocoon; Cricket; Firefly; Flea; Fly; Grasshopper; Ladybug; Locust; Louse; Mosquito; Moth; Spider; Termite; Tick; Wasp**

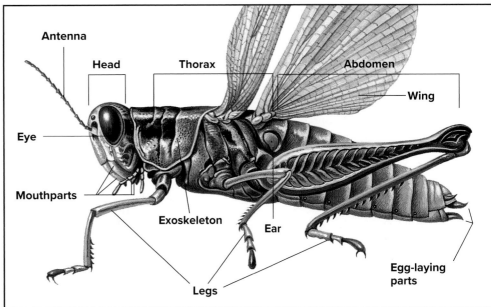

This picture shows the visible parts of an insect. This is a female short-horned grasshopper.

Insects such as these blister beetles use their antennae to smell and feel.

Fun facts about insects

- Over half of all animals are insects.
- Beetle blood may be yellow, green, or orange.
- A dragonfly can reach speeds of up to 38 miles (61 kilometers) per hour.
- Butterflies taste food with their feet.

Flies can walk upside down.

Caterpillars have mouths but butterflies don't.

Some ants can lift objects up to 30 times heavier than themselves.

That's like you lifting up a small car.

- Sometimes a praying mantis attacks creatures larger than itself, such as frogs, mice, or even small birds.

A praying mantis can turn its head almost all the way around.

- Some ants can survive up to 14 days underwater.
- A tiny flea can jump 100 times its own height. That would be like you leaping over an office building.
- Fleas can be made to perform tricks, such as pulling tiny wagons.

If grasshoppers were the size of people, they could leap the length of a basketball court.

- A worker honey bee collects enough nectar in its lifetime to make about 1/10 pound (45 grams) of honey.
- Honey bees can identify a flavor as sweet, sour, salty, or bitter.
- A cockroach can live for weeks without a head.

Instinct

Instincts are natural feelings or knowledge that let living things perform certain actions. These actions do not have to be learned.

Instinctive actions are different from learned actions. Learned actions are a result of what happens to living things as they grow. Most actions are partly instinctive and partly learned. Many kinds of living things, including people, animals, fish, and insects, have instincts to behave in certain ways. Human babies do not have to learn how to suck a bottle. They have the instinct to suck.

When a living thing acts on its instinct, it usually needs something to make it act the way it does. This is called a stimulus (*STIHM yoo luhs*). When winter is near, the shorter days are the stimulus for a certain chemical to go through a bird's body. The chemical, in turn, is the stimulus in the bird's brain that tells it to fly to warmer places.

Most of the actions of insects, spiders, crabs, and lobsters are instinctive. These creatures are called lower animals. They act on instinct more than higher animals do. Higher animals include fish, amphibians, reptiles, birds, and mammals. Higher animals seem to use learning more than instinct as they grow.

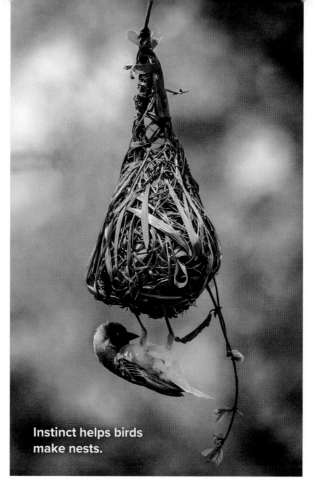

Instinct helps birds make nests.

A baby's smile is part instinct, part learned behavior.

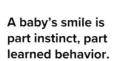

Insurance

Insurance helps protect people against large and unexpected costs. There are several kinds of insurance. Health insurance helps pay doctor and hospital bills when someone gets sick or hurt. Automobile insurance helps pay to fix or replace cars after an accident or a theft. Homeowner's or renter's insurance helps replace things that are stolen or damaged by such things as fire or water. Life insurance pays money to the family of the insured person if he or she dies.

People buy insurance from insurance companies. A person agrees to make regular payments to the insurance company. In return, the company pays if the person suffers a loss.

Insurance helps cover the cost from fire damage.

Intelligence

Intelligence is a word used to describe how quickly people are able to learn and understand things and how well and how long they remember ideas. Teachers may give students an IQ, or intelligence quotient, test to find out how intelligent they are. People have different levels of intelligence in different subjects. For example, someone who is good in mathematics may not be good at learning new words or understanding machinery.

Scientists disagree about where intelligence comes from. Every person is born with a certain amount of brain power. Many events in a child's life can affect that brain power. For example, infants who are poorly fed may not learn well. Also, children who are badly treated may become so upset that their intelligence fails to develop as it should.

Other articles to read: **Artificial intelligence**

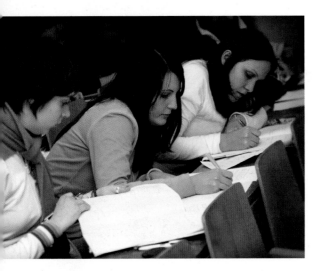

Intelligence is learning and understanding things.

Internal combustion engine.
See Engine.

International Space Station

The International Space Station is a large *artificial satellite* in space. An artificial satellite is an object made by human beings that is flown into space by a rocket. The International Space Station orbits about 250 miles (400 kilometers) above Earth.

More than 15 countries worked together to build the International Space Station. The first part of the station was launched in 1998. The space station was completed in 2011. Astronauts continue to add improvements to the station.

The International Space Station is used to conduct scientific experiments. Some of these experiments measure how conditions in space can affect living things, including the astronauts. Astronauts first lived on the station in 2000. Three astronauts usually live aboard the station at one time.

Spacecraft from several countries regularly visit the station. They bring new supplies and astronauts. In 2012, SpaceX became the first private company to send a spacecraft to the station with supplies. Since then, SpaceX spacecraft have taken supplies to the station many times. In 2020, SpaceX became the first private company to take astronauts into orbit. It carried two U.S. astronauts to the station.

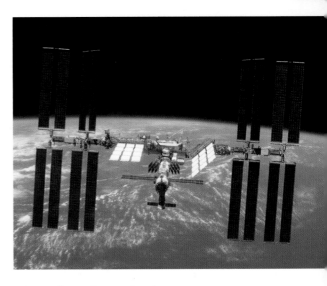

International Space Station

International trade

International trade is the exchange of products between countries, or nations. It is different from domestic trade, which takes place entirely within a single country. International trade is sometimes called world trade or foreign trade.

With international trade, countries produce more of the things they are best able to make or grow. They buy other things they need from other countries. Important trade products include food, machines, and fuel. The things one nation sells to other nations are called exports. The things a nation buys are called imports. International trade makes it possible for people to buy a greater variety of products.

International trade is the exchange of goods and services between countries.

Internet

The internet is a system of computer networks. It links together billions of computers, mobile phones, and other devices. More than half of the world's people have internet access.

The internet is like a vast library. It stores a huge amount of information. This information includes text, such as books and news articles. It includes music, images, and videos. Computer programs are also available on the internet. Such programs include electronic games.

Internet organization and uses

Much information on the internet is organized on *websites.* All the internet's websites, linked together, form the World Wide Web. The web, unlike some other parts of the internet, is easy to use and explore.

The internet does not just store information. People work, shop, and play on the internet. They share artwork and ideas. People use the internet to communicate in many ways. They can e-mail one another. They can also have face-to-face conversations using special cameras. *Social networking websites* help people stay in touch with their friends and families.

People can have face-to-face conversations on the internet using special cameras.

How the internet works

The internet includes computers, mobile phones, other devices, and the wires that connect all these things together. These objects are called *hardware.* They link together, forming a "net." Electronic signals move quickly over the internet's hardware. The signals carry information, such as text, photos, and videos.

The internet's hardware would be useless without *software protocols.* Software protocols are special sets of rules. They control how signals move over the internet. They work much like traffic laws guiding traffic on the streets.

However, information does not move on the internet like a car moves on roads. For example, you might send a photo from

your phone to a friend's computer over the internet. But this photo does not stay in one piece. Instead, the photo is cut up into chunks. The chunks are called *packets.* Each packet can take a different path over the internet. If a path is slow or broken, the packet switches to a new path. This concept is called *packet switching.* Eventually, all the packets arrive at your friend's computer. They are put back together. The computer then displays the photo.

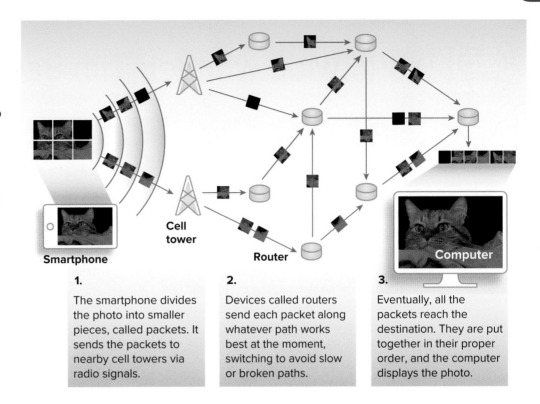

1.
The smartphone divides the photo into smaller pieces, called packets. It sends the packets to nearby cell towers via radio signals.

2.
Devices called routers send each packet along whatever path works best at the moment, switching to avoid slow or broken paths.

3.
Eventually, all the packets reach the destination. They are put together in their proper order, and the computer displays the photo.

The internet links computers all over the world. High-speed communication lines, wireless transmitters, and satellites may all play a part in the exchange of information between two computers over the internet.

Beginnings of the internet

Development of the internet began during the 1960's. At that time, the United States government worried about nuclear attacks from the Soviet Union. Such attacks could have crippled the U.S. communication system. The U.S. military worked with computer scientists. They developed the early internet. With packet switching, communications could still work in case of an attack.

In the 1990's, a computer scientist named Tim Berners-Lee developed the World Wide Web. The web made the internet much easier to use.

Evolution of the internet

During the 2000's, internet connections became much faster. New websites encouraged ordinary people to publish their own writing, photos, and videos. By the 2010's, many mobile phones and other wireless devices could connect to the internet.

Other articles to read: **Cellular telephone; Computer; Computer virus; E-mail; Modem; Multimedia**

World wide wonder: Tim Berners-Lee

Tim Berners-Lee (1955–   ), a British computer scientist, developed the World Wide Web. The World Wide Web (or web for short) is part of the internet, the worldwide network of computers. The web allows computer users to make and view "pages" that may contain pictures, video, animation, and sound, in addition to words.

In 1980, while working at the European Organization for Nuclear Research (CERN) near Geneva, Switzerland, Berners-Lee created a system that linked words in one computer file to those in another. About 1989, he developed the World Wide Web. It was used at first by scientists. In 1991, the web became part of the internet. He created a system that describes how web pages should look using computer programs called web browsers. He also designed a system that assigns each web page a unique address, or location.

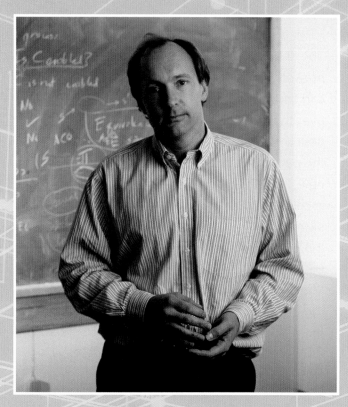

Tim Berners-Lee

A web page is a file represented by its own address on the internet. A special computer language is used to create such files. A web browser displays the elements of pages according to commands called tags.

Inuit

The Inuit (*IHN yoo iht*) are a group of
people who live in the Arctic—the far
northern part of the world. Their homeland
stretches from the northeastern tip of
Russia across Alaska and northern Canada
to Greenland. The Inuit live farther north
than any other people on Earth.

The Inuit used to be called Eskimos.
Many Inuit do not like the word *Eskimo*. It
comes from a Native American word that
means "someone who eats raw meat" or
"someone who speaks a foreign
language." The name *Inuit* comes from the
Inuit-Inupiaq language and means "the
people" or "real people." The Inuit word
for just one person is *Inuk.*

The Inuit live in one of the coldest parts
of the world. Average temperatures in the
Arctic region are below freezing for nine to
ten months each year. The land is covered

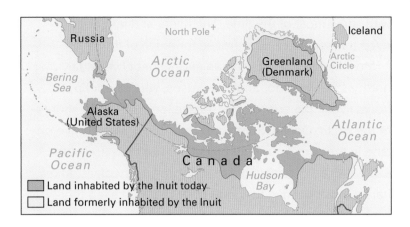

Inuit homeland

Inuit people

Inuit

with snow most of the time. The rivers and lakes—and even the sea itself—stay frozen for much of the year.

Most kinds of plants and animals cannot live as far north as the Inuit do. Seals, walruses, whales, and polar bears live in the sea, on the sea ice, and along the shores of the Arctic Ocean. Some birds and other animals live on land in the Arctic during the summer but then go south for the winter. Animals of the Arctic include wolves, foxes, hares, musk oxen, and a kind of large deer called the caribou (*KAR uh boo*). Arctic fish include arctic char, arctic cod, lake trout, salmon, and whitefish.

The Inuit today

More than 100,000 Inuit live in Russia, Alaska, Canada, and Greenland. Most Inuit speak English, Russian, or Danish as well as their own language. Many Inuit are Christians.

Most Inuit live in towns or in small groups scattered along the coast of the Arctic Ocean. They have wooden homes and wear modern clothing. They travel by motorboat in the water and by snowmobile on land. Many Inuit hunt and fish to feed their families.

Some Inuit have jobs in the fishing industry. Others make soapstone carvings and other artwork and crafts. Some work in mines. But many Inuit cannot find jobs, so the government of the country they live in provides healthcare, homes, and schools for them.

The old way of life

The old, or traditional, Inuit way of life began about 1,000 years ago. At that time, the Inuit lived in what is now the Bering Sea region of Alaska and Siberia. The old way of

Inuit clothing

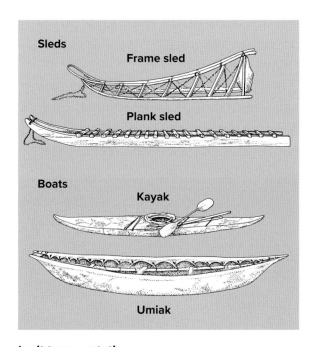

Inuit transportation

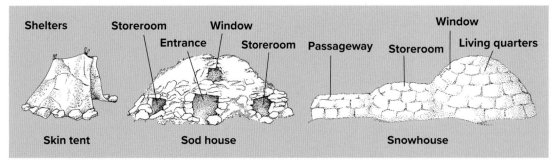

Inuit houses

life lasted until the early 1900's.

The Inuit caught fish and hunted seals, walruses, and whales in the ocean. On land, they hunted caribou, musk oxen, polar bears, and many smaller animals. They ate the meat of these animals and used the skins to make clothes and tents. They made tools and weapons from the animals' bones, horns, and teeth.

Most Inuit families had both a summer house and a winter house. The summer house was a tent framed with wood and covered with seal or caribou skins. The winter house had walls made of rocks and sod, or pieces of dirt covered with grass. The roof was made from wooden boards or whalebone and covered with sod. When they hunted animals during the winter, Inuit hunters built dome-shaped snow houses to live in for a short time as they followed the animals.

During winter months, most Inuit traveled on sleds pulled by dogs. In summer, people walked over land and traveled in long, narrow boats called kayaks (*KY aks*) or larger boats called umiaks (*OO mee aks*).

Other articles to read: **Alaska; Arctic; Arctic Ocean; Canada; Greenland; Russia**

Inuit family in 1929

Invention

An invention is the creation of something new, such as a tool or a machine, or a new way of getting work done. Inventions may give people greater control over their environment and allow them to live better, easier, and happier lives.

An invention is different from a discovery. A discovery is seeing something that exists in nature for the first time. An invention is the creation of something that never existed before. For example, people discovered fire, but they invented the match to start a fire.

Wheel 3500 B.C.

Airplane 1903

Important inventions in history

Plow	5000-3000 B.C.
Wheel	3500 B.C.
Magnetic compass	300's B.C.
Paper	By A.D. 1
Movable type	About 1440
Telescope	1608
Steam engine	1690-1769
Steamboat	1787-1807
Cotton gin	1793
Steam locomotive	1804
Photography	1826
Gas refrigeration	1834
Telegraph	1837
Sewing machine	1846
Dynamite	1867
Typewriter	1867
Electric motor	1873
Telephone	1876
Phonograph	1877
Incandescent light	1879
Gasoline automobile	1885
Zipper	1893
Motion picture	Mid-1890's
Radio	1895
Airplane	1903
Television	1920's
Radar	About 1935
Atomic bomb	1945
Digital computer	1946
Laser	1960
Microprocessor	1971
Cell phone	1979
CD player	1983
Internet	Late 1980's

People may invent things to make money, but the main reason for invention is to help people. An invention must fill an economic, military, or social need. Economic needs have led to the invention of many tools and machines used on farms and in factories and businesses. Military needs have led to the invention of weapons used in war. Social needs have led to the invention of tools used by doctors and products used in people's homes. If an invention does not fill one of these needs, people will not use it.

People have invented things since the earliest times. For example, the plow and the wheel were invented more than 5,000 years ago, and paper was invented about 2,000 years ago. But many important inventions have been developed in the last 600 years. For example, modern printing was invented in about the year 1440.

Thousands of inventions were created in the 1800's to make life at home easier and more comfortable. These inventions included the gas refrigerator (1834), the sewing machine (1846), the safety pin (1849), the telephone (1876), the phonograph (1877), the electric light bulb (1879), the gasoline-powered car (1885), the zipper (1893), and the radio (1895). Important inventions of the 1900's included the airplane (1903), television (1920's), modern plastics (mid-1930's), and the microprocessor used to control modern computers (1971). The world's first commercial cellular telephone system went into operation in Japan in 1979. The internet was invented in the late 1980's and continues to be improved today.

Other articles to read: **Airplane; Automobile; Cellular telephone; Computer; Edison, Thomas; Laser; Motion picture; Photography; Radar; Radio; Telegraph; Telephone; Telescope; Television; Whitney, Eli; Wright Brothers; Zipper**

Invertebrate

Invertebrates (*ihn VUR tuh brihts*) are animals without backbones. The bones that make up the backbone are called vertebrae (*VUR tuh bray*). Invertebrate means *without a backbone*. Animals with backbones are called vertebrates.

There are many kinds of invertebrates. The biggest group includes insects, spiders, and crayfish. Other animals with jointed legs and hard outer skeletons belong to this group too.

Another group includes jellyfish, sea anemones, and coral. Sponges, sea animals with many pores (*pohrz*), or holes, are another kind. Still other groups include flat-bodied worms, round-bodied worms, worms with sections such as earthworms, and sea animals such as starfish.

Other articles to read: **Arthropod; Insect; Mollusk; Sponge; Vertebrate; Worm**

Sally lightfoot crab

Garden snail

Starfish

Iowa

Iowa

Iowa

State flag

State seal

Iowa is a state in the Midwestern region of the United States. Wisconsin and Illinois lie to the east. South Dakota and Nebraska are to the west. Minnesota forms Iowa's northern border. Missouri lies to the south. Iowa produces so much corn that it is called the *Corn State*.

Des Moines is the capital and largest city in Iowa. It lies in the south-central part of the state where the Des Moines and Raccoon rivers meet. Des Moines is an important manufacturing center. Cedar Rapids, Iowa's second largest city, is also a big manufacturing center. Dubuque is a port city on the west bank of the Mississippi River.

Land. A million years ago, glaciers (*GLAY shuhrz*) covered Iowa. These great sheets of ice moved very slowly over the land. They flattened the land and filled the valleys. The glaciers also made the soil very rich. Today, most of Iowa is a flat plain.

Only one glacier moved across the northeast part of Iowa. Here, the land has pine-covered cliffs and hills.

The Mississippi River flows along the eastern border of Iowa. Near the Mississippi are deep valleys and limestone cliffs. Hardwood trees grow in the river valleys. Small lakes and streams are scattered across

Iowa farms produce hogs, corn, beef cattle, and soybeans.

northern and northwestern Iowa. People who love the outdoors enjoy hiking in these areas.

Resources and products. Farms cover almost all of Iowa's land. Corn and soybeans are the most important crops. Much of the corn crop feeds the livestock. Other crops include hay, oats, and wheat.

Iowa farmers also grow many different vegetables, especially cabbage, peas, pumpkins, and sweet corn. Apples are the biggest fruit crop. Iowa farmers also raise such livestock as hogs and cattle.

Many of Iowa's manufacturing plants make food products from the crops and livestock grown in the state. These include cereals, corn oil, corn syrup, and meat. Iowa factories also make farm machinery and concrete.

Other articles to read: **Black Hawk; Louisiana Purchase; Marquette, Jacques; Mississippi River; Mound builders**

Important dates in Iowa

Prehistory	Native Americans lived in the Iowa region long before Europeans arrived. Ancient Native American people known as mound builders buried their dead in large mounds. Many of these mounds can be seen today.
1673	Explorers Louis Jolliet and Jacques Marquette of France traveled into the Iowa region.
1788	Julien Dubuque, Iowa's first white settler, began mining lead near present-day Dubuque.
1803	The United States purchased the Louisiana Territory from France. This huge region, which included present-day Iowa, spread from the Mississippi River to the Rocky Mountains.
1832	Native Americans led by Chief Black Hawk were defeated by the U.S. Army in the Black Hawk War.
1833	Permanent settlements began in the Iowa region.
1838	Congress created the Territory of Iowa.
1846	Iowa became the 29th state on December 28.
1867	The first railroad was completed across Iowa, from the Mississippi River to Council Bluffs.
1917	Iowa began a large road-building program.
1960	The U.S. government reported that, for the first time, more Iowans lived in cities than on farms.
1993, 2008	Heavy rains caused many rivers, including the Mississippi, to flood in Iowa. These floods caused millions of dollars in damages to cities and farms across the state.

Iowa in brief

- **State capital:** Des Moines, Iowa's capital since 1857. Earlier capitals were Burlington (1838–1841) and Iowa City (1841–1857).
- **Area:** 56,273 mi² (145,746 km²), including 415 mi² (1,075 km²) of inland water.
- **Population:** 3,190,369.
- **Statehood:** Dec. 28, 1846, the 29th state.
- **State abbreviations:** Ia. (traditional); IA (postal).
- **State motto:** *Our Liberties We Prize and Our Rights We Will Maintain.*
- **State song:** "The Song of Iowa." Words by S. H. M. Byers; sung to the tune of "Der Tannenbaum."
- **Largest cities in Iowa:** Des Moines (203,433); Cedar Rapids (126,326); Davenport (99,685); Sioux City (82,684); Waterloo (68,406); Iowa City (67,862).
- **Governor:** 4-year term.
- **State senators:** 50; 4-year terms.
- **State representatives:** 100; 2-year terms.

**State bird
Eastern goldfinch
(American goldfinch)**

**State flower
Wild rose**

Iran (*ih RAHN*) is a country in southwestern Asia, in the area of the world known as the Middle East. South of Iran lie the Persian Gulf and the Gulf of Oman, which flow into the Indian Ocean. Iraq and Turkey border Iran to the west. Armenia, Azerbaijan, the Caspian Sea, and Turkmenistan lie to the north. Afghanistan and Pakistan are to the east. Iran is one of the world's oldest countries. Tehran is the country's capital and largest city.

Land. About half of Iran is made up of a high, flat piece of land called a plateau (*plah TOH*). Two huge deserts stretch across the plateau. They are among the world's driest deserts. Few plants and animals, and almost no people, live there.

Two mountain ranges, the Elburz and the Zagros, surround most of the plateau. In the north, a narrow strip of coastland lies between the Elburz Mountains and the Caspian Sea. In the west, a plain lies between the Zagros Mountains and the border of Iraq.

A busy market in Shiraz, Iran

People. More than half of the people in Iran are Persians. Most Iranians speak the Persian language, also called Farsi. It is used in schools and by the Iranian government.

Most Iranians live in the northwestern part of the country, along the Caspian Sea, and in and near Tehran. Some city people live in apartment buildings, and others live in traditional houses. Most families in the countryside live in traditional houses. These houses are made of dried mud or brick and have a flat roof covered with mud or straw. The main foods of Iran's people are rice and bread. Sometimes the rice is mixed with meat and vegetables.

Nearly all the people of Iran are Muslims, people who follow the faith of Islam. The government makes strict laws according to Islam. These laws control much of what people may say or do. The government says that women should wear a long black veil, called a chador. It covers the entire body. It also covers the head and is sometimes drawn across the lower face.

Resources and products. About half of all Iran's workers have service jobs. Service jobs include jobs in the government, in hospitals, in schools, in banks, and in restaurants. Many of Iran's workers hold jobs in factories. The country's main factory products include cars, cement, food products, and petroleum products.

Iran in brief

■ **Capital:** Tehran.

■ **Area:** 636,372 mi² (1,648,195 km²). *Greatest distances*— northwest-southeast, 1,375 mi (2,213 km); northeast-southwest, 850 mi (1,370 km). *Coastline*—1,650 mi (2,655 km).

■ **Population:** *Current estimate*—86,021,000; *2016 census*—79,926,270.

■ **Official language:** Persian, also called Farsi.

■ **Chief products:** *Agriculture*— fruits, milk, nuts, rice, wheat. *Fishing*—caviar. *Manufacturing*— cement, food products, petrochemicals, petroleum products. *Mining*—petroleum.

■ **Money:** *Basic unit*—Iranian rial.

■ **Form of government:** Islamic republic.

■ **Climate:** Hot summers, cooler on Caspian Sea coast and in mountains. Cool winters, cold on plateau and in mountains. Caspian Sea coast is rainy in summer.

Flag

Iran and its neighbors

Iran is one of the world's leading producers of petroleum. People around the world use petroleum for running cars and for other purposes. Nearly all of Iran's income comes from petroleum.

About one-fifth of the workers in Iran are farmers. Most of them live along the Caspian Sea coast or on the plain near Iraq. Farmers raise such crops as barley, corn, cotton, dates and other fruits, nuts, rice, sugar beets, tomatoes, and wheat. Cattle, goats, and sheep provide milk and meat. Iranian fishing crews catch a variety of fish in the Caspian Sea and the Persian Gulf.

History. People have lived in what is now Iran for more than 5,000 years. The greatest early kingdom in Iran was the Persian Empire. It was founded about 2,500 years ago and lasted about 200 years. Persian kings once ruled most of southwestern Asia as well as parts of Europe and Africa.

Other countries have taken over Iran many times during its long history. One of the most important invasions happened in the middle of the 600's, when Muslim Arabs conquered Iran. Under their rule, most of the people became Muslims. From the 1500's to 1700's, the Safavid rulers of Iran controlled a powerful empire.

Crude oil was discovered in southwestern Iran in the early 1900's. When Iran began to sell petroleum to other countries, the nation became rich. In 1979, a group of people led by Ayatollah Ruhollah Khomeini, a Muslim religious leader, took control of the government away from the *shah,* or king, Mohammad Reza Pahlavi. Ayatollah Khomeini set up a new government based on Islamic law, with himself as the most powerful leader.

In 1980, a war broke out between Iran and Iraq. In 1988, the two countries agreed to stop fighting.

Ayatollah Khomeini died in 1989, and another Muslim leader, Ayatollah Ali Khamenei, became an important figure in Iran's government. Iran now has a president who heads the government.

Other articles to read: **Caspian Sea; Islam; Muslims; Persia, Ancient; Tehran**

Zagros Mountains in western Iran

Iraq is a country of southwestern Asia, in the area of the world known as the Middle East. The southeastern tip of Iraq lies on the Persian Gulf. Iraq's neighbors are Iran to the east, Kuwait and Saudi Arabia to the south, Jordan and Syria to the west, and Turkey to the north. Baghdad is Iraq's capital and largest city.

Land. Mountains rise along northeastern Iraq. South of the mountains, a vast plain stretches southeast across the country to the Persian Gulf. Some parts of the plain are dry and hilly, some parts are flat land with farms and oil fields, and other parts are swampland. The Tigris and Euphrates rivers flow through the plain. People use water from the rivers to grow crops. A sandy, hilly desert covers the southwestern and western parts of the country. Iraq gets very little rain.

People. Most of the people in Iraq are Arabs, a Middle Eastern people who speak Arabic. The Kurds, who have their own Kurdish language, make up a smaller group. Most Kurds also speak Arabic, which is Iraq's official language. Nearly all the people of Iraq are Muslims, people who follow the faith of Islam.

Most of Iraq's people live in cities on the plain. Many city people live in apartment buildings.

Most people in the countryside live in small houses. In the north, the houses are made of stone. In the south, the houses are made of dried

Iraq in brief

- **Capital:** Baghdad.
- **Area:** 167,975 mi² (435,052 km²). *Greatest distances*—north-south, 530 mi (853 km); east-west, 495 mi (797 km). *Coastline*—40 mi (64 km).
- **Population:** *Current estimate*—42,053,000; *2016 official government estimate*—37,883,543.
- **Official languages:** Arabic and Kurdish.
- **Chief products:** *Agriculture*—barley, dates, grapes, milk, rice, tomatoes, and wheat. *Mining*—petroleum. *Manufacturing*—cement, chemicals, fertilizer, food products, petroleum refining, textiles.
- **Money:** *Basic unit*—new Iraqi dinar.
- **Form of government:** Federal republic.
- **Climate:** Hot summers, cool winters, and little rain. Hottest temperatures and driest weather in the deserts of the east and southeast.

Flag

Iraq and its neighbors

Iraqi countryside

mud and brick. A few people in western Iraq are nomads, or wanderers, who move from place to place with their camels, goats, and sheep.

In the cities, wealthy people dress in modern clothing like the clothing worn in the United States and much of Europe. Other people wear the kind of clothing that has been worn in Iraq for hundreds of years. Men wear long cotton robes and jackets, and women wear a long robe with a scarf that covers much of the head.

The main foods in Iraq are rice and bread. The people also eat many kinds of fruits, vegetables, meat, and fish. A common food in Iraq is sanbusak, a moon-shaped dough stuffed with cheese or meat. Popular drinks include tea, coffee, and fruit juices.

Resources and products. Oil is important to Iraq's economy. Iraq is an important oil-producing nation. Oil is, by far, Iraq's most important export product. Service industries provide jobs for many of Iraq's workers. Many people work in banks or for the government. Iraq's crops are mainly grown near the Tigris and Euphrates rivers. Important crops include dates, grapes, tomatoes, and wheat. Farmers also raise cattle, chickens, and sheep.

History. The world's first known civilization developed about 5,500 years ago in Sumer, along the Tigris and Euphrates rivers. Sumer was part of Mesopotamia, an area that included most of what is now Iraq and parts of Syria and Turkey. In the year 637, Arab Muslims took over Mesopotamia. In the 700's, the Arabs founded Baghdad as capital of their empire. By 800, Baghdad had grown into a city of more than a million people and was a world center of trade and culture.

In 1258, Mongol warriors from central Asia came to Mesopotamia and destroyed the Arab Empire. From the 1500's through the 1800's, the Ottoman Empire ruled Mesopotamia. The Ottoman Empire was ruled from what is now Turkey. British troops took Mesopotamia from the Ottomans during World War I (1914–1918). Iraq became an independent nation in 1932.

In 1980, a war broke out between Iraq and Iran. In 1988, the two countries agreed to stop fighting. In 1990, troops from Iraq took over Kuwait, a small country south of Iraq. The United Nations (UN) told Iraq to withdraw the troops, but Iraq would not withdraw, and the Persian Gulf War broke out in January 1991. UN forces, led by the United States, defeated Iraq's army. The war ended in April 1991.

In March 2003, a group of countries led by the United States went to war with Iraq. The war led to the downfall of the Iraqi government of dictator Saddam Hussein. The Iraq War officially ended in 2011.

Other articles to read: **Iraq War; Persian Gulf War of 1991**

Baghdad, the capital of Iraq

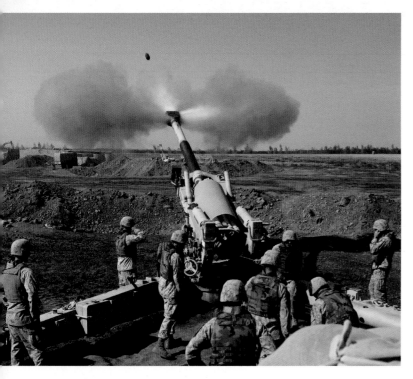

U.S. marines fire a howitzer on Fallujah, Iraq, during the Iraq War.

Iraq War

The Iraq War (2003–2011) was a conflict between Iraq and a group of countries led by the United States.

To help end the Persian Gulf War of 1991, Iraq had agreed to destroy its biological, chemical, and nuclear weapons. But after the war, Iraq would not let United Nations (UN) teams look for weapons. The United Nations is an organization of nations that works for world peace and tries to stop wars between countries.

In 2001, U.S. President George W. Bush said that Iraq's president, Saddam Hussein (*sah DAHM hoo SAYN*), and his government were a threat to the Iraqi people, the United States, and other countries.

On March 20, 2003, a U.S.-led group, including the United Kingdom and Australia, attacked Iraq. The U.S.-led forces controlled most of Iraq by mid-April, after the fall of Hussein's government. Bush declared an end to major combat in Iraq on May 1.

After May 2003, U.S., Iraqi, and allied forces from many countries tried to protect and rebuild the country. However, Iraqi and foreign *militants* (people who engage in war for a cause or belief) carried out attacks against these forces. They also attacked people who were not soldiers.

In December 2003, Hussein was captured by U.S. troops. He was tried and sentenced to death by an Iraqi court in November 2006. Hussein was hanged in December 2006.

From March 2003 through August 2010, the U.S. government referred to the Iraq War as Operation Iraqi Freedom. Some people call it the Second Gulf War or Gulf War II because they see it as a continuation of the Persian Gulf War of 1991. The United States announced an end to combat in Iraq on Aug. 31, 2010. Some U.S. troops remained in Iraq until late 2011 to fight terrorism and perform other duties. In December 2011, the U.S. government declared an official end to the Iraq War.

Other articles to read: **Iraq; Persian Gulf War of 1991**

Ireland

Ireland is a small country in northwestern Europe. It lies on an island in the North Atlantic Ocean. The island is also called Ireland. Dublin is the country's capital and largest city.

Land. Ireland is known as the Emerald Isle because of its beautiful green countryside. Farmlands cover much of the central part of the country, and mountains rise near the coasts.

People. Most of the Irish people descend from peoples who settled in Ireland during the past 10,000 years. These peoples included Celts, Vikings, Normans, Scots, and English. Most of Ireland's people are Roman Catholic Christians. All the people speak English. Many also speak the ancient Irish language. Most of Ireland's people live in cities and large towns. Some live in brick or concrete houses, and others live in apartment buildings.

Potatoes have been an important food in Ireland for several hundred years. One of Ireland's most famous dishes is Irish stew, made with potatoes, onions, and beef or mutton, the meat of sheep.

Resources and products. Most of Ireland's workers have jobs that provide services to people. They work in schools, hospitals, restaurants, hotels, and other businesses. Factories in Ireland make beer, chemicals, clothing, computers, machines, medicines, paper, and processed foods.

Ireland and its neighbors

Ireland in brief

- **Capital:** Dublin.

- **Area:** 27,133 mi² (70,273 km²). *Greatest distances*—north-south, 289 mi (465 km); east-west, 177 mi (285 km). *Coastline*—1,738 mi (2,797 km).

- **Population:** *Current estimate*—5,081,000. *2016 census*—4,761,865.

- **Official languages:** Irish, English.

- **Chief products:** *Agriculture*—apples, barley, beef and dairy cattle, hogs, horses, mushrooms, oats, potatoes, poultry, sheep. *Fishing*—crab, haddock, herring, lobsters, mackerel, whiting. *Manufacturing*—alcoholic beverages, chemicals, computers, machinery, metal products, motor vehicles, paper and paper products, pharmaceuticals, processed foods, textiles, wood products.

- **Money:** *Basic unit*—euro. One hundred cents equal one euro. The Irish pound was taken out of circulation in 2002.

- **Form of government:** Republic.

- **Climate:** Mild and moist, moderated by warm currents from the Atlantic Ocean. Average temperatures are about 59 °F (15 °C) in summer and about 41 °F (5 °C) in winter. The heaviest precipitation is in the western mountains.

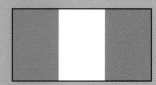

Flag

Ireland, continued

Ireland is called the Emerald Isle because of its lush, green landscape.

Most of Ireland's farmland is used as pasture for cattle and sheep. Farmers also grow barley and potatoes. The waters along Ireland's coasts are excellent fishing areas.

History. The first people to live in Ireland probably came to the island from the European mainland about 9,000 to 10,000 years ago. About 2,400 years ago, people called Celts came to Ireland from England and the European mainland. The Celts spread their religion, language, and knowledge in Ireland. The Celts also created beautiful artwork by carving patterns in stone. Saint Patrick was the most famous of the missionaries who brought Christianity to Ireland about 1,600 years ago.

Over the years, many other groups took control of all or part of Ireland. These groups included the Vikings, the Normans, and the English.

From 1845 to 1848, a plant disease killed Ireland's potatoes, the people's main food. About 1 million Irish people died of starvation or disease. More than 1 million others left Ireland. Many of these people moved to the United States and Canada to look for food and jobs.

In 1919, fighting broke out between Ireland's British rulers and Irish people who wanted the country to be free. In 1920, the British government divided Ireland into two parts. An area in the northeast corner of the island became known as Northern Ireland. Like the British, most of the people in Northern Ireland were Protestant Christians. Under a treaty signed in 1921, the rest of Ireland became the Irish Free State. In 1922 and 1923, supporters and opponents of the treaty fought in a civil war.

In 1949, Ireland cut its remaining ties to the United Kingdom. The country took the name Republic of Ireland. Many people in Ireland wanted Northern Ireland to join with Ireland again. But most of Northern Ireland's people wanted to remain a part of the United Kingdom.

For many years, a lack of jobs led Irish workers to find work in other countries. In the mid-1900's, Irish officials worked to bring new industries to Ireland. By the 1990's and 2000's, Ireland had a strong economy. Many people from Europe came to live in Ireland, and many Irish workers returned home.

Other articles to read: **Blarney Stone; Celts; Dublin; Northern Ireland; Saint Patrick's Day**

Iron and steel

Iron and steel are the cheapest and most useful metals in the world. They are used in thousands of products, from paper clips to cars.

Iron is one of the most common kinds of material in Earth's crust. It is found in minerals or rocks called ores (*ohrz*). People dig huge holes in the ground called mines to get the ores.

To make iron we can use, the ore is heated until it melts. The iron then separates from other materials in the ore.

Many products are made from iron. Steel is made from iron, too. To make steel, the iron is heated again and some materials are added. This produces liquid steel. The liquid steel is then formed into sheets, rods, and other shapes. These shapes are used to make many products.

Other articles to read: **Welding**

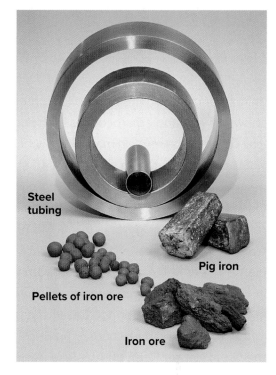

Steel tubing

Pig iron

Pellets of iron ore

Iron ore

Iron ore to steel

Irrigation

Irrigation is the watering of land. People bring water from lakes, rivers, streams, and wells to irrigate land that does not get enough rain.

In desert regions, farming would be impossible without irrigation. In areas where it is rainy part of the year but dry part of the year, irrigation allows farming to continue during the dry season. Even places with regular rainfall sometimes have a drought (*drowt*), or a long period without rain. Irrigation is needed to save the crops.

To irrigate, people must find ways to bring water to where it is needed. Most farms use a network of canals to carry water from streams, rivers, and lakes to ditches that take the water to the fields. Water from wells is often pumped to the surface. The pump in the well lifts the water into a ditch or pipe that carries it to the crops. The water used must be fresh, not salt water.

Irrigation water may be flooded over the surface of the field or sprayed over the field with sprinklers. It may be dripped onto the field through plastic tubes on the ground or soaked into the plant roots from underground pipes.

Sprinkler irrigation spreads water over a field.

Irwin, Steve

Steve Irwin (1962–2006) was an Australian wildlife expert. He hosted several popular TV shows about animals, including "The Crocodile Hunter." On his shows, Irwin handled crocodiles, poisonous snakes, and other dangerous animals with his bare hands.

Stephen Robert Irwin was born on Feb. 22, 1962, near Melbourne, Australia. He grew up in Beerwah, Queensland. There, he cared for the animals in a reptile park that his parents owned. In 1991, he took over the park and named it the Australia Zoo. Irwin married Terri Raines, an American-born wildlife expert, in 1992. They worked together to capture crocodiles and move them to safer *habitats* (living places).

Irwin was killed by a stingray on Sept. 4, 2006, in the Great Barrier Reef, off Australia. A stingray is a fish with a stinger on its tail. Irwin and a crew were filming a show. The stingray's stinger pierced his chest.

Other articles to read: **Crocodile**

Steve Irwin

Muslim pilgrims worship at a mosque at Mecca, the birthplace of Muhammad in Saudi Arabia.

Islam

Islam is one of the world's major religions. People who follow the faith of Islam are called Muslims. About half the world's Muslims live in South and Southeast Asia. Bangladesh, India, Indonesia, and Pakistan have the largest Muslim populations. About one-fifth of all Muslims live in the Middle East. There are many Muslims in parts of Europe and several million in the United States.

Islam was first preached by an Arab *prophet* (holy man) named Muhammad. In about A.D. 610, he began to receive messages from Allah (God). These messages were collected in the Qur'ān (also spelled *Koran*), the holy book of Islam. Muslims believe the Qur'ān contains God's actual words. Muhammad preached that there is only one God and that God wants people to make

The symbol of Islam is a crescent and a star.

Islam, meaning *submission,* to God.

Muhammad died in 632, but the new religion of Islam soon spread. By the mid-700's, Muslims had built an empire that stretched from the Atlantic Ocean to the borders of China. The symbol of Islam is a crescent, or a thin moon, and a star.

Muslims follow the Five Pillars of Islam: (1) saying they believe that there is no God but Allah, and that Muhammad is his messenger; (2) praying five times a day; (3) giving alms, such as money or gifts, to the poor; (4) fasting, or not eating or drinking, from sunrise to sunset every day during Ramadan, a holy month of the Islamic year; and (5) making a pilgrimage, or holy journey, to Mecca, the birthplace of Muhammad in Saudi Arabia, at least once during their life. The building where Muslims worship together is called a mosque (*mahsk*).

Other articles to read: **Mecca; Muhammad; Muslims; Qur'ān; Ramadan**

Island

An island (*EYE land*) is a piece of land that is surrounded by water. Islands are found in oceans, rivers, and lakes throughout the world.

Some islands cover an area smaller than a city block. A small island is called an islet (*EYE liht*). The largest island is Greenland, in the North Atlantic Ocean. Greenland is slightly larger than Mexico. The difference between an island and a continent is its size. Like an island, Australia is surrounded by water. But because of its huge size, Australia is called a continent rather than an island.

Some countries are islands, like Japan and the Philippines. Millions of people live on some islands; other islands have no people. Islands have served as stopping places for travelers in ships. This helped the spread of people, animals, and plants from one continent to another.

Some islands were formed hundreds of millions of years ago. But new ones are forming all the time. There are five main kinds of islands: (1) continental islands, (2) tectonically (*tehk TON ihk uh lee*) formed islands, (3) volcanic islands, (4) coral islands, and (5) barrier islands. Each kind is formed in a different way.

Some continental islands are pieces of land that were once part of a continent. Some of these islands became separated from the

Continental islands are pieces of land that once were connected to a continent.

Barrier islands are created from sand and soil that build up along a shoreline.

Coral islands are created by coral reefs. A reef may grow around a sinking volcano.

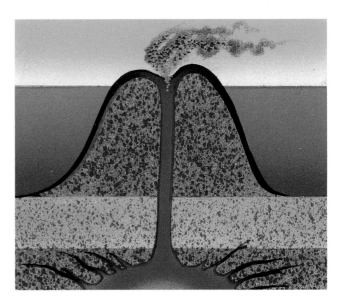

Volcanic islands are formed by volcanoes on the ocean floor.

continent when water covered the land between the continent and the island. Others became separated when their connection with the continent was worn away. Tectonically formed islands are created by movements of Earth's crust. This outer rocky part consists of huge plates that move very slowly. When one plate is pushed under another, the top plate may scrape off pieces of the bottom plate. Over millions of years, this material piles up to form an island. Volcanic islands are formed by volcanoes under the sea. Coral islands are created by coral reefs—limestone formations made by tiny creatures—that grow in a ring around a sinking volcanic island. Barrier islands are formed when winds and ocean waves pile up sand, dirt, and rocks into long, narrow islands along a seacoast.

Israel is a small country in southwestern Asia. It lies on a thin strip of land on the shore of the Mediterranean Sea. It is bordered by Egypt, Jordan, Syria, and Lebanon. Israel identifies Jerusalem as its capital. However, many foreign countries have their embassies in the city of Tel Aviv.

Land. Israel has four major land regions. The coastal plain is a thin strip of land along the Mediterranean Sea. Most of Israel's people live in this area. Most of the nation's factories and farms are here, too.

The Judeo-Galilean Highlands include a series of mountain ranges in northern and central Israel. The highlands include the area known as the West Bank. Galilee is home to most of Israel's Arabs. Jerusalem is located in the northern part of the Judean Hills.

The Rift Valley is a long, thin strip of land in eastern Israel. The area includes the Dead Sea, a saltwater lake. The shore of the Dead Sea is the lowest land area on Earth. The Jordan River flows through the Rift Valley.

East Jerusalem includes the Old City, which dates back to the time of the Bible.

Ancient olive grove in Galilee, Israel

The Negev Desert is a dry area of flatlands and mountains in southern Israel. Water from the Sea of Galilee is now being pumped to parts of the Negev. This allows farmers to grow some crops there.

People. Most of Israel's people are Jews. Some of Israel's Jewish people were born in Israel. Others have come from countries all around the world.

Most of the other people who live in Israel are Arabs. Generally, Israel's Jewish and Arab groups do not trust one another. They live in separate areas, go to separate schools, speak different languages, and follow different traditions.

Resources and products. Israel has few natural resources, but the people of Israel live well. Many people have come to Israel from other countries. They have started businesses that have helped the country. Also, other countries have given money to help Israel grow.

Most of Israel's people make their money in businesses that provide services. These businesses include banks, restaurants, and hotels.

Israel has many modern factories. The goods they produce include chemicals, computers, and food products.

History. Both the Jews and the Arabs trace their history back to Abraham, who settled in what is now Israel nearly 4,000 years ago. Over the centuries, many people have conquered and controlled Israel. About 3,000 years ago, the Kingdom of Israel reached its greatest strength under King David and his son King Solomon. After Solomon died, the kingdom divided into two parts—Israel in the north and Judah in the south. The word *Jew* came from the name Judah. During the next 1,000 years, the Jews were conquered by several empires.

In 63 B.C., the Roman Empire invaded Judah. The Romans eventually forced most Jews to leave the region. The Romans named the region Palestina, which became Palestine in English.

In the 600's, Muslim Arabs took over the area. From that time until the mid-1900's, most of the people in Palestine were Arabs.

In the late 1800's, many European Jews wanted to start a Jewish state in Palestine. Jews began arriving in Palestine in large numbers. By the early 1900's, fights started between the Jews and Arabs. In 1947, the United Nations (UN) decided to divide the area into an Arab state and a Jewish state. Israel was founded in 1948 as a homeland for Jews from all parts of the world. Ever since, there have been problems between Israel and Arab nations and *radical* (favoring extreme change) Islamic groups around Israel. While the two sides have worked for peace over the years, disagreements continue.

Other articles to read: **Gaza Strip; Jerusalem; Jews; Meir, Golda; West Bank**

Israel and its neighbors

Israel in brief

- **Capital:** Jerusalem.
- **Area:** 8,522 mi² (22,072 km²), not including 2,700 mi² (7,000 km²) of Arab territory occupied since 1967. *Greatest distances—*north-south, 260 mi (420 km); east-west, 70 mi (110 km). *Coastline—*170 mi (273 km).
- **Population:** *Current estimate—*9,521,000; *2020 official government estimate—*9,241,200. Population figures do not include people living in occupied Arab territories, except for Israeli citizens.
- **Official languages:** Hebrew.
- **Chief products:** *Agriculture—*beef and dairy cattle, poultry, tomatoes and other vegetables. *Manufacturing—*chemical products, communications products, computer products, finished diamonds, machinery, metal products, plastics, processed foods, textiles and clothing. *Mining—*bromine, copper, clay, gypsum, magnesium, phosphates, potash, salt.
- **Money:** *Basic unit—*new shekel. One hundred agorot equal one new shekel.
- **Form of government:** Democratic republic.
- **Climate:** Hot, dry summers; mild winters. Temperatures are cooler in higher areas. Rain falls mainly from November to March.

Flag

Italy is a country in southern Europe. It is bordered by Austria, France, Slovenia, and Switzerland. It is made up of a boot-shaped peninsula that extends into the Mediterranean Sea. A peninsula is a strip of land with water on three sides. Rome is the capital and largest city of Italy.

Land. Italy has two groups of mountains, the Alps and the Apennines. The Alps form Italy's northern border. The Apennines stretch almost all the way from the north to the south of Italy. Italy also has many valleys and plains. Most of Italy's people live in the Po River Valley in northern Italy. Sicily, the largest island in the Mediterranean Sea, lies off the southwest coast. Mount Etna, one of the largest active volcanoes in the world, is in Sicily.

People. Most Italian people live in apartment buildings. Some people live in single-family homes. Most people live with their parents until they get married. Grandparents often help care for children.

Village in the Dolomites mountain range in northeastern Italy

Italy and its neighbors

Italian people enjoy large meals with several courses or dishes. The first dish is often pasta or soup. The main course may be meat or fish. Pizza is a popular snack or light meal. Fruit is a popular dessert, and wine is often served with the meal.

Many Italians watch and play soccer. On weekends, the parks are filled with soccer teams. Basketball is also popular.

Resources and products. Since 1945, Italy has made most of its money from modern businesses such as automobile factories, banks, and airlines. Millions of tourists come to Italy, so restaurants and hotels are also important. In the past, farming was very important, and the grapes grown in the Po Valley are still important for making wine. Italy has earned more money since it joined the European Union, a group of European countries that trade and cooperate with one another.

History. About 2,500 years ago, the city of Rome started to grow in importance. The Romans built a great empire that ruled many

Italy in brief

- **Capital:** Rome.
- **Area:** 116,630 mi² (302,071 km²). *Greatest distances*—north-south, 708 mi (1,139 km); east-west, 320 mi (515 km).
- **Population:** *Current estimate*—60,172,000. *2019 official government estimate*—59,433,744.
- **Official language:** Italian.
- **Chief products:** *Agriculture*—apples, beef and dairy cattle, grapes, hogs, olives, tomatoes, wheat. *Manufacturing*—chemicals, clothing and shoes, foods and beverages, machinery, motor vehicles, textiles. *Mining*—cement, clay, copper, feldspar, pumice, natural gas.
- **Money:** *Basic unit*—euro. One hundred cents equal one euro. The Italian lira was taken out of circulation in 2002.
- **Form of government:** Parliamentary democracy.
- **Climate:** Central and southern Italy have hot summers—daytime high temperatures of about 86 degrees F (30 degrees C). Winters are mild, with daytime highs reaching about 54 degrees F (12 degrees C). Northern Italy is only slightly cooler than the rest of the country in summer. However, it is much cooler in winter—daytime highs of only about 41 degrees F (5 degrees C). The north receives adequate year-round moisture. Central and southern Italy have dry summers and moderate winter rainfall. In general, total precipitation decreases from north to south.

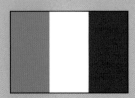

Flag

77

The Grand Canal of Venice, Italy

countries. About 1,500 years ago, groups from northern Europe began fighting the Romans. The last Roman emperor lost his power in the year 476.

For hundreds of years, various groups fought for control of Italy. Emperors from Germany ruled it part of the time. The popes, who headed the Roman Catholic Church, also ruled part of Italy.

After the year 1000, some Italian cities like Venice, Milan, and Florence became powerful and wealthy states. These city-states often fought wars with each other. During the time called the Renaissance—in the 1300's, 1400's, and 1500's—many wonderful artists lived and worked in these city-states. The Italian artists Leonardo da Vinci and Michelangelo were two of the world's greatest painters.

From the 1500's to 1800's, France, Spain, and Austria controlled most of Italy. In 1861, most of Italy was joined together under one Italian king.

In 1922, Benito Mussolini became the prime minister, or leader, of Italy. He became very powerful. By 1925, he completely controlled the country. He was a strong leader but sometimes cruel. Italy and Germany were partners during World War II (1939–1945). They lost the war. In 1945, Mussolini lost his power and was killed by a group of Italians. Soon after the war, Italy became a republic. Today the people of Italy vote to decide who their leaders will be.

Other articles to read: **Alps; Leaning Tower of Pisa; Leonardo da Vinci; Michelangelo; Mount Etna; Pompeii; Rome; Venice; Vesuvius**

Ivory

Ivory is a hard material that makes up the tusks and teeth of certain animals. The tusks of the African elephant are actually long, curved upper teeth. They are the most common source of ivory. Other ivory comes from the tusks of the walrus and the narwhal—a kind of whale—and from the teeth of the hippopotamus and the sperm whale.

Ivory has been carved into objects and works of art for thousands of years. It has also been used to make piano keys. It comes in different colors, from white to pale pink, yellow, or tan.

In 1989, all trade in ivory was banned. Too many elephants were being killed for their tusks. Today, some countries are allowed to sell small amounts of ivory.

A Japanese ivory netsuke was worn on a cord around the waist.

The tusks of elephants are the most common source of ivory.

Ivory has been carved into objects and works of art for thousands of years.

Jj

is the tenth letter of the alphabet for the English language.

Handwritten letters vary from person to person. *Manuscript* (printed) letters (above left) have simple curves and straight lines. Cursive letters (above right) have flowing lines.

The small letter j first appeared about 1200. It developed from the small i.

1200   Today

Special ways of expressing the letter J

Sign Language Alphabet   Braille   International Flag Code

Development of the letter J

The ancient Egyptians	The Semites	The Phoenicians	The Greeks	Medieval scribes
about 3000 B.C., drew this symbol of a hand.	about 1500 B.C., simplified the Egyptian symbol.	about 1000 B.C., changed the letter. They named it *yod,* their word for *hand.*	changed the Phoenician symbol about 600 B.C. They called the letter *iota.* This became the letter I.	sometimes added a tail to I. Over time, this became the letter J.

Jack the Ripper

Jack the Ripper was the name given to an unknown murderer in London in 1888. From August 31 to November 9, he killed five women and cut their bodies into pieces.

At first, the killer was called the Whitechapel murderer. Whitechapel is the district in London where some of the crimes took place. Newspapers followed the crimes and the police investigations closely, capturing public interest. The police received many letters from people claiming to be the killer, including some signed *Jack the Ripper.* Most of these letters were written by attention-seeking people and journalists, but the name Jack the Ripper caught on.

Interest in Jack the Ripper grew over time—partly because of the cruelty of the crimes and partly because the crimes were never solved. Many books have been written about the murders. Also, several motion pictures have been made about the story.

Jackal

Jackal is a wild dog that lives in Asia, Africa, and southeastern Europe. Arabs call it "the howler" because of its mournful cry, usually heard at night.

Jackals are chiefly scavengers that eat animals they find dead. For this reason, they are important as "street cleaners" in some Asian and African cities.

The *common jackal* looks more like a fox than a dog. It is about 14 inches (36 centimeters) high at the shoulder, and 2 to 2 ½ feet (61 to 76 centimeters) long. It has a grayish-yellow or brown coat, and a bushy tail about 8 inches (20 centimeters) long.

The *black-backed jackal* of Africa is prized for its fur, which is more attractive than that of the common jackal. Jackals have a musky smell. Because of this, they do not make good pets.

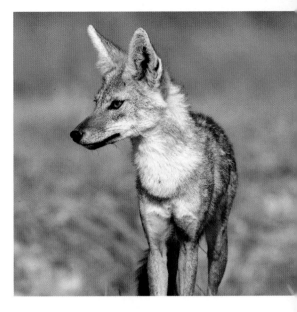

The jackal is a member of the dog family. It feeds mainly on dead animals.

Jackson, Andrew

Andrew Jackson (1767–1845) became the seventh president of the United States in 1829. He served from 1829 to 1837. He was the first U.S. president born in a log cabin.

Andrew Jackson was born on March 15, 1767, along the border between North and South Carolina. His family was poor. His father died before he was born, and his mother died when he was 14 years old.

Jackson became a lawyer in 1787. He worked as a government lawyer in Tennessee and served in the volunteer army. In the War of 1812, he helped the city of New Orleans, Louisiana, fight the British. The British were defeated.

In 1824, Jackson wanted to be the Democratic-Republican Party's candidate for president. But his party chose John Quincy Adams. In 1828, Jackson ran for president and won. As president, he got rid of the Bank of the United States, even though the bank had supporters in Congress. Jackson thought the bank was not handling the nation's money properly.

In 1832, Jackson ran for president again. He won easily. He was the only president to see the national debt paid off.

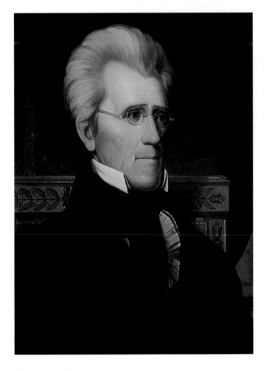

Andrew Jackson

Several states wanted to take over lands that belonged to Native American groups. Jackson would not stop the states, and Congress passed a law ordering the Native Americans to move. Thousands of Native Americans had to leave their homes and move west. Many died on the way.

After his second term, Jackson returned to Tennessee. He remained interested in politics until he died.

Other articles to read: **Trail of Tears**

Jesse Jackson

Jackson, Jesse Louis

Jesse Louis Jackson (1941–   ) is an African American civil rights *activist* and political leader. An activist is someone who fights for a cause. Jackson is also a Baptist minister. In 1989, he was awarded the Spingarn Medal for his achievements in civil rights and politics.

Jackson was born on Oct. 8, 1941, in Greenville, South Carolina. He graduated from North Carolina Agricultural and Technical State University. Much later, in 2000, Jackson received a Master of Divinity degree from the Chicago Theological Seminary.

From 1966 to 1971, Jackson directed Operation Breadbasket, the economic arm of the Southern Christian Leadership Conference. He persuaded many companies owned by white people to hire Black employees and sell products made by Black-owned businesses. In 1971, Jackson founded People United to Save Humanity (PUSH). This organization worked to increase African Americans' economic power. In 1984, Jackson founded the Rainbow Coalition. It aimed to gain political power for Black people and others. The two organizations merged in 1996.

Jackson Five

The Jackson Five were five brothers who became one of the most famous American popular music groups. The Jackson Five, later known as the Jacksons, performed together from the mid-1960's to the early 1990's. The Jackson brothers were born in Gary, Indiana. The Jackson Five were Jackie (Sigmund Esco, 1951–   ); Tito (Toriano Adaryll, 1953–   ); Jermaine (1954–   ); Marlon (1957–   ); and Michael (1958–2009). In 1964, the three older brothers performed as the Jackson Brothers, with Jermaine as lead singer. In addition to singing, Jermaine played rhythm guitar and bass, and Tito played lead guitar. Michael and Marlon later joined the group as singers and percussionists. Michael became the group's lead singer and dancer.

The group became a sensation with the string of hits "I Want You Back" (1969) and "ABC," "I'll Be There," and "The Love You Save" (all 1970). The Jackson Five later had hits with "Never Can Say Goodbye" and "Mama's Pearl" (both 1971) and "Dancing Machine" (1974). In 1976, the Jacksons' youngest brother, Randy (Steven Randall, 1961–), replaced Jermaine. In addition to singing, Randy played a number of instruments. The group then began performing as the Jacksons. The Jacksons' hits included "Enjoy Yourself" (1976), "Shake Your Body (Down to the Ground)" (1978), and "Lovely One" (1980).

Michael Jackson went on to become an international superstar as a solo artist. He died in 2009. The Jackson Five was inducted into the Rock and Roll Hall of Fame in 1997.

Jackson Five

Jade

Jade (*jayd*) is a valuable stone with beautiful colors. It is known for its strength and hardness. The Chinese have used jade for fine carvings and jewelry for more than 3,000 years.

Today, most jade comes from New Zealand. However, a rare and valuable kind of jade is found in Burma, Japan, and California. Jade is usually white or green, but it can be dark green, yellow, red, gray, or black. One rare type of jade is clear, like glass.

Two minerals, jadeite and nephrite, have been called jade. Both minerals are made of very fine needles. These needles are woven tightly together. That is what makes jade good for carving. It can be cut thin and carved with delicate patterns. Today, most jade is carved in China.

Jade elephant

Jaguar

Jaguar

Jaguars (*JAG wahrz*) are the largest, strongest wild cats of North and South America. They live in the Southwestern United States, Mexico, and Central and South America.

Jaguars live in forests, grasslands, and shrubby areas. They hunt many kinds of animals, including deer, fish, turtles, and wild pigs. Jaguars grow up to 8 ½ feet (2.6 meters) long, including the tail. Their fur is golden or brownish-yellow with many spots.

Female jaguars have two to four young, which each weigh about 2 pounds (0.9 kilograms) at birth. They hunt with their mother for two years.

In some areas, very few jaguars are left. Selling jaguars or their skins is against the law in the United States.

Jail. See Prison.

Jakarta

Jakarta

Jakarta (*juh KAHR tuh*) is the capital city of Indonesia, a country in Southeast Asia. Jakarta is also Indonesia's main business center and its largest city. More than 9 million people live there.

Near the center of Jakarta is Medan Merdeka, or Freedom Square. Around it are many modern hotels, offices, and government buildings. Visitors to the national museum can see many ancient Indonesian treasures. Jakarta has a large art center that features art, music, theater, puppet plays, and a planetarium. Jakarta also has a large sports stadium.

People have lived in what is now Jakarta for more than 1,500 years. The Dutch took control of the area in 1619. They named the city Batavia. From 1942 to 1945, during World War II (1939–1945), Japanese forces took over Indonesia. After the war, some Indonesians declared independence in 1945. At first, the Dutch tried to regain control, but then the Netherlands recognized Indonesia's independence in 1949. The name Batavia was changed to Jakarta

Jamaica (*juh MAY kuh*) is a small island nation in the Caribbean Sea, south of Cuba. It is the third largest island in the Caribbean Sea. Kingston is the capital and largest city of Jamaica.

Many people visit Jamaica each year. They come for the island's pleasant weather and beautiful beaches and mountains.

Jamaica is part of a group of islands called the Greater Antilles. The island has three land regions: coastal plains, central hills and highlands, and eastern mountains.

Most of Jamaica's people have a Black African or mixed Black African and European (Afro-European) background. Other groups in the country include Chinese, Indians, Europeans, and Syrians. English is the official language. However, many of the people speak their own form of English. It is different from the English spoken by Americans and English people.

Many of Jamaica's people work on farms. Sugar is the most important crop. Jamaica is among the world's leading producers of bauxite. Bauxite is the material from which aluminum is made. Much of Jamaica's money comes from the many people who visit each year.

Indigenous (native) Arawak people lived in Jamaica when Christopher Columbus arrived there in 1494. The Spaniards controlled Jamaica until the mid-1600's, when the British took over. Jamaica became independent in 1962.

Other articles to read: **Caribbean Sea**

Jamaica and its neighbors

Flag

Jamaica in brief

- **Capital:** Kingston.

- **Area:** 4,244 mi² (10,991 km²). *Greatest distances*—east-west, 146 mi (235 km); north-south, 51 mi (82 km).

- **Population:** *Current estimate*—2,827,000; *2019 official government estimate*—2,734,092.

- **Official language:** English.

- **Chief products:** *Agriculture*—bananas, chickens, citrus fruits, coconuts, coffee, goats, sugar cane, yams. *Manufacturing and processing*—alumina, cement, chemicals, petroleum products, rum, sugar. *Mining*—bauxite, gypsum.

- **Money:** *Basic unit*—Jamaican dollar. One hundred cents equals one dollar.

- **Form of government:** Constitutional parliamentary democracy.

- **Climate:** Hot and wet.

United States

Atlantic Ocean

Gulf of Mexico

Bahamas

Cuba

Mexico

Dominican Rep.

JAMAICA

Haiti

Honduras

Caribbean Sea

Nicaragua

Panama

Venezuela

SOUTH AMERICA

Jamestown

Jamestown was the first permanent English settlement in North America. In May 1607, colonists from England set up a fort and town in what is now southeastern Virginia. The area they settled in was ruled by a powerful Native American chief named Powhatan. The colonists named the settlement Jamestown in honor of King James I of England. Jamestown's lawmaking body, the House of Burgesses, was formed in 1619. It was the first *representative legislature* (group of elected lawmakers) in colonial America.

The first year, disease, attacks from Native American groups, and starvation killed more than half of Jamestown's settlers. More settlers arrived from England in 1608 and 1610. From 1609 to 1614, and in 1622, Native American groups and the settlers fought many battles. The expansion of the tobacco trade helped the colony grow through most of the 1600's. In 1676, the town burned to the ground during a revolt against Virginia's governor.

Other articles to read: **Powhatan; Smith, John; Virginia**

Jamestown in Virginia

Japan is an island country in the North Pacific Ocean. It lies off the east coast of Asia, across from Russia, Korea, and China. Four large islands and thousands of smaller ones make up Japan. Tokyo is Japan's capital and largest city.

Land. Japan is a land of great beauty. Mountains and hills cover most of the country. The Japanese islands are made up of the rugged upper part of a great mountain range that rises from the floor of the North Pacific Ocean.

Japan suffers from many earthquakes. The Japanese islands have about 1,500 earthquakes a year. Most of them are small, but severe earthquakes strike Japan every few years. Undersea quakes sometimes cause huge waves, called tsunami (*tsoo NAH mee*), along the coast of the Pacific Ocean. These waves can cause great damage. The Japanese islands also have more than 60 volcanoes that could erupt at any time.

The four main islands, from largest to smallest, are Honshu, Hokkaido, Kyushu, and Shikoku. Thousands of smaller islands lie near these islands. Japan's land also includes the Ryukyu and Bonin island chains.

Honshu is Japan's largest island. Most of the Japanese people live on this island. Japan's tallest and most famous peak, Mount Fuji, or

Tokyo, Japan

Japan in brief

- ■ **Capital:** Tokyo.

- ■ **Area:** 145,937 mi² (377,974 km²). The four main islands—Hokkaido, Honshu, Kyushu, Shikoku—stretch about 1,200 mi. (1,900 km) from northeast to southwest. *Coastline*—5,857 mi. (9,426 km).

- ■ **Population:** *Current estimate*—125,291,000. *2015 census*—127,100,047.

- ■ **Official language:** Japanese.

- ■ **Chief products:** *Agriculture*—apples, cabbage, cattle, hogs, milk, onions, potatoes, poultry and eggs, rice, sugar beets, tomatoes. *Fishing*—anchovies, crabs, mackerel, oysters, pollock, salmon, sardines, squid, tuna. *Manufacturing*—automobiles, ceramics, chemicals, clothing, computers, electronic products, machinery, plastics, processed foods, steel, textiles, watches. *Mining*—coal, gold, silver.

- ■ **Money:** *Basic unit*—yen.

- ■ **Form of government:** Parliamentary democracy with ceremonial emperor.

- ■ **Climate:** Central and southern Japan have hot summers, mild winters, and moderate precipitation in all seasons. Daytime high temperatures average about 86 °F (30 °C) in the hottest month, August, and about 46 °F (8 °C) in January, the coldest month. Hokkaido, northern Honshu, and high mountain areas are much colder than the rest of the country in winter and cooler in summer.

Flag

Fujiyama, rises on Honshu. It is a volcano, but it is no longer active, which means it does not erupt.

Hokkaido is Japan's second largest island. Many of the people of Hokkaido work in dairy farming, fishing, and forestry. Many people visit the island for fun and relaxation.

Kyushu is the southernmost of Japan's main islands. After Honshu, Kyushu has the most people. Parts of Kyushu have many volcanoes.

Shikoku is the smallest of the main Japanese islands. Most of the people of this island live in the north. Farmers grow rice and different kinds of fruits along the Inland Sea there.

The Ryukyu and Bonin islands belonged to Japan until after World War II (1939–1945), when the United States took control of them. The United States has since returned the islands to Japan.

People. Japan has one of the largest populations in the world. The Japanese people come from groups of people who came to the islands from other parts of Asia. No one knows for sure when people first arrived in Japan, but it was more than 30,000 years ago. Some historians think that a group of people in Japan called the Ainu may

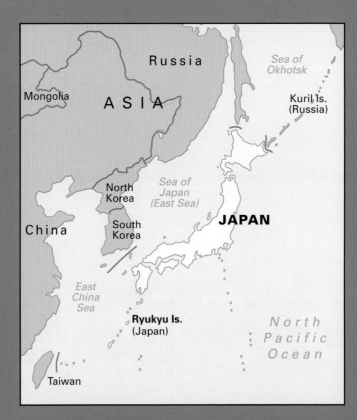

Japan and its neighbors

come from the original settlers of the Japanese islands. Today most Ainu live on Hokkaido. Some Chinese and Koreans also live in Japan.

Resources and products. Japan is one of the world's richest countries, even though it has few natural resources. Japan earns most of its money from the many things it makes and sells. The Japanese make such things

Hozu River in Kyoto, Japan

as cars, computers, food products, steel, and TV sets. Japan buys many of the materials needed to make these products from other countries. Then, its factories make the products and sell them to other countries.

Building is also a big business in Japan. This business grew quickly after World War II, when so much rebuilding was needed. Many of Japan's cities were destroyed during the war. Today, Japanese companies build hotels and office buildings throughout the world.

Throughout most of Japan's history, farming was its main business. But since the 1950's, Japan has become one of the most important manufacturing and fishing nations in the world.

History. The early people of Japan borrowed many Chinese ideas about how to organize society and government. More than 1,000 years ago, warriors called samurai (*SAM uh ry*) became important in Japan. The head of the government was the emperor. But from the 1100's to the mid-1800's, real power was in the hands of a military leader called the shogun (*SHO guhn*).

During the mid-1500's, the first Europeans arrived in Japan. Trade began with several European countries. During the early 1600's, however, the rulers of Japan decided to cut the country off almost entirely from the rest of the world. This lasted until 1853, when Commodore Matthew C. Perry of the United States sailed his warships into Tokyo Bay. A few years later, Japan agreed to trade with the United States.

During the 1870's, the Japanese government began to work toward making the country more modern. By the early 1900's, Japan had become a great business leader and military power.

During the 1930's, Japan's military leaders gained control of the government. On December 7, 1941, Japan attacked the United States at Pearl Harbor in Hawaii. This brought the United States into World War II (1939–1945). In August 1945, the United States dropped the first atomic bomb ever used in a war on the Japanese city of Hiroshima. It dropped an atomic bomb on Nagasaki two days later. On September 2, 1945, Japan gave up, and World War II ended.

After World War II, other countries controlled Japan. The Japanese people worked hard to reconstruct the cities and businesses that had been destroyed in the war. By the 1970's, Japan had become a prosperous and successful nation.

Japan's strong recovery led to economic troubles in the 1980's and 1990's. Manufacturers suffered as their products became too expensive to compete with those of developing nations. Banks lost money on loans as real estate values fell. Japan's economic problems continued in the early 2000's.

In March 2011, a powerful earthquake struck off the coast of Honshu. It was followed by a *tsunami* (series of powerful ocean waves). More than 15,800 people died in the disaster. Water from the tsunami damaged a nuclear power plant, causing dangerous amounts of radioactivity to be released over the surrounding area.

Other articles to read: **Kyoto; Mount Fuji; Osaka; Shinto; Tokyo**

Mount Fuji

Jazz

Jazz is a kind of music that began in the United States in the late 1800's. The music grew from a mixture of different kinds of music, including Black American music and African rhythms.

Jazz musicians often make up music as they play it. Musicians call this improvisation (*ihm pruh vy ZAY shuhn*). Improvisation is part of what makes jazz different from other kinds of music. It makes the person who plays the music the person who creates it. Another important part of jazz is called syncopation (*sihng kuh PAY shuhn*). In syncopation, the musical patterns are uneven and the musical notes are accented, or stressed, in unusual places.

Jazz at Lincoln Center All-Stars Orchestra

Instruments

Jazz may be performed by a single musician or by a small group of musicians called a combo. Sometimes it is performed by a band of 10 or more musicians. Many instruments are used to play jazz. Brass instruments used to play jazz include the trumpet and the slide trombone. Reed instruments include the clarinet and saxophone. Other instruments include the piano, drums, and bass. Guitar is also used in some types of jazz.

History of jazz

The earliest jazz was performed by African Americans who had not gone to music school. They listened to ragtime, a type of music that has great energy and syncopation. They also listened to the blues, a sad kind of music with much repetition. They listened to band music played at African American funerals and in parades. And they knew many folk songs and pieces of dance music. From all these types of music, jazz was born. Jazz probably started in New Orleans in the early 1900's. Today, this style of jazz music is called Dixieland Jazz.

Jazz saxophonist Charlie Parker (center), trumpeter Miles Davis, and bassist Tommy Potter perform in 1947.

Jelly Roll Morton was the first important jazz pianist and the first great jazz composer.

Wynton Marsalis is a leading jazz trumpeter and composer. He is shown here performing with his brothers saxophonist Branford, trombonist Delfeayo, and drummer Jason.

In time, other types of jazz came about. The 1920's is often called the golden age of jazz or the jazz age. Jazz spread from New Orleans to other cities, such as Memphis, St. Louis, Kansas City, Chicago, Detroit, and New York City. It began to be played on the radio. Jazz stayed popular after this golden age. In the 1930's, big bands formed with both Black and white musicians. Jazz singers sang popular songs. Many ordinary people, both Black and white, enjoyed the bands and the singers and danced to the music.

Swing jazz was popular with the big bands of the 1930's. It had its own special rhythm. The name "swing" came from the song "It Don't Mean a Thing If It Ain't Got That Swing," which was recorded in 1932 by Duke Ellington.

In the 1940's, bebop was a new jazz style. It was a difficult style, and the musicians who played it had great skill. Each phrase, or part, of the music had many notes and many surprises. Cool jazz, popular in the 1940's and 1950's, had a soft sound. Hard bop, in the 1950's, added blues music and church music to jazz.

In the 1970's, fusion jazz became popular. It combined jazz with rock music. Some jazz musicians used electronic instruments, and some even used computers to create new sounds.

Today, many styles of jazz are popular. Many musicians play swing and bebop. Others play fusion jazz. Electronic technology is also being used more in jazz music today.

Other articles to read: **Armstrong, Louis; Blues; Brass instruments; Ellington, Duke; Fitzgerald, Ella; Guitar; Piano**

Jefferson, Thomas

Thomas Jefferson (1743–1826) served as the third president of the United States from 1801 to 1809. Before becoming president, Jefferson was vice president to John Adams and held many other government offices, including governor of Virginia. He is best remembered for writing the Declaration of Independence in 1776. The Declaration of Independence announced that the 13 American colonies were free from British control.

Jefferson had many interests and great talents. He designed buildings, including his own home, called Monticello. He loved art, music, and reading. In addition, he was an inventor. He invented a plow, a lap desk, and a machine that could figure out codes.

He thought and wrote about politics and government. He believed that most people could govern, or rule, themselves without much government control. He also believed in freedom of religion and freedom of speech, including ideas printed in newspapers.

During Jefferson's time as president, he almost doubled the size of the United States. He did this in 1803 with the Louisiana Purchase. He agreed to buy a huge area of land from France. That land was called the Louisiana Territory. It stretched from the Mississippi River to the Rocky Mountains.

After he left the presidency, Jefferson continued to work for the American people. He advised the presidents who followed him, James Madison and James Monroe. He also started the University of Virginia. He was proud of this school, saying that it was based on the "freedom of the human mind to explore."

Other articles to read: **Declaration of Independence; Louisiana Purchase**

Thomas Jefferson

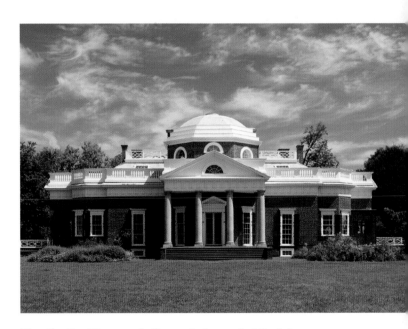

Monticello, Thomas Jefferson's home in Virginia

Jellyfish

Jellyfish

Jellyfish are sea animals. They are filled with a jellylike material that helps them hold their shape and float. Some kinds of jellyfish are as small as a pea. Others are as much as 7 feet (2.1 meters) across.

The body of a jellyfish is umbrella-shaped. A tube with a mouth and four short arms hangs down underneath it. Long tentacles dangle around the edges of the body. The tentacles have stinging cells.

Jellyfish swim by opening the body like an umbrella and then quickly shutting it. This movement squeezes out water and makes them shoot upward. When they stop moving, they sink slowly. As they sink, they catch small animals, sting them, and swallow them.

Some jellyfish are very dangerous. Their sting can be painful or even poisonous to people.

Jemison, Mae Carol

Mae Carol Jemison (1956–) is an American engineer and doctor who became an astronaut. She was the first African American woman to travel in space.

Jemison was born in Decatur, Alabama. She grew up in Chicago and studied engineering at Stanford University. She then received a degree in medicine from Cornell University. For two years, she worked for the Peace Corps in Africa.

Jemison joined the National Aeronautics and Space Administration's (NASA's) astronaut corps in 1987. In September 1992, Jemison flew on the space shuttle Endeavour. She spent eight days in space. While on the Endeavour, she performed many scientific experiments.

Jemison left the space program in March 1993. She went to work on other projects, including the improvement of health care in western Africa and advancing technology in developing countries. She is also a strong supporter of STEM education. STEM stands for *S*cience, *T*echnology, *E*ngineering, and *M*athematics. In 2011, Jemison helped found 100 Year Starship. The goal of the 100 Year Starship is for humans to travel beyond our solar system.

Mae Carol Jemison

Jerusalem

East Jerusalem includes the Old City, which dates back to the time of the Bible.

Jerusalem is a historic city that has long been a spiritual center to Jews, Christians, and Muslims. It is the largest city in Israel. People have lived in Jerusalem for thousands of years. Israel identifies Jerusalem as its capital. However, many foreign countries have their embassies in Tel Aviv, Israel's next largest city.

In 1948, Jerusalem was divided between Israel and Jordan. Jordan is a neighboring country of Israel. Israel held West Jerusalem. Jordan controlled East Jerusalem. Israel captured East Jerusalem in the Arab-Israeli war of 1967 and gave its people the same rights as other Israelis. West Jerusalem is the modern part of the city. East Jerusalem includes the walled Old City, a part of the city that dates back to the times of the Bible.

Today, most of Jerusalem's people are Jews. The rest are Muslims and Christians. Jerusalem is a city of three Sabbaths—Friday for Muslims, Saturday for Jews, and Sunday for Christians. The Sabbath is the day of the week on which the faithful rest from work and gather for worship. Businesses in Jerusalem may be closed on any of these days.

Other articles to read: **Israel; Jews**

Jesus Christ

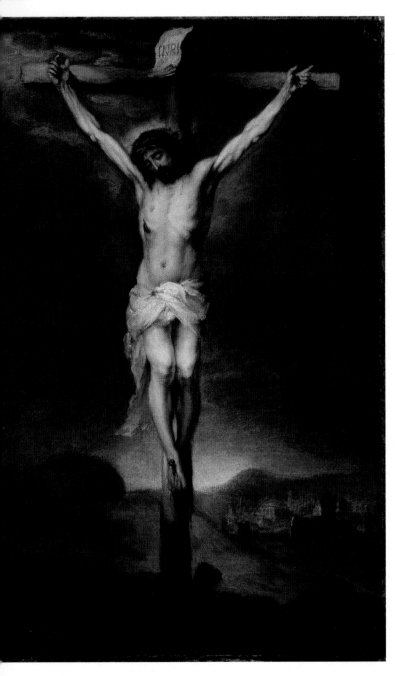

The Crucifixion of Jesus Christ

Jesus Christ was one of the world's greatest religious leaders. The Christian religion was founded on His life and teachings. Most Christians believe that He is the Son of God sent to Earth to save all people. Even many people who are not Christians believe that He was a great and wise teacher.

Four books of the New Testament tell almost all we know of Jesus. These are the Gospels of Matthew, Mark, Luke, and John. Jesus was born in Bethlehem, a small town in Judea, a small country in southern Palestine in ancient times.

No one is sure exactly when Jesus was born, but it was probably no later than 4 B.C. The day of Jesus's birth was first celebrated on December 25 in the early 300's. Mary was the mother of Jesus. Joseph was Mary's husband. Jesus was raised in Nazareth, a town in Galilee, the northernmost part of Palestine in Roman times.

Jesus's mission, or work on Earth, was to tell the world that the Kingdom of God was coming. The "Kingdom of God" meant that God was going to change the way of life on Earth.

Jesus's announcement was good news for many people. But rulers and religious leaders were unhappy with Him. They were afraid of Him. They captured Him and took Him to Pontius Pilate, the Roman governor of Judea. Pilate sentenced Jesus to die by being nailed to a cross.

According to the Bible, Jesus arose from His grave shortly after His death. He then stayed on Earth during the next 40 days and taught His followers. Then He rose into heaven.

Other articles to read: **Christianity; Christmas; Easter**

Jews

Jews are people who came from an ancient people called the Hebrews. The Hebrews were founded by a shepherd named Abraham, who lived between 3,500 and 3,800 years ago. Abraham settled in what is now Israel, where he established the Hebrews. Over a period of hundreds of years, Jews moved to different places throughout the world.

The Jews have been important people in world history. They made the Hebrew Bible. The Hebrew Bible, with its belief in one God, became an important part of three world religions—Judaism, Christianity, and Islam.

Jewish history has been full of sad events. The Jews made up a very small group almost everywhere they went to live, and they often were treated cruelly. In Europe, during World War II (1939–1945), about 6 million Jews were killed in the Holocaust. The Holocaust was the planned murder of Jewish people by the German government of that time, which was known as the Nazi government.

Three generations of a Jewish family read from the Torah, the oldest part of the Bible.

Beginning in the late 1800's, many Jews from Eastern Europe moved to Israel. At that time, Israel was called Palestine. Many more Jews came to Palestine after the Holocaust. The nation of Israel was founded in 1948.

There are about 15 million Jews in the world today. The United States is home to the largest number of Jews. About 6.5 million Jews live in the United States. About 6 million Jews live in Israel. Other countries with large numbers of Jews include Argentina, Canada, France, Russia, and the United Kingdom.

Other articles to read: **Abraham; Hanukkah; Holocaust; Israel; Judaism; Passover; Pentateuch; Rosh Ha-Shanah; Yom Kippur**

Saint Joan of Arc

Joan of Arc, Saint

Saint Joan of Arc (1412?–1431) was a French national hero. She became a saint of the Roman Catholic Church. She was a peasant girl who helped rescue France from defeat against England in the Hundred Years' War, which was fought from 1337 to 1453.

Joan of Arc, or Jeanne d'Arc (*zhahn dahrk*), was born at Domrémy in France. By the time she was 13, she had seen religious visions and heard strange voices. Joan believed these voices came from saints. The voices said God had chosen her to help King Charles VII of France force the English out of France.

When Joan was 17, she went to see the king. Charles gave her soldiers to command. In April 1429, she set out to rescue the city of Orléans from the English. In 10 days, her soldiers saved the city.

Charles had never been crowned king. Joan led Charles and his followers safely to Reims, France, where Charles was crowned on July 17, 1429.

Charles allowed Joan to try to free Paris. In May 1430, she was captured by French people called

Burgundians, who supported the English. The Burgundians handed her over to the English for a large amount of money. She was tried for witchcraft and for not believing in the accepted religion. Joan said that the voices she heard had come from God, and she would not change her mind. She was sentenced to death.

Joan was tied to a wooden post and burned to death in Rouen, France on May 30, 1431. In 1455, her family asked for a new trial. In 1456, the pope said she was innocent. Joan of Arc was made a saint in 1920. May 30 is her feast day.

Job. See Careers.

Jobs, Steve

Steve Jobs (1955–2011) was the cofounder of Apple Inc. (originally Apple Computer, Inc.). He also was one of two men who started the company. Apple makes personal computers and also develops and publishes computer software. Under his leadership, Apple introduced the iMac computer and iPod music player.

Steven Paul Jobs was born in Los Altos, California, on Feb. 24, 1955. Paul and Clara Jobs of Mountain View, California, adopted Steve that same year. While in high school, Jobs took a summer job at a company where he met Stephen Wozniak, an engineer. In 1975, Jobs and Wozniak started Apple Computer. In 1984, Apple introduced the popular Macintosh personal computer. In the late 1990's and early 2000's, Jobs oversaw the development of many popular Apple devices. These included the iMac, the iPod, and the iPad tablet computer. Jobs died on Oct. 5, 2011.

Steve Jobs

Johannesburg, South Africa

Johannesburg

Johannesburg (*joh HAN ihs BURG*) is the largest city in South Africa. It is also the most important business center in Africa south of the Sahara.

Johannesburg is in the northeastern part of South Africa. It stands on the world's richest gold field. Gold mining is an important industry in Johannesburg, though not as important as it used to be. Today, there are many kinds of businesses in the city.

Johannesburg was founded in 1886. The city has a stock exchange and two universities. It also has several art galleries and museums.

Andrew Johnson

Johnson, Andrew

Andrew Johnson (1808–1875) became the seventeenth president of the United States in 1865, after President Abraham Lincoln was shot.

Johnson was born in Raleigh, North Carolina, on December 29, 1808. He became a tailor and settled in Greeneville, Tennessee. His wife taught him to write and do arithmetic. He built a good business, became the mayor, and was elected to the state government in 1835. He was elected to Congress in 1843.

Abraham Lincoln was elected president in 1860. In 1861, the American Civil War (1861–1865) began. The Southern States seceded (*seh SEED uhd*) from, or left, the nation.

Lincoln was elected again in 1864, with Johnson as his vice president. On April 14, 1865, only five days after the war ended, President Lincoln was shot. Lincoln died the next day, and Johnson became president.

When the war ended, Congress could not agree on how to treat the Southern States. Some felt the South should be treated harshly. Johnson did not agree. Soon Congress and Johnson were fighting over laws that Congress passed. On February 24, 1868, the United States House of Representatives voted to impeach (*ihm PEECH*) Johnson, or accuse him of crimes. The trial was held in the Senate. A two-thirds vote was needed to find him guilty. He was found not guilty by one vote.

After the trial, Johnson finished his term and went back to Tennessee. In 1875, he was elected to the U.S. Senate. Many senators welcomed him back. He died a few months later.

Johnson, Lyndon Baines

Lyndon Baines Johnson (1908–1973) became the 36th president of the United States in 1963 after President John F. Kennedy was murdered.

Lyndon Johnson was born on August 27, 1908, near Stonewall, Texas. He became a high school teacher. In 1931, he worked to get Richard Kleberg, a local Democrat, elected to Congress. Kleberg won and took Johnson to Washington, D.C., as his secretary.

Johnson ran for Congress in 1937 and won. During World War II (1939–1945), he served in the U.S. Navy. After the war, he returned to Congress.

Johnson was skillful at getting laws passed and soon became a Democratic leader. In 1960, John F. Kennedy was elected president and Johnson became vice president.

On November 22, 1963, President Kennedy was shot in Dallas, Texas. Johnson became president when Kennedy died. In 1964, Johnson ran for president and won.

Johnson asked people to work toward the Great Society. He wanted to improve education, help poor people, and help the cities. But the Vietnam War, which

President Lyndon B. Johnson in the Oval Office at the White House

began in 1957 and involved U.S. troops, was getting worse. Some people felt U.S. soldiers should leave Vietnam. Others felt the United States should send more troops to end the war.

In March 1968, Johnson said he would not run for president again. Richard M. Nixon, a Republican, was elected in November. After Nixon took office, Johnson retired to his ranch in Texas.

Johnson is sworn in as president of the United States aboard Air Force One in Dallas, Texas. Jacqueline Kennedy, the widow of President John F. Kennedy, is at right in the photograph.

Johnson, Magic

Earvin "Magic" Johnson (1959–   ) is one of the greatest players in basketball history. He played guard for the Los Angeles Lakers of the National Basketball Association (NBA).

Earvin Johnson, Jr., was born in Lansing, Michigan. He went to Michigan State University. In 1979, his team won the National Collegiate Athletic Association (NCAA) tournament, the national college championship.

Johnson joined the Lakers in 1979. He helped that team win five NBA championships, and he won the Most Valuable Player award three times.

In the 1991–1992 season, Johnson learned that he had HIV, the virus that causes AIDS. He retired from basketball. However, he played on the United States "Dream Team" in the 1992 Summer Olympics. The team won a gold medal. Johnson returned to the Lakers for a short time in 1996. In 2012, Johnson became a part owner of the Los Angeles Dodgers major league baseball team. In 2017 to 2019, Johnson was the Lakers' president of basketball operations.

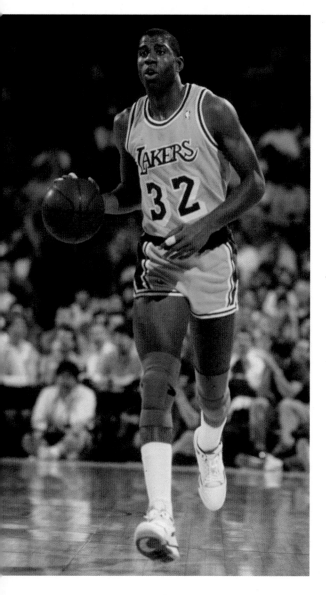

Magic Johnson

Jones, John Paul

John Paul Jones (1747–1792) is often called the *Father of the American Navy.* When the British asked him to surrender in battle, he replied, "I have not yet begun to fight."

Jones was born in Scotland. His name was John Paul. He went to sea when he was 12 years old. In 1769, he was put in charge of a ship. A few years later, he was accused of killing one of his crew. He fled to America and added Jones to his name.

When the American Revolution started in 1775, Jones went back to sea. He commanded many ships. In one attack, his ship was so close to a British ship that their guns touched. The sailors on the two ships fought hand to hand. After three hours, the British surrendered.

A few years after the war ended, Jones served in the Russian navy. In 1789, he moved to Paris.

John Paul Jones

Joplin, Scott

Scott Joplin (1868–1917) was an American musician who wrote lively music called ragtime.

Joplin was born in Texarkana, Texas. About 1894, he settled in Sedalia, Missouri. He played piano at the Maple Leaf Club. The owner of a music store published Joplin's "Maple Leaf Rag" (1899) and many other pieces.

In 1907, Joplin moved to New York City. He had written an opera, *Treemonisha,* and other works for the stage. He wanted to get them performed. He did not succeed. Joplin died in a mental hospital.

In the 1970's, people began to play Joplin's music again. His music was used in *The Sting,* a popular movie, and *Treemonisha* was performed. In 1976, the Pulitzer Prize officials gave Joplin a special award for his contribution to American music.

Scott Joplin

Jordan is a country in southwestern Asia, in the region known as the Middle East. It lies on the East Bank of the Jordan River. The country is bordered by Iraq, Israel, Saudi Arabia, Syria, and the West Bank, an area of land west of the Jordan River. Amman is Jordan's capital and largest city.

Land. Jordan's land includes deserts, mountains, deep valleys, and rolling plains. The country has a warm, pleasant climate, but some parts get very little rain.

Jordan's largest cities and most of the country's farmland are on the Transjordan Plateau (*plah TOH*), an area of high, flat land in western Jordan.

People. Most of the people of Jordan are Jordanian Arabs, people who speak the Arabic language and whose ancestors were from Jordan. The rest of the people are mainly Palestinian Arabs. They or their families came to Jordan to escape the Arab-Israeli wars of 1948 and 1967. Other Palestinians moved from the West Bank to Amman between the wars, when the West Bank was part of Jordan.

Most of the people of Jordan follow the religion of Islam. A few are Christians.

Many Jordanians work in hotels, restaurants, and banks. Others have jobs in government and the military. Some people work in factories in

Amman is Jordan's capital and largest city.

Amman. Many Jordanians work in oil-producing Arab countries. These workers send money to their families in Jordan.

Resources and products. Much of Jordan's money comes from such businesses as hotels, restaurants, and banks. Tourism helps support many of the nation's businesses.

Jordan gets some income from factories that make fertilizer and cement. Mines produce phosphates and potash used to make fertilizer.

History. The first writings that tell about the area come from about 4,000 years ago. Many groups and empires ruled the land in ancient times, including the Israelites, Egyptians, Assyrians, and Persians. The Romans took control of it just over 2,000 years ago. It was part of the Ottoman Empire from the 1500's to the early 1900's. The Ottoman Empire was based in what is now Turkey.

After World War I (1914–1918), Britain was in charge of what is now Jordan. In the 1920's, Britain let Jordan—then called Transjordan—be partly responsible for its government. Transjordan became independent in 1946. Its name was changed to Jordan in 1949.

From 1948 to 1973, Jordan fought in several wars with Israel. In 1949, Jordan gained control of an area just west of the Jordan River called the West Bank, including part of the city of Jerusalem. Israel captured the West Bank in a war in 1967. Later, Jordan gave up its claim to the West Bank. Jordan and Israel signed a peace treaty in 1994.

Other articles to read: **Dead Sea; Jerusalem; West Bank**

Jordan and its neighbors

Jordan in brief

- **Capital:** Amman.

- **Area:** 34,495 mi² (89,342 km²).

- **Population:** *Current estimate*—10,852,000; *2015 census*—9,531,712.

- **Official language:** Arabic.

- **Chief products:** *Agriculture*—citrus fruits, cucumbers, goats, melons, olives, potatoes, poultry, sheep, tomatoes. *Manufacturing*—cement, chemicals, clothes, fertilizer, pharmaceuticals, refined petroleum. *Mining*—phosphate, potash.

- **Money:** *Basic unit*—Jordanian dinar. One thousand fils equal one dinar.

- **Form of government:** Constitutional monarchy.

- **Climate:** Hot and dry in Jordan River Valley and Syrian Desert. Milder and wetter on the plateau.

Flag

Michael Jordan

Jordan, Michael

Michael Jordan (1963–) became one of the most exciting players in the National Basketball Association (NBA). Jordan stands 6 feet 6 inches (198 centimeters) tall. He played guard and forward for the Chicago Bulls in the 1980's and 1990's. His spectacular shooting, especially his leaping shots near the basket, thrilled fans throughout the world. Jordan became one of the highest-scoring players in basketball history.

Michael Jeffrey Jordan was born in New York City and grew up in Wilmington, North Carolina. While he was a freshman at the University of North Carolina, he made the winning shot in the championship game of the 1982 National Collegiate Athletic Association (NCAA) basketball tournament. He joined the Bulls in 1984. In the 1984–85 NBA season, Jordan scored 2,313 points, more than any other player that season. He was named Rookie of the Year. A rookie is a new player. Jordan played on the United States teams that won first place in men's basketball at the 1984 and 1992 Summer Olympic Games. He was named the NBA's Most Valuable Player five times between 1987 and 1998. He helped lead the Bulls to six NBA championships from 1990 to 1998.

In 1993, Jordan retired from basketball to play professional baseball. He played minor league baseball as an outfielder for the Chicago White Sox in 1994. He returned to the Bulls in March 1995, then retired from basketball again in 1999.

In 2000, he became part owner and president of basketball operations of the NBA's Washington Wizards and part owner of the National Hockey League's Washington Capitals. Jordan resigned as Wizards manager and joined the team as a player in 2001. He played the 2001–2002 and 2002–2003 seasons and then announced his retirement.

Joseph, Chief

Chief Joseph (1840?–1904) was a chief of the Nez Perce, a Native American people. He was famous for leading his people away from battle.

The United States government ordered Joseph's people to move from Oregon to a reservation in Idaho. In June 1877, war broke out between Joseph's people and the U.S. Army. Joseph's people won several battles. But Joseph knew they could not defeat the Army. He led his people toward Canada, hoping to join with Sioux bands that had fled there.

Joseph led his people for more than 1,000 miles (1,600 kilometers), fighting off Army troops along the way. Finally, not far from the Canadian border, he surrendered. The U.S. government then sent Joseph and his people to the Indian Territory in Oklahoma. Joseph later lived on a reservation in Washington state.

Chief Joseph

Judaism

Judaism (*JOO dee ihz uhm*) is the religion of the Jewish people. Judaism is the world's oldest major religion.

The most important teaching of Judaism is that there is one God. Judaism teaches that God wants people to do what is right and to be fair and kind to other people. Many Jewish people believe that someday God will send a special person, called a Messiah (*muh SY uh*), to Earth. The Messiah will bring the Jews together, lead them in God's way, and defeat their enemies.

The Jewish Sabbath, or day of worship, begins at sundown every Friday and ends at nightfall on Saturday. On the Sabbath, many Jewish people attend services and have special meals at home. Important holy days

A girl reads from the Torah at her bat mitzvah, the Jewish coming-of-age ceremony for girls.

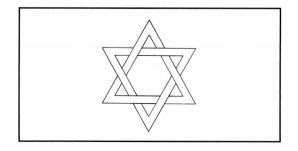

The Star of David is the symbol of Judaism.

and festivals of Judaism include Rosh Ha-Shanah, Yom Kippur, Passover, and Hanukkah.

The synagogue is the Jewish house of worship. It is also a center for Jewish education and social activities. A rabbi is a Jewish leader and teacher. A cantor chants the prayers during worship in the synagogue.

The teachings of Judaism are described in two important collections of writings—the Hebrew Bible and the Talmud. The Hebrew Bible is what Christians call the Old Testament. The first five books of the Hebrew Bible make up the Torah. The Torah is the most important of all Jewish holy writings. It contains the basic laws of Judaism and tells about the history of the Jews. The Talmud is a guide to the laws that Jewish people are supposed to live by.

Other articles to read: **Abraham; Hanukkah; Holocaust; Israel; Jews; Passover; Pentateuch; Rosh Ha-Shanah; Yom Kippur**

Judo

Judo

Judo is a sport in which a person uses balance and timing to defeat an opponent. People learn judo for exercise, relaxation, and self-protection.

The Japanese word *judo* means *the gentle way.* Judo contestants use "gentle" methods to make an opponent become off balance. In this way, a skilled contestant can throw or pin a stronger opponent.

Judo contestants wear a costume called a *judogi,* with a white cotton jacket and pants and a colored belt. Judo techniques are divided into three groups: (1) *nagewaza,* techniques of throwing; (2) *katamewaza,* techniques of choking and holding; and (3) *atemiwaza,* techniques of striking.

Judo developed from an ancient form of self-defense called *jujutsu* or *jujitsu.* It was practiced by the Japanese warrior class called *samurai.* In 1882, Japan's Jigoro Kano developed a modern form of judo education.

Other articles to read: **Karate; Martial arts**

Julian, Percy Lavon

Percy Lavon Julian (*JOOL yuhn*) (1899–1975) was a famous American scientist. He was a chemist (*KEHM ihst*), a scientist who studies substances and how they change.

Julian created a drug used to treat an eye disease called glaucoma (*glah KOH muh*). He also found a way to make a drug called cortisone (*KAWR tuh zohn*). Cortisone is made naturally in the human body. With Julian's method, cortisone could be made from chemicals at low cost. Doctors use cortisone to treat eye and skin disorders, some kinds of cancer, and other diseases.

Julian was born in Montgomery, Alabama. He graduated from DePauw University and got a master's degree from Harvard University. Then he earned a Ph.D. degree from the University of Vienna, Austria.

Julian created more than 100 new chemical products. Many of them were made from soybeans. One product was a fire-fighting liquid that saved many lives during World War II (1939–1945). In 1947, Julian received the Spingarn Medal, a medal given each year by the National Association for the Advancement of Colored People (NAACP) to an outstanding African American.

In 1953, Julian founded, or started, Julian Laboratories. The business had branches in Mexico and South America. In 1964, he became the head of the Julian Research Institute. The institute does research on chemicals made from soybeans.

Percy Lavon Julian

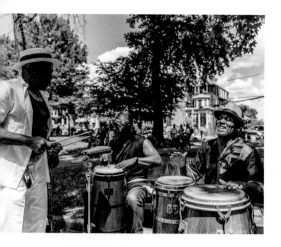

Musicians perform during Juneteenth celebrations in Philadelphia, Pennsylvania.

Juneteenth

Juneteenth is the oldest known celebration that honors the end of slavery in the United States. This festival is held each year in many African American and other communities. The name of the festival refers to its date, June 19. Some communities hold longer festivals that span several days.

Juneteenth originated in Texas at the end of the American Civil War (1861–1865). In 1863, President Abraham Lincoln issued the Emancipation Proclamation. The proclamation declared freedom for enslaved people in the Southern states. However, many slaveowners in Texas kept this information secret. On June 19, 1865, Union General Gordon Granger entered Galveston, Texas. He ordered that all enslaved people in the state be freed. About 250,000 people were then freed.

Juneteenth has become a popular celebration of freedom and African American culture in many communities. Texas became the first U.S. state to recognize Juneteenth officially, in 1980. Today, all of the states recognize Juneteenth in an official capacity. Juneteenth became a federal holiday in 2021. Juneteenth festivities often include family reunions, parades, plays, and storytelling. In some places, Juneteenth is called Black Independence Day, Emancipation Day, Freedom Day, or Jubilee Day.

Other articles to read: **African Americans; Civil War, American; Lincoln, Abraham; Slavery**

Jungles are parts of rain forests where sunlight reaches the forest floor.

Jungle

Jungles are wild areas that have a thick tangle of tropical plants. Jungles are found in tropical rain forests.

Tropical rain forests have huge trees, long vines, and such animals as parrots and monkeys. In many parts of a rain forest, the trees are so dense, or thick, that sunlight never reaches the ground.

Jungles are the parts of rain forests where sunlight reaches the forest floor. Such jungles grow along rivers and in clearings. Jungles often grow in places where trees have been cut down. Sometimes, people have to cut paths through jungles with long knives called machetes (*muh SHEHT eez*).

Jupiter

Jupiter was the king of gods in Roman myths (*mihths*), or stories of gods and goddesses. He was a son of Saturn, the ruler of the universe. At first Jupiter was the god of the sky, thunder, and lightning.

Jupiter's wife, Juno, was queen of the gods. Their children included the gods Mars and Vulcan. Many other gods, goddesses, and heroes were Jupiter's children. Some myths say that one goddess, Minerva, sprang full grown from Jupiter's head. Jupiter was also the father of the nine Muses. They were spirits who helped people create art and poetry.

Jupiter's symbols were the oak tree, the eagle, and the thunderbolt. The largest planet is named after him.

Other articles to read: **Mars**

Jupiter

Jupiter

Jupiter is the fifth planet from the sun and the largest planet in the solar system. More than 1,000 Earths would fit inside Jupiter. When viewed from Earth, Jupiter appears brighter than most stars. Among the planets, only Venus is brighter. Jupiter is named after the king of the Roman gods.

Jupiter is a giant ball of gas and liquid. It has little or no solid surface. Instead, the planet's surface is made of thick red, brown, yellow, and white clouds. The clouds have dark and light-colored areas. These areas circle the planet and give it a striped appearance.

Jupiter's most outstanding surface feature is the Great Red Spot, a swirling mass of gas. It is a long-lived storm similar to a hurricane. The color of the Great Red Spot varies from brick-red to brownish.

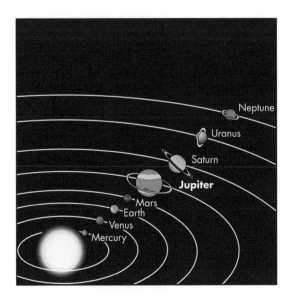

Jupiter in the solar system

Jupiter is a giant ball of gas and liquid.

Jupiter has three thin rings around its middle. They seem to be made mostly of dust particles.

Jupiter rotates, or spins, faster than any other planet. Jupiter's day—that is, the time it takes to spin around once—is only about 10 hours long. By comparison, Earth's day is 24 hours long. Jupiter takes about 12 years to travel once around the sun, while Earth takes one year.

Jupiter has many satellites, or moons, that rotate around it the way our moon rotates around Earth. The planet has 16 moons that measure at least 6 miles (10 kilometers) in diameter and dozens of smaller satellites. Scientists have discovered volcanoes on the moon called Io. They believe the moon called Europa contains liquid water. The Galileo spacecraft orbited Jupiter in December 1995. The Cassini spacecraft, designed to study Saturn, flew by Jupiter in December 2000. The two craft helped astronomers study the planet's moons, atmosphere, and weather from two locations.

Jupiter's Great Red Spot looks like a hurricane in a photograph taken by the Voyager 2 spacecraft.

Jute

Jute (*joot*) is a long, soft, shiny fiber from the jute plant. It can be woven into rough, strong threads.

Most jute is used to make cloth for wrapping bales, or bundles, of cotton, and to make rough cloth bags called gunny sacks. Jute fibers are also used in curtains, chair coverings, carpets, and coarse cloth called burlap. Jute is used in making twine and rope, too.

Jute grows best in warm, damp areas. China, India, and Bangladesh are the world's biggest growers. Jute fibers are off-white to brown and grow 3 to 15 feet (0.9 to 4.5 meters) long.

Jute plant and twine made from jute

Juvenile delinquency

Juvenile delinquency refers to crimes committed by a *juvenile* (youth). Juvenile delinquency includes such adult crimes as car theft and burglary. It also includes acts that are illegal only for children. Some examples are staying out after a curfew and drinking alcoholic beverages.

The legal age at which a person is considered a juvenile is different from place to place. Most states in the United States consider anyone under 18 years of age to be a juvenile. In Canada, juveniles may be those under the age of 16. Juvenile delinquency is a serious problem in all countries. It is more common in nations that have large cities.

Experts have done studies to try to understand the causes of juvenile delinquency. Research has focused on family relationships and neighborhood conditions. These studies have shown that there are many reasons why a child might become a delinquent.

Kk

is the eleventh letter of the alphabet for the English language.

Handwritten letters vary from person to person. *Manuscript* (printed) letters (above left) have simple curves and straight lines. Cursive letters (above right) have flowing lines.

The small letter k first appeared during the A.D. 800's as a rounded letter. By about 1500, the letter had developed into its present shape.

K	k
A.D. 800	Today

Special ways of expressing the letter K

Sign Language Alphabet	Braille	International Flag Code

Development of the letter K

The ancient Egyptians	The Semites	The Phoenicians	The Greeks	The Romans
about 3000 B.C., drew this symbol of a cupped hand.	about 1500 B.C., simplified the Egyptian symbol. They called the letter *kaph,* their word for *palm of the hand.*	about 1000 B.C., wrote the letter like this.	gave the letter its present form about 600 B.C. They called the letter *kappa.*	began using the Greek letter about A.D. 114.

Kabuki

Kabuki

Kabuki (*kah BOO kee*) is a kind of Japanese drama, or play. It has been performed the same way for hundreds of years.

Kabuki plays are popular in Japan. Some of them are about history, and others are about people in everyday life. The scenery is beautiful, and the actors wear colorful costumes and makeup. The acting in kabuki plays is very lively. Chanting and music are part of the plays.

Kabuki began in the 1600's. Some of its style was copied from puppet plays, which were very popular. In kabuki theater, men play all the parts.

Kahlo, Frida

Frida Kahlo (1907–1954) was an important Mexican painter. She was best known for painting pictures of herself that showed her feelings.

Frida Kahlo was born on July 6, 1907, in Coyoacan, a part of Mexico City. When she was 18 years old, she was badly hurt in a bus accident. She had many operations and lost one leg.

Kahlo wanted to be a doctor, but her injuries were too great. She taught herself to paint. In 1929, she married the famous Mexican artist Diego Rivera.

Most of Frida Kahlo's paintings are pictures of herself that show her suffering. She used strong colors and included things that were part of Mexican history. She sometimes painted herself wearing *Indigenous* (native) Mexican costumes. Kahlo died on July 13, 1954.

Other articles to read: **Rivera, Diego**

Frida Kahlo

Kaleidoscope

A kaleidoscope (*kuh LY duh skohp*) is a viewer that shows beautiful colors and designs.

A kaleidoscope has a tube that is closed at both ends. One end has a peephole. The other end has two pieces of glass. A space between them holds bits of colored glass. When you turn the kaleidoscope, the colored bits tumble into different places and form a new design.

Inside the kaleidoscope are two long mirrors. They are slanted in a V shape, and they reach all the way down the tube. The bits of colored glass are reflected in the mirrors. The reflections make the design you see when you look through the peephole.

Other articles to read: **Mirror**

Kaleidoscope image

The mirrors of a kaleidoscope reflect bits of glass in colorful patterns.

Kangaroo

A kangaroo is a type of furry animal that hops on its hind legs. Kangaroos live mainly in central, southern, and eastern Australia.

Kangaroos are mammals. They feed their young with mother's milk. They are a kind of mammal called a marsupial (*mahr SOO pee uhl*). Marsupials give birth to very small babies. Most baby marsupials live in a pocket, or pouch, on the mother's belly until they grow larger.

The two main kinds of kangaroos are red kangaroos and gray kangaroos. A full-grown male kangaroo stands about as tall as a man. Female kangaroos are smaller.

Kangaroos have a small head, a pointed nose, and large ears. They have a long tail and large, powerful hind legs. Kangaroos can hop as fast as 30 miles (48 kilometers) per hour. They use their long tails for balance when they hop.

Kangaroos usually rest in the shade during the day. At night, they feed on grass and small plants. They usually spend their time in small groups.

Female kangaroos give birth to one very tiny baby at a time. The baby is called a joey. A newborn joey is only about 1 inch (2.5 centimeters) long. It fastens itself to a nipple in its mother's pouch and stays there for about six to eight months.

Kangaroos usually live six to eight years. Their only enemies are people and wild dogs called dingoes. Kangaroos are protected by law. But when there are a great many kangaroos, some hunting is allowed.

Kangaroos carry their babies in a pouch.

Kansas

Kansas is a state in the Midwestern region of the United States. It lies in the center of the country between Colorado and Missouri. Nebraska lies to the north, and Oklahoma lies to the south.

Kansas is called the *Sunflower State* for the yellow prairie flowers that grow there. Kansas is also called the *Wheat State* because it is a leading wheat-producing state.

Topeka is the capital of Kansas. The city lies in northeastern Kansas, an area of gently rolling hills. Topeka is an important trade center. The city's factories make farm machinery, pet foods, potato chips, steel products, and tires. Wichita, the largest city in Kansas, is a major manufacturing center. Many airplanes are made in Wichita. The Arkansas River flows through the middle of the city.

Land. Most of Kansas is a rolling plain, with some low hills. Long ago, huge sheets of ice called glaciers covered Kansas. The glaciers moved very slowly, flattening the land and filling the valleys. The glaciers also made the soil very rich for farming.

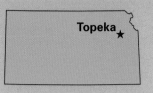

Kansas

Kansas

State flag

State seal

Tallgrass Prairie National Preserve lies in the Flint Hills region in Kansas's southeastern plains.

Kansas, continued

Kansas in brief

- **State capital:** Topeka, since 1861. Earlier capitals were Fort Leavenworth (1854), Shawnee Mission (1854–1855), Pawnee (1855), and Lecompton (1855–1861).

- **Area:** 82,278 mi² (213,099 km²), including 516 mi² (1,336 km²) of inland water.

- **Population:** 2,937,880.

- **Statehood:** Jan. 29, 1861, the 34th state.

- **State abbreviations:** Kans. or Kan. (traditional); KS (postal).

- **State motto:** *Ad Astra per Aspera* (To the Stars Through Difficulties).

- **State song:** "Home on the Range." Words by Brewster Higley; music by Daniel Kelley.

- **Largest cities in Kansas:** Wichita (382,368); Overland Park (173,372); Kansas City (145,786); Topeka (127,473); Olathe (125,872); Lawrence (87,643).

- **Governor:** 4-year term.

- **State senators:** 40; 4-year terms.

- **State representatives:** 125; 2-year terms.

**State bird
Western meadowlark**

**State flower
Sunflower**

Kansas has many rivers and streams. The Kansas River flows through northern Kansas. The Arkansas River flows through the southern part of the state. Huge cottonwood trees line the banks of the streams and rivers.

Resources and products. Kansas grows many kinds of crops in its rich soil. Wheat, one of the state's leading crops, is grown in every part of Kansas. Farmers also grow corn, hay, grain, sorghum, soybeans, and sunflowers. Hay and grain sorghum are used to feed beef cattle and hogs. Kansas is a leading cattle state.

Manufacturing plants in Kansas make airplanes, truck parts, snowplows, and trailers. Also, many plants make food products from the state's crops and livestock. Kansas also produces oil and natural gas.

Other articles to read: **Coronado, Francisco Vásquez de; Louisiana Purchase**

Important dates in Kansas

Prehistory	Before white settlers came, several Native American groups lived in what is now Kansas. These included the Kansa, Pawnee, and Wichita.
1541	Spanish explorer Francisco Vásquez de Coronado entered Kansas.
1803	The United States purchased the Louisiana Territory, which included what is now Kansas, from France.
1821	William Becknell set up the Santa Fe Trail. Many early settlers crossed the Kansas region along this trail.
1850's	People in the Kansas region fought over whether slavery should be legal in the region. This fighting gave the area the nickname Bleeding Kansas.
1854	Congress established the Territory of Kansas.
1861	Kansas became the 34th state on January 29.
1870's	Immigrants from Russia planted and raised the first Turkey Red wheat in Kansas. This kind of wheat could be farmed easily in the state. Kansas became the leading U.S. producer of wheat.
1894	People began mining oil and natural gas, two major sources of energy, in Kansas. The state became an important mining center.
1934–1935	Dust storms damaged large areas of Kansas farmland.
1990–1995	Joan Finney became the first woman to be elected governor of Kansas.

Karate

Karate (*kuh RAH tee*) is a form of combat in which a person kicks or strikes with the hands, elbows, knees, or feet. Karate is one of many forms of combat called *martial arts*. The Japanese word *karate* means *empty hand.* Many men and women learn karate for self-defense.

There are four major types of karate—Chinese, Japanese, Korean, and Okinawan. All use the same basic techniques, but each stresses certain skills and movements.

Students and teachers of karate wear a uniform called a *gi* that consists of a loose cotton jacket tied with a colored belt, and pants with an elastic waist. They train in bare feet. As karate students become more skilled, they earn belts of a different color. Beginners wear a white belt, and experts wear a black one.

Other articles to read: **Judo; Martial arts**

Karate

Kazakhstan in brief

- **Capital:** Nur-Sultan.

- **Area:** 1,052,091 mi² (2,724,902 km²). *Greatest distances*—north-south, 1,000 mi (1,600 km); east-west, 1,800 mi (2,900 km).

- **Population:** *Current estimate*—19,280,000; *2020 official government estimate*—18,785,000.

- **Official language:** Kazakh.

- **Chief products:** *Agriculture*—beef, milk, potatoes, wheat. *Manufacturing*—chemicals, food products, processed metals. *Mining*—coal, copper, lead, natural gas, petroleum.

- **Money:** *Basic unit*—tenge.

- **Form of government:** Republic.

- **Climate:** Dry, with cold winters and long, hot summers.

Flag

Kazakhstan (*kah zahk STAHN*) is a country that lies mostly in west-central Asia. It borders the Caspian Sea in the southwest. Russia lies to the west and north. China is to the east. Turkmenistan, Uzbekistan, and Kyrgyzstan lie to the south.

Kazakhstan's land varies greatly from west to east. Dry lowlands cover much of the western and southwestern regions. High, grassy plains called steppes (*STEHPS*) blanket large areas of the north, and sandy deserts cover much of the south. Northeastern Kazakhstan has high, flat lands that are good for farming. Mountain ranges form the nation's eastern and southeastern borders. Nur-Sultan is the capital, but Almaty is the largest city.

In the cities, most Kazakhs live in modern apartments or houses. In the villages, most people live in houses. But some Kazakh shepherds still live in tentlike houses called yurts, which can be moved from place to place.

Agriculture is a major money-making activity in Kazakhstan. Important industries in Kazakhstan include those that make food and mine minerals. Coal and copper are mined in Kazakhstan. Petroleum and gas are found near the Caspian Sea. People use coal, petroleum, and gas for heating homes, running machines, and other purposes.

For hundreds of years, the Kazakh people worked as herders. They were nomads who wandered across the plains with their sheep, camels, cattle, and horses. They relied on their animals for food, clothing, and transportation. This lifestyle began to change in the 1800's, when Russia conquered the Kazakh region. Kazakhstan became part of the Soviet Union in 1920. While Kazakhstan was under Soviet rule, industry grew steadily. Most of the Kazakh people stopped working as herders and settled in villages or cities. In 1991, Kazakhstan declared its independence from the Soviet Union.

Kazakhstan and its neighbors

Keller, Helen

Helen Keller (1880–1968) is a great example of a person who overcame disabilities. Although she was blind and deaf, she became a famous author and speaker. Keller worked all her life to help other blind and deaf people.

Helen Keller was born in Tuscumbia, Alabama. As a baby, she developed a serious illness that destroyed her sight and hearing. Because of this, she was completely shut off from things around her. For almost five years, she was a wild child. She could only scream, giggle, kick, and scratch to make her feelings known.

When Helen was about 7 years old, her father hired a teacher named Anne Sullivan. Sullivan made contact with Helen through the sense of touch. The teacher used a sign-language alphabet to spell words into Helen's hand. Slowly, Helen understood that certain hand movements stood for letters, that groups of letters made words, and that words stood for people and things. Once she understood this, Helen made fast progress. Within three years, she could read and write in braille, the form of reading and writing used by blind people. By the time she was 16, she had learned to speak. She went to college and graduated with top grades.

After college, Helen worked to better the lives of blind and deaf people. She appeared before government leaders. She gave speeches and wrote many books and articles. During World War II (1939–1945), she worked with soldiers who had been blinded in battle. Wherever she spoke, she brought new courage to blind and deaf people.

Other articles to read: **Blindness; Braille; Sign language**

Helen Keller

John Fitzgerald Kennedy

Kennedy, John Fitzgerald

John Fitzgerald Kennedy (1917–1963) served as the 35th president of the United States, from 1961 to 1963. He was assassinated, or murdered, after serving less than three years as president.

Kennedy was the youngest man ever elected to be the U.S. president, and he was the youngest to die in that office.

John Kennedy was born in Brookline, Massachusetts. He came from a political family whose ancestors were farmers in Ireland. During World War II (1939–1945), he was the skipper of a U.S. Navy boat in the South Pacific. A Japanese destroyer cut the boat in two, and Kennedy led his crew to safety. He returned home as a war hero. Kennedy was elected to the U.S. House of Representatives in 1946. He served until 1952, when he was elected to the Senate.

Kennedy became president in 1961. He was a strong leader and won great respect throughout the world. In 1962, the United States learned that the Soviet Union had set up nuclear missiles in Cuba. People feared that the Soviet Union might use these missiles to bomb the United States. But Kennedy demanded that the Soviets take out the missiles, and they were removed.

At home, the United States was very prosperous. African Americans made great progress in their struggle for equal rights. While Kennedy was president, the United States made its first manned

John Fitzgerald Kennedy is shown with his wife, Jacqueline; their son, John, Jr.; and their daughter, Caroline.

space flights and prepared to send astronauts to the moon.

On November 22, 1963, Kennedy visited Dallas, Texas. As he rode in an open car with his wife, Jacqueline, three shots rang out. The president was struck in the head and neck and died soon after. The murder of this young, popular president shocked the world.

President Kennedy belonged to an important political family. His grandfather, Patrick J. Kennedy, was a state senator. The president's brother Robert F. Kennedy became attorney general and later served as U.S. senator from New York from 1965 until he was killed in 1968. Another brother, Edward M. "Ted" Kennedy, served as a U.S. senator from Massachusetts from 1962 until 2009.

Kennedy, Robert Francis

Robert Francis Kennedy (1925–1968) served as attorney general of the United States from 1961 to 1964. As attorney general, he was the chief law officer of the United States. He helped make sure that people obeyed the country's laws. Robert Kennedy also served in the U.S. Senate from 1965 to 1968.

Kennedy was born in Brookline, Massachusetts. Many members of his family held public office. His brother, John F. Kennedy, was president of the United States from 1961 to 1963. Robert—also known as Bobby—acted as his brother's closest personal adviser when John Kennedy was president. Another brother, Edward M. "Ted" Kennedy, was a member of the U.S. Senate from 1962 to 2009.

Robert F. Kennedy was murdered in Los Angeles in June 1968. At the time, he was trying to run for president of the United States.

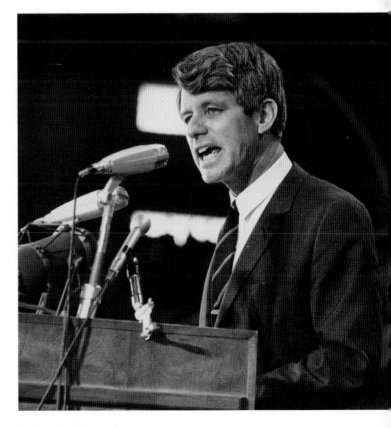

Robert F. Kennedy

Kentucky

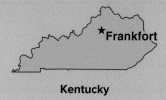

Kentucky

Kentucky

State flag

State seal

Kentucky is one of the Southern States of the United States. Illinois, Indiana, and Ohio lie to the north. Tennessee borders Kentucky on the south. Virginia and West Virginia lie to the east. Missouri lies to the west.

Kentucky is often called the *Bluegrass State* for the bluish-green grass that grows there. The state also has many horse farms where race horses graze in fields of bluegrass.

Frankfort, the capital of Kentucky, lies in north-central Kentucky, just east of Louisville. Louisville is Kentucky's largest city and an important center for trade and industry. It is also known for Churchill Downs, where the Kentucky Derby, a famous horse race, is run every year. Lexington, another large city, is the home of the University of Kentucky.

Kentucky is also known for two natural wonders—Mammoth Cave and Cumberland Falls.

Land. North-central Kentucky has rich farmland and the state's biggest cities. The northwestern region is rich in coal. The state's westernmost

Kentucky horse farms produce some of the world's finest Thoroughbred horses.

region has low hills and some swamps and lakes. Southern Kentucky has flat farmland and some rocky ridges. The Appalachian Mountains rise in the southeast.

Resources and products. Many areas of Kentucky have rich soil, and farming is a leading industry. Tobacco is one of Kentucky's most important farm products. Farmers also grow corn, wheat, and other grains; soybeans; and fruits and vegetables.

Livestock farmers raise beef cattle, chickens, and hogs. Around Lexington, they breed and sell race horses. The grass and water in this area have many minerals that give horses strong bones and muscles.

Kentucky also has many coal fields. These large coal deposits make Kentucky a leading coal producer.

Kentucky factories make many products, such as cars, trucks, and airplane parts. They also make chemicals, food products, and machinery.

Other articles to read: **Appalachian Mountains; Boone, Daniel**

Important dates in Kentucky

Prehistory	Native Americans lived in the Kentucky region for thousands of years before the first Europeans arrived. These peoples included the Cherokee, Delaware, Iroquois, and Shawnee.
1750	American pioneer Thomas Walker explored what is now eastern Kentucky.
1767	American pioneer Daniel Boone made his first journey to Kentucky.
1774	Harrodsburg, Kentucky's first permanent white settlement, was founded.
1775–1783	Frontier leaders defended Kentucky settlements against attacks from Native American groups during the American Revolution.
1792	Kentucky became the 15th state on June 1.
1815	The *Enterprise*, the first steamboat to travel up the Mississippi and Ohio rivers, reached Louisville from New Orleans.
1861–1865	Kentucky remained part of the United States during the Civil War.
1936	The U.S. government established a gold vault at Fort Knox.
1955	Kentucky allowed 18-year-olds to vote.
1990	Kentucky launched reform of its public school system with the passage of the Education Reform Act.
2000	Voters approved a constitutional amendment allowing the state legislature to meet every year.

Kentucky in brief

- **State capital:** Frankfort, Kentucky's capital since 1793. Lexington served as the temporary capital in 1792.

- **Area:** 40,411 mi^2 (104,664 km^2), including 919 mi^2 (2,380 km^2) of inland water.

- **Population:** 4,505,836.

- **Statehood:** June 1, 1792, the 15th state.

- **State abbreviations:** Ky. or Ken. (traditional); KY (postal).

- **State motto:** *United We Stand, Divided We Fall.*

- **State song:** "My Old Kentucky Home." Words and music by Stephen Collins Foster.

- **Largest cities in Kentucky:** Louisville (597,337); Lexington (295,803); Bowling Green (58,067); Owensboro (57,265); Covington (40,640); Hopkinsville (31,577).

- **Governor:** 4-year term.

- **State senators:** 38; 4-year terms.

- **State representatives:** 100; 2-year terms.

**State bird
Northern cardinal**

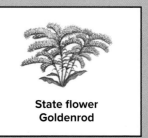

**State flower
Goldenrod**

Kenya (*KEHN yuh* or *KEEN yuh*) is a country on the east coast of Africa. It stretches west from the Indian Ocean to Uganda. Tanzania lies to the south, Ethiopia lies to the north, and Somalia lies to the northeast.

Land. Kenya's coastal area is hot and humid. Beautiful sandy beaches, swamps, and patches of rain forest line the coast. Inland, huge grassy plains stretch over most of the land. This area of scattered bushes, shrubs, and grasses is the driest part of Kenya. A highland region of mountains, valleys, and high, flat plains rises in the southwest. Forests and grasslands cover much of this region. The highland has good farmland, and most of Kenya's people live there.

Kenya is famous for its wildlife. Its plains and highlands are home to antelope, buffaloes, cheetahs, elephants, giraffes, leopards, lions, rhinoceroses, and zebras. Crocodiles and hippopotamuses live where there is plenty of water. Many large birds, such as eagles, ostriches, and storks, and dozens of species of small, brightly colored birds also live in Kenya.

People. Almost all Kenya's people are Black Africans. They belong to about 40 different ethnic groups. These groups speak different languages and have many different ways of life. Kenyans value large families. Many Kenyan families have six or more children.

Most of Kenya's people live in the rural areas, or the countryside. The rest live in cities and towns. Most of the rural people live on small farm settlements. They raise crops and animals for a living. A small number of people are nomads who move from place to place in search of grazing land and water for their animals. Most city people work in stores, factories, and business or government offices.

Resources and products. Agriculture is the most important part of Kenya's economy. Tea is the leading money-making crop. Many farmers raise beef and

Lake Turkana in northern Kenya

dairy cattle. Manufacturing is growing in importance in Kenya. Service industries, such as banking, government, tourism, and trade, are also important.

Tourism is a major source of money for Kenya. Numerous tourists visit Kenya every year. They come to enjoy its scenic coast and especially to see its amazing wildlife.

History. Scientists have found the bones of some of the earliest known human beings in Kenya. The scientists think that people probably lived there about 2 million years ago.

About 3,000 years ago, people from other parts of Africa began moving into the Kenya area. These groups became the ancestors of today's Kenyans. They included farmers, herders, and hunters.

Traders from Arabia came to Kenya's coast about 2,000 years ago. Arabs took control of the coastal area in the 700's and ruled it for hundreds of years.

The British ruled Kenya from 1895 to 1963. They set up schools in Kenya like the schools in the United Kingdom, and many Europeans started large farms in Kenya.

In 1963, Kenya became independent, or free from British rule. Since independence, the leaders of Kenya have encouraged people from the country's many ethnic groups to join together as Kenyans.

Other articles to read: **Lake Victoria; Nairobi**

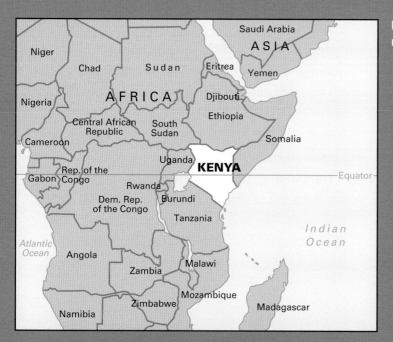

Kenya and its neighbors

Kenya in brief

- **Capital:** Nairobi.

- **Area:** 228,561 mi² (591,971 km²). *Greatest distances*—north-south, 640 mi (1,030 km); east-west, 560 mi (901 km). *Coastline*—284 mi (457 km).

- **Population:** *Current estimate*—56,295,000; *2019 census*—47,564,296.

- **Languages:** *Official*-English; *National*-Swahili (or Kiswahili).

- **Chief products:** *Agriculture*—bananas, beef, coffee, corn, milk, pineapples, pyrethrum, sisal, sugar cane, tea, tomatoes, wheat. *Manufacturing*—beer, chemicals, cigarettes, motor vehicles, processed foods, textiles.

- **Money:** *Basic unit*—Kenyan shilling. One hundred cents equal one shilling.

- **Form of government:** Republic.

- **Climate:** Tropical, with wet and dry areas; mild and wet in the highlands.

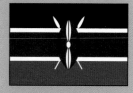

Flag

Johannes Kepler

Kepler, Johannes

Johannes (*yoh HAHN uhs*) Kepler (1571–1630) was a German astronomer (*uh STRON uh muhr*). An astronomer is a scientist who studies the planets, stars, and other objects in the sky. Kepler also studied math.

Kepler discovered three laws that explained how the planets move. The English scientist Sir Isaac Newton later used Kepler's three laws to come up with his own laws about gravity. Gravity is the force that keeps us on Earth. Without gravity, we would float away.

Kepler was one of the first astronomers to support the ideas of the Polish astronomer Copernicus (*koh PUR nuh kuhs*). Copernicus showed Earth's motion could explain the movements of other objects in space. Also, Kepler showed how our eyes work.

Kepler was born on Dec. 27, 1571, in Weil (near Stuttgart), Germany. He died on Nov. 15, 1630.

Other articles to read: **Copernicus, Nicolaus; Gravity; Newton, Sir Isaac; Planet**

Francis Scott Key

Key, Francis Scott

Francis Scott Key (1779–1843) became famous for writing the words of "The Star-Spangled Banner"— the national anthem, or official song, of the United States.

Francis Scott Key was born in what is now Carroll County, Maryland. While he was working as a lawyer in Washington, D.C., the War of 1812 broke out between the United States and the United Kingdom. One night, Key watched from a ship while British ships attacked Fort McHenry in Baltimore Harbor, Maryland. He knew that the fort had little defense.

The next morning, when he saw that the American flag still flew above the fort, he was overjoyed. Key wrote a poem about the experience. He made it into a song by borrowing a tune from a popular song of the time. In 1931, the U.S. government chose the song as the U.S. national anthem.

Other articles to read: **National anthem**

Francis Scott Key observes the British attack on Fort McHenry from a ship in Baltimore Harbor.

Keyboard instruments

Keyboard instruments make music by means of keys arranged in rows. The keys are usually pieces of wood, plastic, or other material. They are connected with a device that can make sounds. A person plays musical notes by pressing a key.

The most popular keyboard instruments include the piano, harpsichord, and pipe organ. The keys on a piano make small hammers inside the piano move. The hammers make sounds by striking the strings. On a harpsichord, the keys control a small piece of leather or other material that makes sounds by plucking, or pulling, the strings. Pressing a key on a pipe organ opens a pipe through which a column of air vibrates, or moves quickly back and forth, and produces sounds.

Other articles to read: **Piano**

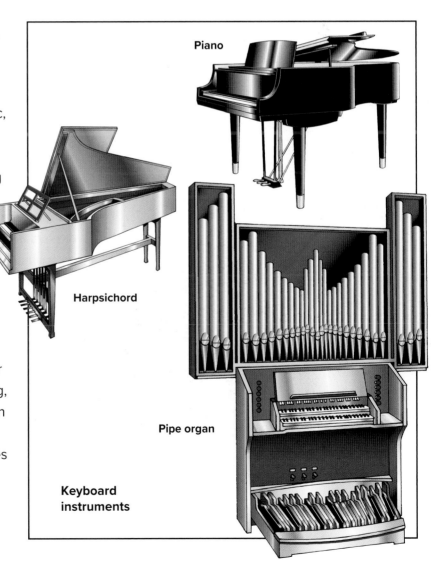

Piano

Harpsichord

Pipe organ

Keyboard instruments

Cross section of left kidney

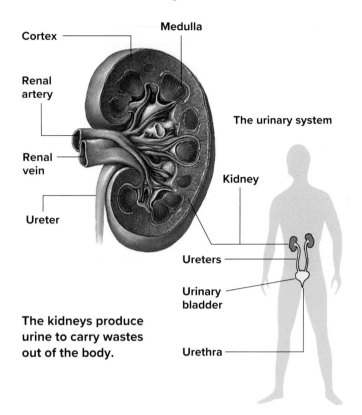

Cortex

Medulla

Renal artery

Renal vein

Ureter

The urinary system

Kidney

Ureters

Urinary bladder

Urethra

The kidneys produce urine to carry wastes out of the body.

Kidney

Kidneys are organs, or body parts, in human beings and in all other living things that have backbones. The most important job of the kidneys is the production of urine. Urine is a fluid that carries wastes out of the body. If one kidney is lost in an accident or by disease, the other may grow larger and do the work of both. If both kidneys are damaged or lost, poisons build up in the person's body, leading to death. However, many people with damaged kidneys are kept alive by a dialysis machine. It does the work of the kidneys. Some people get a kidney transplant. Then they have a healthy kidney again.

The kidneys of human beings look like large purplish-brown kidney beans. They are about the size of a grown-up's fist. They lie below the middle of the back on each side of the backbone.

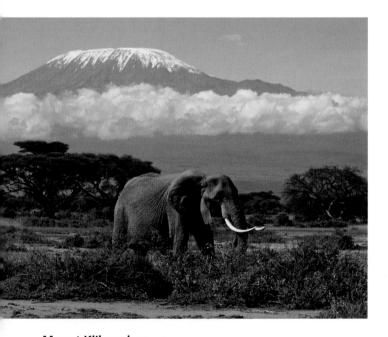

Mount Kilimanjaro

Kilimanjaro

Kilimanjaro (*KIHL uh muhn JAHR oh*) is Africa's highest mountain. It is in northern Tanzania, on the Kenya border.

Kilimanjaro has two mountaintops. The higher one, Kibo, rises 19,340 feet (5,895 meters) high at Uhuru Peak. It is always covered by snow and ice, even though it is near the equator. The other mountaintop, Mawensi, stands 16,890 feet (5,148 meters) high and has no snow or ice.

Kilimanjaro is a volcano, but it is not active. It has rich soil on its slopes and receives heavy rainfall. Farmers raise bananas and coffee on the lower slopes.

Many people visit the wildlife parks around Kilimanjaro. Ernest Hemingway, an American author, used it in a famous short story, "The Snows of Kilimanjaro."

Killer whale

Killer whales, also called orcas (*AWR kuhz*), are large sea animals. They live in all the oceans, especially in cold waters. They are mammals, animals that feed their young on mother's milk.

Killer whales are up to 30 feet (9 meters) long. They weigh up to 10 tons (9 metric tons). They have shiny black backs, and they are white underneath.

Killer whales have teeth. They feed on salmon, other fish, and sometimes small seals, dolphins, and whales. They have not been known to attack people, however.

Killer whales often travel in groups called pods. Each pod is made up of several females and their young. Every pod has its own "language," or set of underwater sounds.

Killer whale

Kindergarten

Kindergarten is the grade before first grade in school. In kindergarten, children learn by talking, playing, and doing many other things. In many kindergartens, time is set aside every day to talk about interesting things the children have seen and done. They are also given special jobs to do, like helping with snacks. The teacher helps children learn to work together.

Kindergarten children often take trips to learn about things. They may look at plants and animals, go through a supermarket, or visit a post office. They learn numbers by counting, measuring, and comparing things.

Kindergarten teachers talk with parents about how their children are growing and learning. Teachers may visit the children's homes, or parents may visit the school.

Other articles to read: **Preschool**

A kindergarten teacher works on a computer with her student.

King Louis XIV of France

King

Kings are men who hold titles of great power or honor. A king's wife is called a queen. In many countries, people believed that the king came from a family of gods. In the ancient tribes of Europe, a king was elected by the people during times of war. When these people became Christians, the king's power grew greater. He was thought to speak and act for God. It was his duty to make sure the people followed God's teachings.

Today, some areas are ruled by powerful kings. In other places, such as the United Kingdom and other European countries, kings or queens have little real power. But they do have important positions in their countries.

Other articles to read: **Crown; Monarchy; Queen**

Coretta Scott King

King, Coretta Scott

Coretta Scott King (1927–2006) was an African American supporter of civil rights and the wife of civil rights leader Martin Luther King, Jr. She was president of the King Center in Atlanta, which works to remember and celebrate her husband's achievements. She and her husband are buried at the center.

Coretta Scott was born on April 27, 1927, near Marion, Alabama. She graduated from Antioch College and studied concert singing at the New England Conservatory of Music. She and Martin Luther King, Jr., were married in 1953. Mrs. King helped her husband in his civil rights work by giving speeches and musical programs. She continued these activities after King was murdered in 1968. She wrote *My Life with Martin Luther King, Jr.* (1969). She died on Jan. 30, 2006.

Other articles to read: **Civil rights; King, Martin Luther, Jr.**

King, Martin Luther, Jr.

Martin Luther King, Jr., (1929–1968) was an important civil rights leader in the United States. He fought for the freedoms and rights of African Americans and other people. King won the 1964 Nobel Peace Prize for leading peaceful protests. Today, the United States celebrates King's birthday with a national holiday on the third Monday in January.

King was born on January 15, 1929, in Atlanta, Georgia. He became a Baptist minister in 1948. In 1955, King received a Ph.D. degree from Boston University in Massachusetts. At that time, African Americans were treated unfairly in many ways. In some parts of the United States, they were not allowed to use the same schools, hotels, and restaurants as white people. Many people also tried to keep Black people from voting. King worked in peaceful ways to fight against this unfair treatment.

In 1955, King led a protest against the bus system of Montgomery, Alabama. That year, a Black passenger named Rosa Parks was arrested for disobeying a state law that said Black passengers had to give up their seats to white passengers. In 1957, King received the Spingarn Medal, a medal given each year by the NAACP to an outstanding African American.

Martin Luther King, Jr.

King was a great speaker. He opposed the use of violence as a way to get fair treatment for African Americans. Through the work of King and others, the Civil Rights Act of 1964 and other laws were passed to protect people's rights.

Though King encouraged peaceful action, many people used violence against him. Some people threw rocks at him and bombed his home. On April 4, 1968, King was shot and killed in Memphis, Tennessee. His widow, Coretta Scott King, continued King's civil rights work after he died. She died in 2006.

Other articles to read: **Civil rights; Martin Luther King, Jr., Day; Parks, Rosa Louise**

King, William Lyon Mackenzie

William Lyon Mackenzie King (1874–1950) was a prime minister of Canada. He headed Canada's government for 21 years, longer than any other prime minister. King was the leader of Canada's Liberal Party.

Mackenzie King was born in Berlin (now Kitchener), Ontario, on December 17, 1874. He received a degree from the University of Toronto, and he also studied in the United States and England. While in college, King developed an interest in the problems of workers and the poor.

As deputy minister of labour in 1900, King helped workers. He helped organize Canada's first Department of Labour. King was elected to Parliament, Canada's lawmaking body, in 1908. He lost his seat in Parliament in 1911, but he continued to work for the Liberal Party.

King became prime minister on Dec. 29, 1921. He served from 1921 to 1926, from 1926 to 1930,

William Lyon Mackenzie King

and from 1935 to 1948. As prime minister, King helped guide Canada to independence from the United Kingdom (UK). Canada became an independent country in 1931. King made important trade agreements with the United States and the UK. He skillfully led Canada through World War II (1939–1945) and helped English-speaking and French-speaking Canadians understand one another better.

King retired as prime minister in November 1948. But he remained a member of Parliament until April 1949. He died on July 22, 1950.

King Arthur. See Arthur, King.

King Tut. See Tutankhamun.

Kipling, Rudyard

Rudyard (*RUHD yuhrd*) Kipling (1865–1936) was a leading English short-story writer, poet, and novelist. He is best known for his stories about India during the late 1800's, when India was a British colony. Kipling wrote more than 300 short stories. In 1907, Kipling became the first English writer to receive the Nobel Prize in literature.

Several of Kipling's most popular poems were published in *Barrack-Room Ballads* (1892), including "Danny Deever," "Fuzzy Wuzzy," "Gunga Din," and "Mandalay." Kipling also wrote *The Jungle Book* (1894) and *The Second Jungle Book* (1895). These collections of children's stories describe the adventures of Mowgli, an Indian child who gets lost in the jungle and is raised by a family of wolves. His novels include *Captains Courageous* (1897) and *Kim* (1900).

Joseph Rudyard Kipling was born on Dec. 30, 1865, to English parents in Bombay (now Mumbai), India. He died on Jan. 18, 1936.

Rudyard Kipling

Kiribati in brief

- **Capital:** Tarawa.
- **Area:** 313 mi² (811 km²).
- **Population:** *Current estimate*—123,000.
- **Official language:** English; Gilbertese is also spoken.
- **Chief products:** Bananas, breadfruit, chicken, copra (dried coconut meat), giant taro, pandanus fruit, papaya, pigs, sweet potatoes.
- **Money:** Australian dollar.
- **Form of government:** Republic.
- **Climate:** Hot and wet. Northern islands receive more than twice as much rainfall as the other islands.

Flag

Kiribati (*KIHR uh BAS*) is a small country in the middle of the Pacific Ocean. It is made up of 33 islands. Kiribati has three island groups: (1) the Gilbert Islands and Banaba, (2) the Phoenix Islands, and (3) the Line Islands. Most of the country's people live in the Gilbert Islands. Tarawa, an island in the Gilbert Islands, is Kiribati's capital.

Almost all the islands of Kiribati are coral islands. Coral is a stony substance made of the skeletons of tiny sea creatures. The islands are low and flat. Many are ring-shaped.

The language of the islanders is Gilbertese, but most people also speak some English. English is the official language, used in government and business. Many of the people live in small villages. Many homes are made of wood and leaves from coconut trees. Some people have cement-block houses with iron roofs.

Fishing is an important part of life for the people of Kiribati. They also make and sail canoes. The islanders grow most of their own food, which includes bananas, breadfruit, papaya (*puh PY uh*), sweet potatoes, and a plant with a starchy, underground stem called giant taro (*TAH roh*). They also raise pigs and chickens.

People have lived on what is now Kiribati for hundreds of years. Great Britain took control of much of what is now Kiribati in 1892. Kiribati became independent on July 12, 1979.

Kiribati and its neighbors

Kite

A kite is an object that is flown in the air at the end of a string. Kites may be made of paper, cloth, or plastic. Many have a light frame made of wood. The frame may also be plastic, fiberglass, or aluminum. Kites should be flown in open spaces, far from electric lines or antennas. The name *kite* comes from a graceful, soaring bird called a *kite*.

Kites probably were first used in China more than 2,000 years ago. Most people fly kites for fun, but kites are also flown in contests. They have been used in scientific experiments, too.

Kites can be made in hundreds of sizes, shapes, and colors. The flat kite is the oldest and simplest kind. It has a tail that helps keep the kite pointed upward. A simple tail consists of cloth strips tied together and attached to the bottom of the kite. The more wind there is, the longer the tail should be.

To fly a kite, one person holds the kite while another, called the flier, holds the string and walks about 50 steps away. The wind should be blowing at the back of the flier and in the face of the person holding the kite. The flier pulls the string tight, and the kite is released. The kite rises while the flier lets out the string slowly. If the kite begins to fall, the flier should loosen the string. To bring the kite down, the flier walks toward the kite while pulling in the string.

For safety reasons, kites should never be flown in stormy or wet weather.

Flying a kite

Kiwi

A kiwi (*KEE wee*) is a type of bird that lives in the country of New Zealand. It is one of the few birds that cannot fly.

Many kiwis live in the forests. The birds are shy, and will run away if anyone comes near them.

The kiwi is about the size of a chicken. It has a thick body covered with shaggy, brown feathers. The legs and neck of the kiwi are short, but its bill is long and flexible. It has tiny wings and no tail.

The kiwi is the only bird that has nostrils at the end of its bill. The bird uses them to smell food in the thick, wet forests. At night, it feeds on berries, earthworms, and insects.

Kiwi

Kiwi fruit

A kiwi (*KEE wee*) fruit is a berry with brown, fuzzy skin. Inside, it has bright green pulp, or soft flesh, and tiny black seeds. A kiwi fruit is about the same size and shape as an egg. The fruit has a pleasant flavor, but some are a bit sour. Kiwi fruit is rich in vitamin C, like oranges.

People eat kiwi fruit fresh, frozen, or canned. Kiwi fruit is often used in fruit salads, pies, ice cream, and wine.

Kiwi fruit grows on vines. The plants grow best in places where the weather is not too hot or too cold. New Zealand is the world's biggest producer of kiwi fruit.

Kiwi fruit

Klondike River

Klondike

The Klondike (*klon DYK*) is a region in Yukon, a territory in northwestern Canada. The Klondike covers about 800 square miles (2,070 square kilometers), including the Klondike River and its streams. The Klondike has long, cold winters and short, warm summers. Dawson is the Klondike's main town.

On Aug. 17, 1896, a team of explorers discovered gold in Rabbit Creek (later named Bonanza Creek). The team included George W. Carmack, his First Nations wife Kate, and her relatives Skookum Jim and Tagish Charlie. A Canadian miner named Robert Henderson had directed Carmack's team to Rabbit Creek. News of the discovery spread quickly. Many people traveled to Klondike in 1897 and 1898 to search for gold. By 1930, about $200 million worth of gold had been mined from the region. Large mining companies eventually bought out most of the original mines. They produced millions more dollars' worth of gold.

Today, mines in the Klondike yield millions of dollars worth of gold each year. Other minerals in the area include silver, lead, and zinc.

Other articles to read: **Yukon; Yukon River**

Knight

Knight was a male soldier who fought on horseback. Knights lived in Europe many years ago. A knight wore a suit of metal called armor to protect him. He rode a huge war horse. Knights fought with swords, shields, and wooden spears called lances.

The best knights were brave, good, well-mannered, and kind. They were faithful to God and their country. They treated women with respect, protected the weak, and were fair to enemies. Some knights did not behave this way, however. Some were very cruel, especially toward people of low rank.

The best knights were brave, good, well-mannered, and kind.

A joust is a fight between two knights on horseback who are armed with lances.

Medieval knights engaged in single combat on foot.

Knights lived during the later part of the Middle Ages. The Middle Ages lasted between the 400's and the 1400's. Between 1100 and 1300, most knights became servants to lords, or people of high rank.

Some men were made knights on the battlefield if they had shown great bravery. But most began training as boys. When a boy reached the age of 7, he left home and lived in the home of a knight or person of high rank. There, he learned the skills and behavior of a good knight.

A knight's job was to fight in times of war. In the early days of knighthood, the knight wore heavy clothing of padded fabric or leather, covered with mail, or chains of metal rings. His helmet had a flap that covered his nose.

Later, armor became heavier and covered more of the body. In the 1400's, metal armor covered the knight's body completely. On a knight's shield and outer clothing, he wore a coat of arms. The coat of arms identified his family. When the face of a knight in battle was completely covered, the coat of arms was the only way to recognize him.

In times of peace, knights passed the time by practicing for war. They took part in tournaments, which were fights between two groups of knights. These fights were like real battles, and they provided valuable training. But kings did not like tournaments, because they were bloody and wasteful. Kings also feared the power of large groups of knights. As a result, tournaments could be held only with permission from the king.

Knights also had jousts (*jowsts*), which were fights between two knights. Many people liked to watch jousts. Tilting also became popular. In tilting, two knights on horseback galloped toward each other in narrow lanes. Each knight tried to knock the other off his horse.

Other articles to read: **Armor; Arthur, King; Crusades; Heraldry**

Knitting

Knitting is a way of making fabric by looping yarns around each other. The yarn is linked together by knitting needles. Much of our clothing is knitted, including sweaters, scarves, and hats. Knitted clothes are popular because they are warm and comfortable. They can stretch, too.

People who knit use two long, pointed knitting needles to make a flat piece of fabric. They use three or four needles to knit round, hollow items, such as socks. They may also use needles with a circle shape. Knitters may use slender needles and lightweight yarn for baby clothes. They use thick needles and heavy yarn to make a heavy sweater.

Knitting machines use many needles. They can knit much faster than a person can.

People who knit use two long, pointed knitting needles to make a flat piece of fabric.

Knot

A knot is a way to tie ropes, cords, or threads, or to fasten them together. People use knots for many things. Sailors use knots to tie ropes on things that are lifted on or off boats, and to tie the lines attaching their sails. Doctors tie tiny knots in threads used for stitching cuts. Farmers use knots to tie animals to posts. In arts and crafts, people use knots to make clothing, belts and purses, and decorations. Knots are used to tie shoelaces, set up tents, prepare fishing tackle, and many other jobs.

There are many types of knots. The square knot is probably the best known and most widely used knot. It joins the ends of two ropes, cords, or threads. It is strong and easy to tie and untie.

Early people used knots to tie arrowheads to arrow shafts and to tie bowstrings to bows. They also used knots to make clothes and fishing nets and to bind wood together to make a shelter.

The carrick bend is used to tie large ropes together.

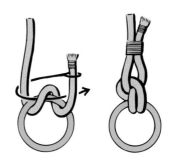

The fishermen's bend is a strong, safe knot used to tie anchors and fishhooks.

A joey rides on his mother's back.

Koala

A koala (*koh AH luh*) is a small animal found in Australia. It is sometimes called a bear, but it is not really a bear. Koalas are marsupial (*mahr SOO pee uhl*) mammals. The young koala, called a joey, is carried in a pouch on its mother's belly, and it drinks its mother's milk.

A koala has soft gray or brown fur on its back and white fur on its belly. It has round ears, long toes, and sharp, curved claws. A full-grown koala is 25 to 30 inches (64 to 76 centimeters) tall.

Koalas live in trees and sleep most of the day. They are active at night. Koalas eat the leaves and shoots of eucalyptus (*yoo kuh LIHP tuhs*) trees.

A koala mother carries its baby in its pouch for about seven months. The young koala spends the next six months riding on its mother's back.

Kolkata

Kolkata *(kawl KUHT uh)* is one of the largest cities in India. Kolkata lies along the Hooghly *(HOO glee)* River north of the Bay of Bengal. Kolkata is the world center of jute production. Jute is a plant material used to make rope and cloth. Many ships enter and leave Kolkata's busy port every year.

Rich Kolkatans live near the center of the city in pleasant neighborhoods with wide streets and modern houses. But most people in Kolkata live in poor, run-down areas called bustees. Many bustee houses have no electricity or running water.

In 2001, the city's official name was changed to Kolkata from Calcutta.

Kolkata, India

Elaine Konigsburg

Konigsburg, Elaine

Elaine Konigsburg *(KOH nihgz BURG)* (1930–2013) wrote and illustrated children's books. One of her best-known books, *From the Mixed-Up Files of Mrs. Basil E. Frankweiler* (1967), won the 1968 Newbery Medal. It describes the adventures of two children who explore the Metropolitan Museum of Art in New York City.

Konigsburg also won the 1997 Newbery Medal for *The View from Saturday* (1996), a book about a group of sixth-graders and their teacher. In 2001, she received the Catholic Library Association's Regina Medal.

Konigsburg was born on Feb. 10, 1930, in New York City. Her other books include *Jennifer, Hecate, Macbeth, William McKinley, and Me, Elizabeth* (1968), *A Proud Taste for Scarlet and Miniver* (1973), *Up from Jericho Tel* (1986), *Silent to the Bone* (2000), and *The Mysterious Edge of the Heroic World* (2007). Selections of her short stories were published as *Altogether, One at a Time* (1971, 1989) and *Throwing Shadows* (1979). Konigsburg died on April 19, 2013.

Kookaburra

The kookaburra (*KUK uh bur uh*) is the name of a group of birds that live in Australia and New Guinea. Kookaburras are known for their unusual call, which sounds like a loud laugh. The kookaburra is a kind of kingfisher. It is one of Australia's best-known birds.

Kookaburras have large heads, long bills, and brown, black, or white feathers. They are about 17 inches (43 centimeters) long. These birds live in the woods and nest in tree holes. The male birds are fierce, and they defend their homes from enemies.

Kookaburras enjoy a wide variety of foods. They eat caterpillars, fish, frogs, insects, small mammals, snakes, worms, and even small birds.

Kookaburra

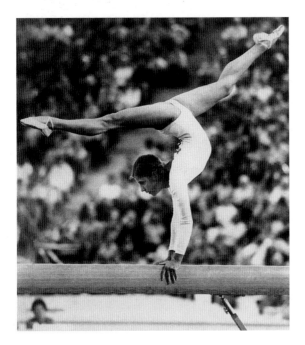

Olga Korbut

Korbut, Olga

Olga Korbut (1955–   ) is a famous gymnast from the former Soviet Union. She became a star at the 1972 Olympic Games in Munich, Germany. Korbut was known for her daring back flips. She became the first person ever to do a back flip in the gymnastics event called the uneven parallel bars. In this event, gymnasts perform on two bars, one of which is higher than the other.

Korbut was born in Grodno in what is now Belarus. She entered a special school for athletes when she was 11. Korbut won three gold medals and a silver in the 1972 Olympic Games, and a gold and a silver at the 1976 Olympics in Montreal, Canada.

In 1977, Korbut graduated from a teaching school in Grodno. In 1991, she moved to the United States. She coached gymnastics in Atlanta, Georgia.

Korea, North. See North Korea.

Korea, South. See South Korea.

United States soldiers prepare for battle during the Korean War.

Korean War

Korean War (1950–1953) was the first war in which the United Nations (UN) played a military role. The Korean War began on June 25, 1950, when troops from Communist-ruled North Korea invaded South Korea. The UN demanded that the Communists withdraw from South Korea. But the Communists kept fighting, and a number of UN countries sent troops and supplies to help the South Koreans. The United States provided about 90 percent of the troops and supplies that were sent to South Korea. China fought on the side of North Korea, and the Soviet Union gave military equipment to the North Koreans.

The Korean War ended on July 27, 1953, when the UN and North Korea signed an *armistice* (cease-fire) agreement. Neither side won complete victory. A permanent peace treaty between South Korea and North Korea has never been signed.

Other articles to read: **North Korea; South Korea; United Nations**

Kosovo (*KOH soh voh*), also spelled *Kosova,* is a country in southeastern Europe. Priština *(PRISH tih nah)* is the capital of Kosovo. Kosovo is bordered by Albania to the southwest, Montenegro to the northwest, Serbia to the north, and North Macedonia to the southeast.

Land. Kosovo covers a mostly mountainous area. There are some areas of flatlands and valleys that are used for farming. Winters are cold, with heavy snowfall. Summers are hot and dry.

People. The earliest group of people who lived in the region that is now Kosovo were the Illyrians. A group called the Slavs first arrived in the Kosovo area in the A.D. 500's. Historical records first mention Albanians in Kosovo around 1043. The Albanian population in the region grew steadily.

  Most of the people living in Kosovo today are Albanians. Others include Croats, Egyptians, Montenegrins, Roma, Serbs, and Turks. The country's main languages are Albanian and Serbian. The major religions of Kosovo are Christianity and Islam.

Resources and products. Kosovo is one of the poorest countries in Europe. Farming is important to Kosovo's economy. Crops grown in the country include corn, potatoes, tomatoes, and wheat. Farmers also raise chickens, dairy cattle, and sheep. Manufacturing and mining are also important.

History. From the 850's to the early 1900's, many different empires ruled Kosovo. Serbia took control of it in 1912. In 1918, Kosovo became part of the Kingdom of the Serbs, Croats, and Slovenes——later renamed Yugoslavia.

Priština, the capital of Kosovo

Yugoslavia's government took away many rights of the Albanians in Kosovo and drove thousands from their homes.

In 1946, Yugoslavia became a nation with six republics: Bosnia-Herzegovina, Croatia, Macedonia, Montenegro, Serbia, and Slovenia. Kosovo became a self-governing region in Yugoslavia and later a self-governing province of the republic of Serbia. In 1989 and 1990, however, Serbia ended Kosovo's self-governing powers. Serbia also took away the rights of many Albanians in Kosovo. In 1992, the republics of Serbia and Montenegro formed a new Yugoslavia after the other four republics declared independence.

After the early 1990's, most of Kosovo's Albanians wanted independence for the province. In 1997, groups seeking Kosovo's independence attacked Serbian police stations and vehicles. In response, Serbian forces launched military strikes against Kosovo's Albanians. These strikes caused many Albanians to leave their homes.

In 1999, North Atlantic Treaty Organization (NATO) forces attacked military targets in Serbia to end the fighting. Serbian forces left Kosovo later that year. The United Nations (UN) then sent officials to form a temporary government in Kosovo.

Yugoslavia changed its name to Serbia and Montenegro in 2003. In 2006, Montenegro declared independence, after its citizens voted to separate from Serbia. Serbia then declared its own independence.

In 2007, officials from the UN and the European Union (EU) failed to settle an agreement between Serbia and Kosovo. The Serbian government wanted Kosovo to remain a province of Serbia. Serbia offered Kosovo some self-governing powers, but Kosovo's leaders wanted complete independence for the province.

Kosovo declared its independence on Feb. 17, 2008. The United States and most European countries supported Kosovo's independence.

Other articles to read:

Serbia; Yugoslavia

Kosovo and its neighbors

Flag

Kuwait in brief

- **Capital:** Kuwait.

- **Area:** 6,880 mi² (17,818 km²), including offshore islands. *Greatest distances*—east-west, 95 mi (153 km); north-south, 90 mi (145 km). *Coastline*—120 mi (193 km).

- **Population:** *Current estimate*—4,591,000; *2019 official government estimate*—4,420,110.

- **Official language:** Arabic.

- **Chief products:** Petroleum, natural gas.

- **Money:** *Basic unit*—Kuwaiti dinar. One thousand fils equal one dinar.

- **Form of government:** Nominal constitutional monarchy.

- **Climate:** Hot from April to September, often above 120 °F (49 °C). Coolest in January, averaging between 50 and 60 °F (10 and 16 °C). A little rain falls from October to March.

Flag

Kuwait (*koo WYT or koo WAYT*) is a small country at the north end of the Persian Gulf, an inlet of the Indian Ocean. Its neighbors are Iraq and Saudi Arabia. The capital is the city of Kuwait.

Kuwait is mostly waterless desert, but there is water underground. Drinking water is made from seawater by a process called distillation (*dihs tuh LAY shuhn*).

Most of the Kuwaiti people are Arabs. Their religion is Islam. Groups of Palestinians, Egyptians, Asian Indians, and Iranians also live in Kuwait.

Beneath Kuwait's desert is one-tenth of the world's oil. People use oil for heating homes, running machines, and other purposes. Its oil has made Kuwait one of the world's richest nations. Kuwait's people enjoy free education, receive free health and social services, and pay no income tax.

Kuwait's second most important product is natural gas. Natural gas is also used as fuel to heat buildings and run machines. The government has started new industries. There are plans to turn the desert into farmland for crops.

Hardly any people lived in Kuwait before the 1700's, when the British set up a mail service there. Britain took responsibility for Kuwait's defense from 1899 to 1961. After drilling for oil began in 1936, Kuwait changed rapidly from a poor land to a wealthy one. In 1961, Kuwait became independent, or free from British rule.

In August 1990, Iraq invaded Kuwait and tried to make it part of Iraq. This attack led to the Persian Gulf War of 1991. Allied forces freed Kuwait in February 1991.

Kuwait and its neighbors

148

Kwanzaa

Kwanzaa (*KWAHN zuh*) is an African American holiday. It is based on an African harvest festival. Kwanzaa begins on December 26 and lasts for seven days.

The idea for the holiday came in 1966 from Professor Maulana Karenga, a teacher of African studies. He listed seven principles, or important ideas, of Black culture. They are *Umoja,* meaning unity; *Kujichagulia,* meaning self-determination; *Ujima,* meaning collective work and responsibility; *Ujamaa,* meaning cooperative economics; *Nia,* meaning purpose; *Kuumba,* meaning creativity; and *Imani,* meaning faith.

On each day of Kwanzaa, people think about one of the seven principles. At a feast called *karamu,* people eat typical African food and honor their ancestors. They think back on the old year and enjoy music, songs, and dancing.

Kwanzaa celebration

Kyoto

Kyoto (*kee OH toh*) is one of Japan's largest cities. It stands on Honshu Island, the largest of the four main islands of Japan.

Kyoto was the capital of Japan from 794 to 1868. The word *Kyoto* is Japanese for *capital city.* The city has many fine, old palaces and religious buildings. One of the most beautiful sights is the Golden Pavilion, built in 1397 as part of a palace and rebuilt in the 1950's. Nijo Castle was built in the 1600's. The Imperial Palace was built for the emperor in 794 and rebuilt in 1855.

Kyoto has many colleges. Its small factories make fine pottery and silk cloth.

The Golden Pavilion in Kyoto, Japan

Kyrgyzstan in brief

- **Capital:** Bishkek.

- **Area:** 77,201 mi² (199,949 km²). *Greatest distances—* east-west, 580 mi (935 km); north-south, 270 mi (435 km).

- **Population:** *Current estimate*—6,762,000; *2019 official government estimate*—6,523,500.

- **Official languages:** Kyrgyz and Russian.

- **Chief products:** *Agriculture*—apples, cattle, cotton, onions, potatoes, sheep, tomatoes, wheat. *Manufacturing*—clothing and textiles, construction materials, food products, machinery. *Mining*—coal, gold, mercury, petroleum.

- **Money:** *Basic unit*—Kyrgyz som. One hundred tyin equal one Kyrgyz som.

- **Form of government:** Parliamentary republic.

- **Climate:** Warm, dry summers in lowlands, cool in winter. Cold winters in the mountains.

Flag

Kyrgyzstan (*kihr guh STAHN*) or *(KIHR guh stahn)* is a country in central Asia. It lies in the high Tian Shan and Alay mountains. Peak Pobedy, the highest mountain, rises 24,406 feet (7,439 meters), close to the border with China. Bishkek is the capital city and main industrial center.

Most of the country's people live in the lower plains and mountain valleys. Summers are warm and dry there, and winters are less cold than in the mountains. In the north is a large lake called Issyk-Kul.

About two-thirds of the people of Kyrgyzstan are Kyrgyz. The others are Russians, Uzbeks, Dungan (ethnic Chinese Muslims), and Ukrainians. The Kyrgyz and Uzbeks are Muslims. Most of the other people are Christians.

The Kyrgyz are farmers and herders. Some live in villages, and others are nomads who wander from place to place for at least part of the year. The nomads carry their tentlike homes, called yurts, with them. They herd sheep, cattle, and yaks.

Kyrgyzstan's factories make clothing, food products, and machinery. Its mining products include coal, gold, mercury, and oil.

Beginning in the 1200's, Kyrgyzstan was ruled for hundreds of years by central Asian peoples called the Mongols. During the 1800's, the region became part of the Russian Empire. Kyrgyzstan was part of the Soviet Union from 1924 until 1991. In 1991, Kyrgyzstan became an independent country.

Kyrgyzstan and its neighbors

Ll

is the twelfth letter of the alphabet for the English language.

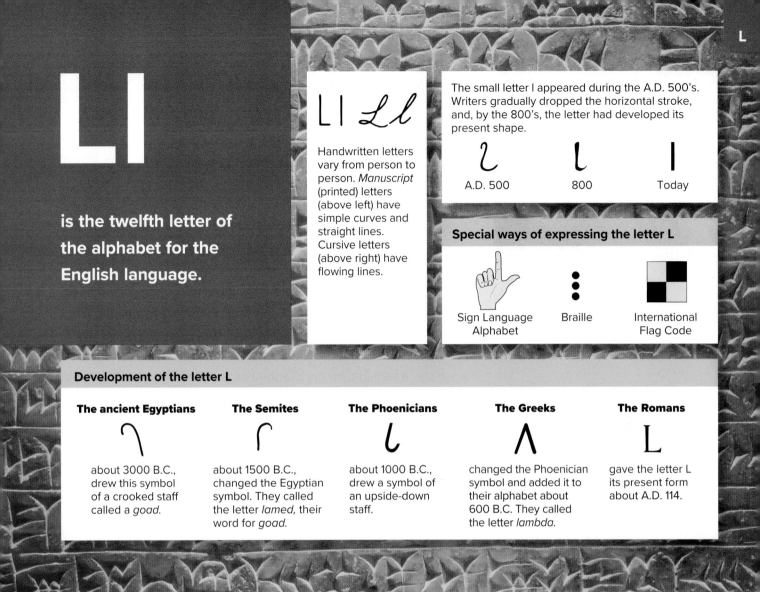

Ll *Ll*

Handwritten letters vary from person to person. *Manuscript* (printed) letters (above left) have simple curves and straight lines. Cursive letters (above right) have flowing lines.

The small letter l appeared during the A.D. 500's. Writers gradually dropped the horizontal stroke, and, by the 800's, the letter had developed its present shape.

A.D. 500   800   Today

Special ways of expressing the letter L

Sign Language Alphabet   Braille   International Flag Code

Development of the letter L

The ancient Egyptians
about 3000 B.C., drew this symbol of a crooked staff called a *goad*.

The Semites
about 1500 B.C., changed the Egyptian symbol. They called the letter *lamed,* their word for *goad*.

The Phoenicians
about 1000 B.C., drew a symbol of an upside-down staff.

The Greeks
changed the Phoenician symbol and added it to their alphabet about 600 B.C. They called the letter *lambda*.

The Romans
gave the letter L its present form about A.D. 114.

Labor Day

Labor Day is a holiday that honors working people. It is observed as a legal holiday on the first Monday in September throughout the United States, Puerto Rico, and Canada. Labor organizations sponsor various celebrations, but for most people, it is a day of rest and recreation. In Europe, Labor Day is observed on May 1. In Australia, the holiday is called either Labour Day or Eight-Hour Day.

Two men have been credited with suggesting a holiday to honor working people in the United States—Matthew Maguire, a machinist from Paterson, New Jersey, and Peter J. McGuire, a New York City carpenter who helped found the United Brotherhood of Carpenters and Joiners. They helped stage the first Labor Day parade in New York City in September 1882. In 1887, Oregon became the first state to make Labor Day a legal holiday. President Grover Cleveland signed a bill in 1894 making Labor Day a national holiday.

Bobbin lace

Lace

Lace is a lovely, netlike fabric made from threads. Today, most lace is made by machines, but some lace is still handmade. There are two main kinds of handmade lace. One kind is called needlepoint lace, and the other is called bobbin lace.

To make needlepoint lace, a drawing of the design is sewn onto a piece of linen. Then the lacemaker fills in the design with a needle and thread.

To make bobbin lace, the drawing is sewn onto a pillow. Then pins are stuck into the lines of the design. The lacemaker works threads from bobbins, or spools, around the pins to make the lace.

Lacemaking began in Europe about 500 years ago. Many kinds of lace are named for the place where they were first made. For example, a well-known needlepoint lace called Venetian lace was first made in Venice, Italy. A well-known bobbin lace called Chantilly was first made in Chantilly, France.

A lacrosse player catches a ball in a pocket.

Lacrosse

Lacrosse (*luh KRAWS*) is a fast team sport. It is played on a field with goals at either end. Each player carries a stick called a crosse, which has a net pocket at the end. Players use the pocket to catch and throw the ball down the field. Each player may pass, catch, or run with the ball in the pocket. Players on the opposing team may try to gain the ball by knocking it out of the pocket with their own sticks. Only the goalkeeper may touch the ball with the hands. A team scores by putting the ball into the opponent's goal.

A game like lacrosse was played by Native Americans hundreds of years ago. In 1867, the modern rules for the game were set by a Canadian lacrosse player named George Beers. The game is popular in colleges and high schools in the United States, where men's collegiate lacrosse began in 1877. The first U.S. women's lacrosse team was formed in 1926.

Lacrosse rules are not the same in every country where the game is played. In U.S. men's lacrosse, there are 10 players on a team. Men may body check, or bump, an opponent, and players wear gloves, helmets, and face masks for protection. A women's team has 12 players. In women's lacrosse, no body contact is allowed.

Lady Gaga

Lady Gaga (1986–   ) is an American pop singer, songwriter, and musician. She became enormously popular in the first decade of the 2000's.

Lady Gaga was born on March 28, 1986, in New York City. Her real name is Stefani Joanne Angelina Germanotta. She began studying piano as a child. A music producer gave her the name Lady Gaga in 2006. The name was inspired by the song "Radio Ga Ga" (1984) by the British rock band Queen.

In 2008, Lady Gaga's first single, "Just Dance," was released. The song became a worldwide hit. Her first album, *The Fame* (2008), featured the song "Poker Face." Both also became huge worldwide hits. Her other hits include "Paparazzi" (2008), "Bad Romance" and "Telephone" (both 2009), "Born This Way" (2011), and "Applause" (2013). In 2014, Lady Gaga and the American singer Tony Bennett had a number-one hit with *Cheek to Cheek,* a duets album of jazz standards. She has won a number of Grammy Awards for her music.

In 2019, Lady Gaga won an Academy Award as co-writer for best original song for "Shallow," from the motion picture *A Star Is Born* (2018). She also starred in the film. Lady Gaga has also acted in a number of other motion pictures and TV programs.

Lady Gaga

Ladybug

Ladybugs are small beetles known for their bright colors. They are also known as ladybirds or lady beetles. The round body of a ladybug is shaped like half of a pea. Ladybugs have stiff, leathery wings. The wings are often bright red or yellow. They have black, red, white, or yellow spots. Like other insects, ladybugs have six legs.

Ladybugs feed mainly on small insects, including pests. People use ladybugs to remove insect pests from garden plants and crops.

There are thousands of kinds of ladybugs. Some kinds harm beans, melons, squashes, and other garden plants. But there are many helpful kinds, and ladybugs do much more good than harm.

Ladybug

Portrait of the Marquis de Lafayette

Lafayette, Marquis de

The Marquis de Lafayette (*mahr KEE deh LAH fih EHT*) (1757–1834) was a French soldier and leader. He helped the Americans in the American Revolution (1775–1783), when the thirteen colonies fought for their freedom from British rule.

Lafayette was born in Chavaniac, France, on September 6, 1757. His name was Marie Joseph Paul Yves Roch Gilbert du Motier. His parents and grandfather died when he was young. He received a great fortune from his family and studied at a military academy.

Lafayette did not enjoy the life of a rich man in France. He wanted to win fame by fighting against Great Britain. He bought a ship and sailed to America in 1777 with a group of French soldiers.

Lafayette served with General George Washington through the long winter at Valley Forge, Pennsylvania. He led soldiers in several battles. He went back to France in 1779 but returned in 1780. The next year, his troops helped defeat British troops and force Britain's General Cornwallis to give up.

Lafayette returned to France. In 1789, the French Revolution broke out. The people rebelled against their government. Lafayette was in charge of the troops sent to keep order, so he was unpopular with the French people. The king and queen did not trust him, either. In 1792, he left France. When he returned in 1800, he found out that his fortune had been taken by the French government.

Lafayette later was elected to the government by the French voters. He worked to help the American government, and he worked for the independence of many other countries, including Greece, Poland, and South American nations.

Lake

A lake is a body of water with land all around it. Lakes are found in all parts of the world. Some large bodies of water that are called seas are really lakes. These include the Salton Sea in California and the Sea of Galilee in Israel.

How do lakes come to be? Some lakes were made by glaciers (*GLAY shuhrz*). These slowly moving rivers of ice cut deep valleys into the land. When the ice melts, the valleys fill up with water, becoming lakes. Glaciers made the Great Lakes thousands of years ago.

Sinkholes can also make a lake. Under the ground, a soft rock called limestone can slowly melt away with the rain. When it does, the ground can fall in and make a hole.

Crater Lake, Oregon

Moraine Lake, Banff National Park, Alberta, Canada

As water from a stream or river fills the hole, it becomes a lake. Some lakes in Florida were made this way.

Lakes can form in other ways, too. For example, rain water can collect in the craters, or hollows, of dead volcanoes. This is how Crater Lake in Oregon was formed.

A lake creates a wonderful world of its own where animals and plants live and grow. Some lake plants float freely, but some are rooted to the bottom of the lake. Snails, bugs, and fish feed on the plants. Ducks, geese, swans, and other birds swim on the lake. Deer and bears come to the edge of the lake to drink water.

A large lake can affect the climate of land nearby. It can make the climate milder. Then it is not so cold in winter, and not so hot in summer.

Lakes are important for trade and travel, too. Native Americans and early European explorers used canoes to explore North America's Great Lakes. Today, tugboats, barges, and ships carry coal, iron, and corn on these lakes.

People use lake water to drink and to water crops. Lakes also give people pleasure. People go to lakes all year to enjoy fishing, swimming, boating, and ice skating.

Other articles to read: **Great Lakes; Lake Victoria; Ocean; River**

Lake Victoria

Lake Victoria is the biggest lake in Africa. It is also the second largest freshwater lake in the world. Only Lake Superior, in the United States, is larger.

Lake Victoria lies partly in Kenya, partly in Tanzania, and partly in Uganda. The equator crosses the lake. The equator is an imaginary line around the middle of Earth. The lake is the main source, or the starting point, of the Nile River. At its deepest point, Lake Victoria is about 270 feet (82 meters) deep. More than 200 kinds of fish live in its waters.

In 1858, John Hanning Speke, an English explorer, became the first European to reach the lake. He named it after Queen Victoria of the United Kingdom.

Lake Victoria

Lamp

Lamps are things people use to make light. People have used lamps for thousands of years. With lamps, people can work, read, or do other activities after the sun goes down.

Long ago, lamps burned oil or fat. A wick, or cord, made of fibers soaked up the oil or fat. When the wick was lit, it burned and gave off light.

Gas lamps were used in the 1800's. The gas was piped into the lamp. It burned as it rushed out of a small opening and mixed with the air. Today, gas lamps are often used by campers. Such lamps provide light in places that have no electricity.

Thomas Alva Edison, an American inventor, made the first workable electric lamp in the late 1800's. Electric lamps give more light than earlier lamps. They also cost less and are easier to use.

Other articles to read: **Electricity**

Electric lamp

A language laboratory helps these military troops learn to speak and understand a foreign language.

Language

Language allows people to talk to each other. It also allows people to write their thoughts and ideas. Wherever there are people, there is language. People who cannot hear or speak may use sign language. They use their hands to make words.

Around 7,000 languages are spoken in the world today. Chinese is the language spoken by the greatest number of people. People in different parts of China speak different forms of Chinese. These different forms are called *dialects.* The most common dialect is called Northern Chinese or Mandarin. Other languages that are spoken by many of the world's people include Arabic, Bengali, English, Hindi, Portuguese, Russian, and Spanish.

How children learn language

Children learn language by hearing and repeating sounds. Babies like to make all kinds of sounds. They hear the people around them speak. They imitate the sounds they hear from the people around them and begin to say words. When they are a little older, they learn that these words have meanings. For example, when a child sees a dog, the child will say the word "dog."

The parts of language

We talk about three things when we talk about language— sounds, words, and structure. Most languages have about 20 to 60 sounds. All languages have words. Words stand for objects, actions, or ideas. Languages also have structure, such as word order. Words come in a certain order: first, second, third, and so on. For example, in English we can say,

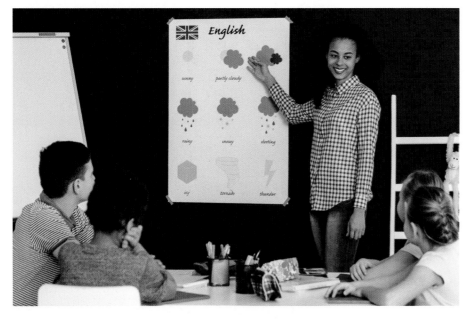

Children who move to English-speaking countries attend English as a Second Language (ESL) classes.

"The lion roared." First, we must say "the"; then "lion"; and finally "roared." We cannot change the words around. In some other languages, word order is different.

Writing is a part of some languages, but not of all languages. No language began with writing. Writing always comes after speaking.

The beginning of language

Nobody really knows how language began. It is a mystery. Language probably began very slowly and very early in human history. First, people might have made sounds such as barks, grunts, and hoots. In time, the sounds might have become more exact. Then the sounds came to mean certain things. However, there is no record of early spoken languages. We can only guess about how language began.

We know more about early writing. People have found examples of writing that are over 5,000 years old. Early writing came from Egypt, China, and Sumeria. The earliest writing was in word-pictures.

Language families

Languages are grouped into families. For example, German and English have many words that are similar. They are both Germanic languages. Long ago, they came from the same parent language, which changed over time.

Italian, French, and Spanish all come from the same parent language. They belong to the Romance group. Hebrew and Arabic belong to the Afro-Asian family.

Other articles to read: **Alphabet; Communication; Dictionary; English language; Hieroglyphics; Punctuation; Sign language; Writing**

Children learn language by hearing and repeating sounds.

Laos in brief

- ■ **Capital:** Vientiane.

- ■ **Official language:** Lao.

- ■ **Area:** 91,429 mi² (236,800 km²). *Greatest distances*—northwest-southeast, 650 mi (1,046 km); northeast-southwest, 315 mi (510 km).

- ■ **Population:** *Current estimate*—7,455,000; *2015 census*—6,492,228.

- ■ **Chief products:** Cattle, coal, coffee, copper, corn, gold, gypsum, hogs, poultry, rice, rock salt, silver, teak, vegetables, water buffalo.

- ■ **Money:** *Basic unit*—kip.

- ■ **Form of government:** Communist state.

- ■ **Climate:** Hot and wet, with a rainy season from November to March.

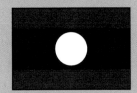

Flag

Laos (*LAH ohs*) is a country in Southeast Asia. It is a tropical land of mountains and thick forests. Laos is bordered by China on the north, Vietnam on the east, Cambodia on the south, and Thailand and Myanmar on the west. Vientiane (*vyehn TYAHN*) is the capital and the largest city.

The Lao, Hmong, and Tai people of Laos speak languages similar to Chinese. Other people speak languages similar to those spoken by other people in Southeast Asia and parts of India. They include the Kha people.

About half the people of Laos are Lao. The Lao people are leaders in business and government. Many Hmong helped the United States and South Vietnam during the Vietnam War. After the war ended in 1975, thousands of Hmong fled to other countries. The Kha were the first people to live in Laos. Until recently, they were treated badly and had few rights.

Many of the people live in villages and farm for a living. Many farms are on the lowlands along the Mekong River and other rivers. Farmers there raise mainly rice. Most villagers are poor, and some villages have no schools.

Most of the nation's resources have not been developed, and the country has few factories. Old-fashioned methods hold back its farm production.

Ancestors of the Lao and Tai people probably moved into Laos about 1,200 years ago. About 600 years ago, most of what is now Laos was joined together in a kingdom called Lan Xang, which means "land of a million elephants." France took control of Laos in the late 1800's. Laos became an independent country in 1953.

Other articles to read:
Vietnam War

Laos and its neighbors

La Salle, Sieur de

Sieur de La Salle (*syur deh luh SAL*) (1643–1687) was a French explorer. He was the first European to follow the Mississippi River to the Gulf of Mexico.

La Salle was born in Rouen, France. His real name was Rene-Robert Cavelier, but he was known by the name of his family's property. La Salle studied to be a priest. However, he left in 1665 to seek adventure.

La Salle sailed to French Canada and became a wealthy fur trader. *Indigenous* (native) people told him of two great rivers, the Mississippi and the Ohio. La Salle thought one of the rivers might lead to the Pacific Ocean. After he explored the Ohio River, he became sure that the Mississippi River flowed into the Gulf of Mexico instead.

The king of France gave La Salle permission to explore the Mississippi. In 1681, La Salle led a group of explorers down the Illinois River and the Mississippi. They reached the Gulf of Mexico on April 9, 1682. La Salle claimed all the land drained by the Mississippi—and the rivers that ran into it—for France.

In 1684, La Salle sailed from France to start a colony at the point where the Mississippi River flows into the Gulf of Mexico. But he sailed past it, and the settlers landed much farther west. They were attacked by Native American groups, and many colonists died from disease. La Salle led a group of people to seek help. Some of the men rebelled against him and killed him.

Sieur de La Salle

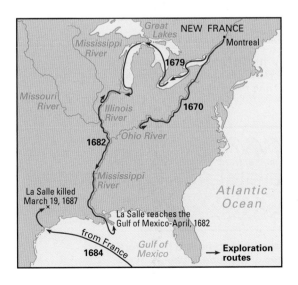

Sieur de La Salle's explorations

Laser

A laser ranging facility directs a laser toward a spacecraft in orbit around the moon.

A laser is something that makes strong, narrow beams of light. A laser beam is powerful enough to burn a hole in a diamond. A laser beam is narrow enough to drill 200 holes on a pinhead.

The direction of lasers

Most light travels in many directions. For example, light from a light bulb travels in all directions. It shines on all parts of a room. Light from the sun also travels in all directions. When the sun shines, its light covers half of Earth's surface. Light from a laser is a different kind of light. Laser light travels in only one direction. It travels in a narrow beam like an arrow of light.

The frequency of lasers

Light travels in waves that cannot be seen with the eye alone. Most light travels in waves that move at many different speeds. These wave movements are vibrations—they move quickly back and forth. Most light waves vibrate at different times per second, or at different frequencies.

How does a laser work?

In one type of laser, a powerful flash tube is coiled around a crystal, such as a ruby crystal.

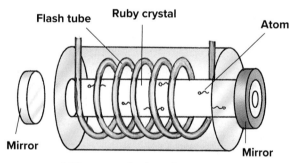

1. The atoms in the ruby crystal contain energy.

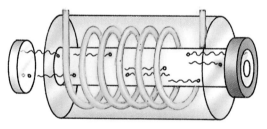

2. When a strong light shines through the ruby crystal, the atoms take up more energy and become excited.

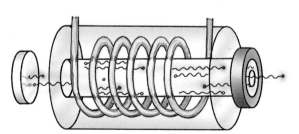

3. The excited atoms give off light. Most of the light comes out of the end as laser light.

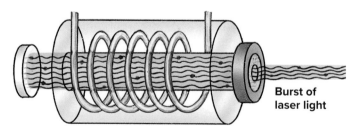

4. The laser light is reflected by mirrors at each end of the tube. It causes other excited atoms to give off light, too.

In other words, most light has many frequencies. But the light from a laser usually has only one frequency. Its waves usually move the same number of times per second.

Atoms and lasers

To understand lasers, you have to know something about atoms. Everything in the world is made from atoms. They are like building blocks. Atoms are extremely small. You cannot see them with the eye alone. Atoms store energy, including light. Sometimes atoms give off energy in the form of light, for example. Sometimes they give off this light in such a way that the light goes in only one direction. This is the kind of light a laser makes.

Parts of a laser

To make a laser work, you need power. The power causes atoms to become excited, or move quickly, and give off light. You also need a certain material and a container for the material. The material must have atoms that will easily get excited and give off light in one direction. Crystals or glass are usually used.

The history of lasers

The famous scientist Albert Einstein was the first person to describe the laser. Scientists began to use the idea in the 1950's. The first laser used a ruby rod as the source of power. It was built in 1960. In 1969, space scientists put a special kind of mirror on the moon. They wanted to see if a laser could measure the distance between Earth and the moon. They sent a laser beam from Earth to the moon. The mirror on the moon sent the beam back. Scientists on Earth measured the time it took the beam to travel to the moon and come back. That allowed them to figure out the distance from Earth to the moon more exactly. Scientists keep finding new ways to use lasers.

Other articles to read: **Bar coding; Compact disc; Holography**

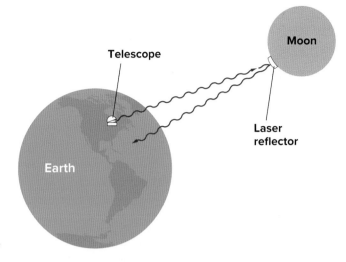

The distance to the moon can be measured precisely using a laser beam sent from Earth to a reflector on the moon and bounced back to Earth.

A laser reflector placed on the moon by astronauts

Uses of lasers

Lasers can be used for many different purposes. The images on these two pages show some of the uses of lasers in communication, industry, medicine, war, art, business, and police work.

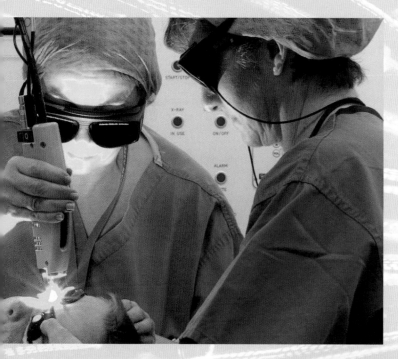

Lasers for industry

Lasers can cut tools, such as the teeth in saws. They can drill eyes in needles. They can even guide ships and airplanes with their light. Lasers also create great heat. This heat can be used to melt hard rocks and metals. Welders use laser torches to cut metal and then weld, or melt, it together in a new form.

Lasers in medicine

A laser beam can burn away sick or dead parts from the body. A laser can also seal up veins so they will not bleed when a doctor does an operation. Eye doctors can fix eye problems with laser beams.

Lasers for art

Lasers can gently clean old works of art that might be harmed by ordinary cleaning. Lasers are also used in holography, a type of photography. The images from holography have three dimensions—they are high, wide, and deep. You may see these images on fancy belt buckles or on advertising posters. You may also see them on credit cards.

Lasers to send messages

A laser can be used to send voice messages and television signals. Its frequency allows it to carry many television programs or telephone voices at the same time. Because its light goes in only one direction, it avoids unwanted noise or interference. Laser light is also used to play compact discs (CD's) and DVD's.

Lasers during war

Lasers are also used by military forces. Soldiers can measure distances and make maps by bouncing light from a laser. They can also bounce laser light off an enemy target to find out how far away it is. Pilots can bounce laser light off an enemy airplane to find out how far away it is and to measure its speed.

Lasers in stores

A type of laser is used in supermarket and department stores every day. Laser scanners read the bar codes that tell the price of the items we buy. The scanner also records the items sold by the store. It helps the store clerks keep track of what they need to reorder.

Lasers to solve mysteries

Police officers who work in crime labs use lasers to help them solve crimes. They shine laser beams on guns and other objects to look for fingerprints. If the laser beam shows fingerprints, the lab worker photographs them. The fingerprints might help find a criminal or solve a mystery.

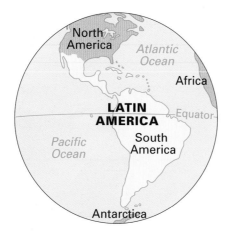

Latin America

Latin America

Latin America is a large region, but it is not a continent. Latin America includes Mexico, Central America, South America, and the Caribbean Islands. Brazil is the largest country in Latin America. Mexico City, Mexico, is Latin America's largest city. Mexico City is also one of the largest cities in the world. Today, most of the people of Latin America speak Spanish or Portuguese. These languages are European, and they came from the Latin language used in ancient Rome. Because of its languages, this part of the world is called Latin America.

Before 1492, however, Latin languages were not spoken in Latin America. *Indigenous* (native) people in this part of the world spoke their own languages. Indigenous peoples in Latin America included the Aztec, the Maya, and the Inca. Some of these Indigenous people created art, studied the stars, built roads, and invented ways to write.

Shortly after the first Europeans arrived in Latin America, they brought enslaved African people to work the land. Today, Latin America has a mixture of customs and people—Africans, Indigenous people, Europeans, and mixed ancestry.

For hundreds of years, Latin American countries were ruled by European countries, especially Spain and Portugal. In the 1800's, many countries fought for freedom and won. Most were not democracies at first. The people had few rights. For example, they did not vote for their leaders. Today, many Latin American countries are democracies.

Other articles to read: **Central America; Mexico City; South America**

Latitude. See Longitude and latitude.

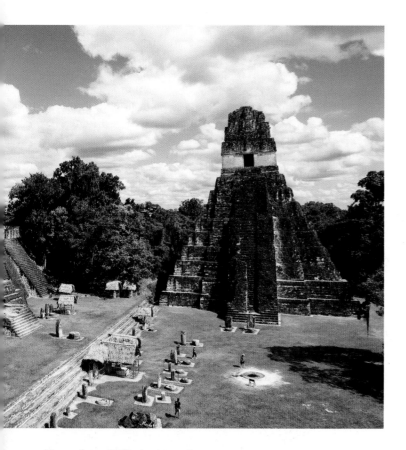

The ruins of Tikal, a great Maya city in Guatemala

Latvia (*LAT vee uh*) is a country that lies in northern Europe along the Baltic Sea. Estonia and Lithuania border Latvia. Together, these three countries are called the Baltic States. In the east, Latvia also borders Russia and Belarus. Riga is Latvia's capital and its largest city.

A large plain with many low hills and valleys covers most of Latvia. Almost half of the country has forests. There are small lakes and swamps throughout the land.

More than half of Latvia's people are Latvians. They have their own culture and language. The Latvian language is one of the oldest in Europe. Most of the rest of Latvia's people are Russians. Other people in Latvia include Belarusians, Lithuanians, Poles, and Ukrainians.

The people of Latvia like folklore, especially folk songs. They enjoy song festivals, opera, drama, and dance. For special times, they dress in colorful clothing of red, white, and gold. But most of the time, they dress in modern clothes. Most people belong to the Lutheran, Roman Catholic, or Russian Orthodox church.

Most of Latvia's workers are in service industries—industries that provide services, or help, to people. The country's factories produce clothes, food products, and wood products.

For more than 1,000 years, Latvia was ruled by different countries. They included Russia, Lithuania, Poland, Sweden, Germany, and the Soviet Union. Latvia won its independence from the Soviet Union in September 1991, and the Soviet Union broke apart later that year.

Latvia and its neighbors

Latvia in brief

- **Capital:** Riga.

- **Area:** 24,932 mi² (64,573 km²). *Greatest distances*—north-south, 170 mi (270 km); east-west, 280 mi (450 km). *Coastline*—330 mi (530 km).

- **Population:** *Current estimate*—1,864,000; *2020 official government estimate*—1,907,675.

- **Official language:** Latvian.

- **Chief products:** *Agriculture*—barley, beef and dairy cattle, chickens, hogs, potatoes, rye, wheat. *Manufacturing*—clothing, processed foods, textiles, transportation equipment, wood products.

- **Money:** *Basic unit*—euro. One hundred cents equal one euro. The euro replaced the Latvian lat in 2014.

- **Form of government:** Parliamentary democracy.

- **Climate:** Cold winters and mild summers, with 20 to 31 in (51 to 80 cm) of rainfall per year.

Flag

Sir Wilfrid Laurier

Laurier, Sir Wilfrid

Sir Wilfrid Laurier (*WIHL frihd LAW rih ay*) (1841–1919) was prime minister of Canada, or Canada's head of government, from 1896 to 1911. He was the first French Canadian to become a prime minister. Queen Victoria of the United Kingdom (UK) knighted Laurier, or made him Sir Wilfrid, in 1897.

Laurier spoke both English and French very well. He was known for his great speeches.

Wilfrid Laurier was born on Nov. 20, 1841, in Saint-Lin, Quebec. He studied law at McGill University in Montreal. Laurier graduated in 1864.

After graduation, Laurier became a successful lawyer in Quebec. He was elected to the Quebec legislature, or lawmaking group, in 1871. Three years later, he was elected to the Canadian Parliament, or government. Laurier served in Parliament for a total of 45 years. He was leader of the Liberal Party for 32 years.

Laurier worked to settle conflicts between the French-speaking and English-speaking Canadians. He also tried to make Canada more independent from the UK. At that time, Canada was part of the UK.

Laurier became prime minister on July 11, 1896. In 1905, during Laurier's term as prime minister, Alberta and Saskatchewan became Canadian provinces. Laurier's government helped many people from different countries settle in the prairies of the new provinces.

In 1911, the Conservative Party gained control of the government. Sir Wilfrid Laurier continued to serve as leader of the Liberal Party. He died on Feb. 17, 1919.

Lava. See Volcano.

Law

The law is the set of rules under which a society lives. No society could exist if people always did whatever they wanted, without thinking about the rights of others. A society also could not exist if people did not understand that there are things they should do for others. The law sets the rules that explain a person's rights—the fair treatment that a person deserves. The law also spells out a person's duties toward others.

The law sets punishments for people who do not follow its rules. Most societies use police, courts, and other government bodies to make sure that people obey the law.

There are two main types of law: public law and private law. Public law explains the rights and duties people have as members of society and as citizens. It includes laws dealing with crimes, such as robbery, and laws about taxes and the government. A constitution—a written set of rules saying what the government can or cannot do—is also public law. Private law, also called civil law, sets the rights and duties people have in their dealings with others. Such dealings include borrowing or lending money, buying a home, settling a divorce, or running a business.

Each country sets its own laws, and so the laws may be different from one place to another. But in many societies, governments try to make the laws fair to all people.

The earliest known set of written laws was developed about 4,100 years ago in the ancient Middle Eastern land of Babylonia, in what is now southeastern Iraq. The ancient Greeks began to develop laws about 2,600 years ago. The ancient Romans began writing laws about 2,450 years ago. Many later laws of Europe were based in part on Roman law.

The Court of King's Bench was a court of common law in the English legal system.

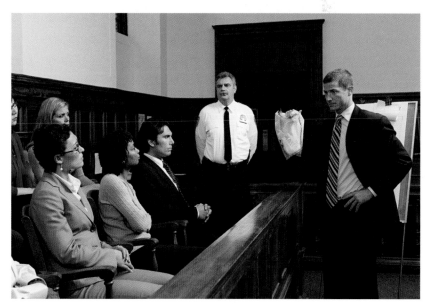

A lawyer offers advice on legal matters and represents clients in courts of law.

Lead (front) and lead ore

Lead

Lead (*lehd*) is a soft, heavy, bluish-gray metal. It can be hammered easily into different shapes. It does not rust and is not harmed by powerful chemicals. Lead has been used as a building material and to make pottery for thousands of years.

People use lead in batteries, paints, insect poisons, glass, and other products. Lead also stops X rays. It is used as a shield in rooms with X-ray machines.

People get lead from an ore, or mineral, that is mined underground. But people use much more lead than they mine each year. Much of it comes from recycling, or reusing, the lead in old batteries.

Too much contact with lead can be dangerous. Breathing too much lead dust or fumes, or eating bits of lead, can cause lead poisoning, a serious illness.

Two workers remove lead paint from an old house.

Lead poisoning

Lead poisoning is a sickness that people can get if their bodies take in too much lead. Lead is a metal found underground that is made into many different products.

People can get lead poisoning by swallowing objects made of lead, breathing in lead dust or *fumes* (gases), or taking in lead through their skin. Children can get lead poisoning by eating chips of lead paint or breathing in lead paint dust. Such paint was once used in older houses and has been found in some manufactured products. Lead poisoning also strikes adults who work to manufacture batteries or in other industries that use lead. Lead can damage blood cells and the brain, liver, and other organs.

Doctors can check people's blood to see if they have too much lead. People can take medicine to help to clean the lead from their bodies.

Other articles to read: **Lead**

Leaf

A leaf is the main food-making part of almost all plants. Leaves come in many different shapes. Many are oval, but others are shaped like arrowheads, feathers, hands, hearts, and countless other objects. Leaves may be flat or thick. Some leaves look like thick sewing needles. The number of leaves on plants ranges from several to thousands.

Most leaves are 1 to 12 inches (2.5 to 30 centimeters) long. But some plants have huge leaves. The largest leaves grow on the raffia (*RAF ee uh*) palm. The leaves of this tree grow up to 65 feet (20 meters) long. And some plants have tiny leaves. The leaves of asparagus plants are so tiny that they are hard to see without a magnifying glass.

The importance of leaves

Leaves are important to people. They are eaten as food and used to flavor foods and make such drinks as tea. Some drugs come from leaves. People use certain leaves to make rope. Leaves also help make the air that we breathe. When leaves make the plant's food, they give off a gas called oxygen. People and other animals must breathe oxygen to live.

A leaf makes its food out of energy from sunlight, water from the soil, and carbon dioxide, a gas in the air. This food-making process is called photosynthesis (*FOH tuh SIHN thuh sihs*). Plants need food to grow. Plants also use food to produce flowers and seeds. They store the food made by leaves in their fruits, roots, seeds, stems, and even in the leaves themselves.

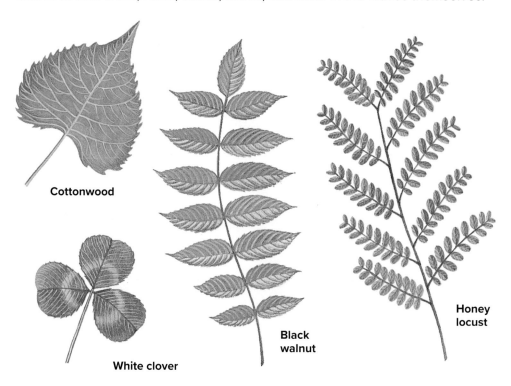

Cottonwood

White clover

Black walnut

Honey locust

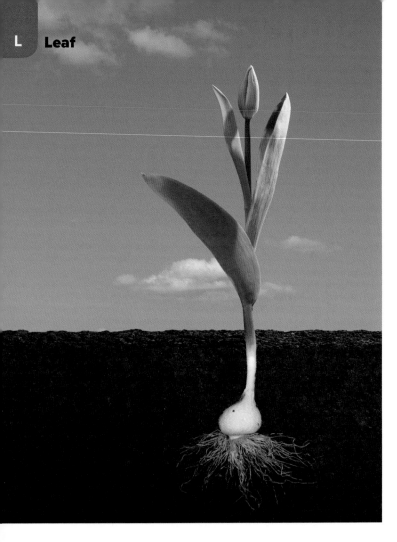

Tulip bulbs are made up of special leaves that store food underground in winter.

Some leaves have special jobs other than making food. The spines of a cactus keep animals from eating the plant. The fat leaves on a tulip bulb store food underground in winter. Many plants that grow in dry places have thick leaves that store water. Tendrils are special leaves that hold climbing plants in place. Some leaves attract, trap, and digest insects.

The life of a leaf

A leaf begins its life in a bud. Buds are the growing parts of a stem. They form along the sides and at the tip of the stem. The bud contains a tightly packed group of very tiny leaves. These leaves unfold and make food for the plant.

The leaf is green because it contains a green substance called chlorophyll (*KLAWR uh fihl*). Chlorophyll helps the leaf make food. The leaf also has other colors, but they are hidden by the green. In cool weather, the green color disappears. The leaf may then show its other colors, such as yellow or orange-red. Some dying leaves turn red and purple. When the leaf dies, it dries up and drops to the ground.

On the ground, the dead leaf becomes part of the soil. It then helps provide nourishment for new plant growth.

Other articles to read: **Chlorophyll; Photosynthesis**

Leaves develop on a lilac bush. First, a bud develops, then the bud opens and the leaves unfold. Finally, a twig develops.

Leaning Tower of Pisa

The Leaning Tower of Pisa is a bell tower in Pisa, Italy. It leans because it was built on soil that was not firm. The tower has eight floors. Each floor has arches all the way around it. A staircase on the inside leads to the top.

The tower is one of three buildings that make up the cathedral of Pisa. These buildings are known for their colorful marble and beautiful arches.

People began building the tower more than 800 years ago and finished it almost 200 years later. After the first three floors were built, the tower began to sink and lean over.

Each year, the tower has leaned a little more. In 1990, the tower was closed for repairs. Engineers worked on the tower's foundation, or base. They straightened the tower enough to keep it from falling. The tower opened again in June 2001.

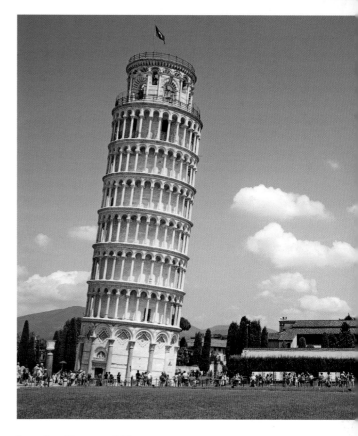

Leaning Tower of Pisa

Leap year

A leap year is a special year that has 366 days. That is one more day than an ordinary year. The extra day is February 29. A leap year occurs in every year that can be divided evenly by four, except for some years that mark an even century.

The calendar year is only 365 days long. But a *solar year* is slightly longer. A solar year is the time Earth takes to revolve around the sun—365 days, 5 hours, 48 minutes, and 46 seconds. We have to add an extra day every four years to make up the difference between the calendar year and the solar year.

Adding an extra day every fourth year would make the average calendar year a few minutes too long. So, the years that mark an even century are not leap years, unless they can be divided evenly by 400. The year 1900 had only 365 days, but 2000 had 366 days.

Other articles to read: **Year**

Leather

Leather is a strong material made from the skin of animals. Most leather comes from cattle hides. But the thinner skins of deer, goats, pigs, and sheep are also widely used. Fancy leathers are made from alligator, shark, and snake hides.

Leather is strong, and it lasts a long time. It can be made as soft as cloth or as stiff as wood. Some kinds of leather are thick and heavy, but others are thin. Leather can be dyed in different colors or polished until it is shiny.

Many things that people use every day are made of leather. They include shoes, belts, gloves, jackets, pants, shirts, and purses. Leather is also used to make baseballs, basketballs, and footballs. Most leather is made into shoes.

There are four main kinds of leather: shoe sole leather, shoe upper leather, chamois (*SHAM ee*), and suede (*swayd*). Shoe sole leather is made from the thick skins of cattle and other large animals. Shoe upper leather is produced from the thinner skins of calves and other smaller animals. Some people split thick hides into thin layers.

Most chamois leather is made from split sheepskin. It is as soft as cloth and soaks up water like cloth does. Chamois leather is good for washing and polishing things.

Suede is made from the inside of a cow's skin. Suede is soft and warm. It is used to make clothing and the tops of shoes.

People have used leather since prehistoric times. The process of turning animal skin to leather is called tanning.

Leather products

Lebanon (*LEHB uh nuhn*) is a small country in western Asia. It lies at the eastern end of the Mediterranean Sea. Israel lies to the south, and Syria lies to the north and east. Beirut, the capital and largest city of Lebanon, is on the coast. About half of Lebanon's people live in the Beirut area.

Land. Sandy beaches stretch along the Mediterranean coast. East of the coast, farmers raise fruit on a narrow plain. Most of Lebanon's cities are in this area.

Rugged mountains rise east of the plain. They extend down most of the length of the country. Farmers raise fruit in the mountains. Mountains also run along the country's eastern border.

A valley lies between the two mountain ranges. Many vegetables are grown there. The ruins of several ancient cities also are in this valley.

People. Most of Lebanon's people are Arabs. A large number are Palestinian Arabs, who once lived on land that is now part of Israel. Many of them came to Lebanon during the wars between Arabs and Israelis. Other groups in Lebanon include Kurds, people of a mountainous region of southwest Asia, and Armenians. Almost all Lebanese speak Arabic, the national language.

More than half of the people of Lebanon are Muslims. They follow the religion of Islam. Almost all the rest are Christians.

Resources and products. A war between Christians and Muslims in the 1970's and more fighting in the 1980's hurt Lebanon's industries and closed many businesses. Many people had no work.

Today, many people work in service industries. They work in banks, stores, hospitals, and hotels. Many people also work in factories and on farms.

History. People have lived in what is now Lebanon for thousands of years. About 4,000 years ago, the Phoenicians (*fih NEE shuhnz*) lived in cities along the coast. They were sailors, traders, and explorers. The

Lebanon and its neighbors

Lebanon in brief

■ **Capital:** Beirut.

■ **Area:** 4,036 mi² (10,452 km²). *Greatest distances*—north-south, 120 mi (193 km); east-west, 50 mi (80 km). *Coastline*—130 mi (210 km).

■ **Population:** *Current estimate*—5,566,000; *2018 official government estimate*—4,842,000.

■ **Official language:** Arabic.

■ **Chief products:** *Agriculture*—almonds, apples, beef and dairy cattle, cherries, chickens, cucumbers, grapes, lemons, olives, potatoes, tomatoes. *Manufacturing*—cement, chemicals, furniture, jewelry, processed foods, textiles.

■ **Money:** *Basic unit*—Lebanese pound. One hundred piasters equal one pound.

■ **Form of government:** Republic.

■ **Climate:** Coast—warm, humid summers and mild winters. Mountains—cooler and less humid than coast, but greater rainfall. Valley between mountains—less rainfall than mountains.

Flag

175

Beirut, Lebanon

Roman Empire gained control of the area a little over 2,000 years ago. Ruins of Roman temples and a Roman town still stand in Lebanon.

Christianity came to Lebanon about 1,700 years ago. Many Lebanese became Christians. In the early 600's, Muslims came to Lebanon. Many people along the coast became Muslims. But most people in the mountains remained Christians.

The Ottomans took over Lebanon in 1516. They ruled until World War I (1914–1918), when Britain and France took control of the country.

France helped set up Lebanon's government. The country became independent in 1943. Christian and Muslim leaders agreed to share power in the government.

In the mid-1970's, fights between Christians and Muslims led to civil war. The war ended in 1976. But fighting between Christians, Muslims, and other groups in Lebanon continued. The fighting caused many deaths and destroyed much of Lebanon. A peace plan ended most of the fighting in 1991.

In July 2006, Israel began bombing Lebanon after an anti-Israeli group based there, called Hezbollah (*HEHZ buh LAH*), captured two Israeli soldiers. Hezbollah fired missiles into northern Israel. In August, a peace agreement ended most of the fighting. Over 1,000 people died in the conflict, most of them Lebanese.

Lee, Robert E.

Robert E. Lee (1807–1870) was a great general. He commanded the Confederate Army of the South during the Civil War (1861–1865). For his military achievements and his character, Lee won the respect of Northerners as well as Southerners.

Robert Edward Lee was born near Montross, Virginia, on January 19, 1807. He graduated from the U.S. Military Academy at West Point in 1829 and served as an engineer in the Army. He helped to lay out the boundary line between Ohio and Michigan. Later, he was superintendent of West Point for three years. Then he served in Texas.

In 1861, Texas, Lee's home state of Virginia, and other Southern States seceded (*suh SEED ed*) from, or left, the United States. The Civil War began that same year. Lee resigned from the U.S. Army to defend Virginia, even though he did not want to see the country divided.

Lee took command of the Army of Northern Virginia. The Union, or Northern, forces had more soldiers, more supplies, and more weapons. However, Lee won several important battles. In July 1863, his soldiers fought at Gettysburg, Pennsylvania. After three days of bitter fighting, they lost.

Early in 1865, Lee was made chief of all the Confederate armies. By this time, the Confederate troops were exhausted and battered. Eventually, they had to retreat. Lee surrendered to General Ulysses S. Grant of the Union, or northern, Army on April 9, 1865, at Appomattox Court House, Virginia.

Lee spent his last years as president of Washington College, now Washington and Lee University. His home has been preserved in Arlington National Cemetery, near Washington, D.C.

Other articles to read: **Civil War, American**

Robert E. Lee

Leg

Legs are parts that support the bodies of people or animals. They are used to stand and move.

In people, the thigh has the longest, strongest bone in the body. The lower leg has two long bones. The largest one is the shinbone. The knee joint is like a hinge between the thigh bone and lower leg bones. A small bone called the kneecap is in front of the knee joint.

Muscles are attached to the bones. In the front of the thigh, a big muscle straightens the knee and bends the thigh at the hip. Muscles in the back of the thigh bend the knee and straighten the thigh.

Muscles in the lower leg bend and straighten the ankles and toes. They also bend the foot side ways.

Other articles to read: **Foot; Human body; Muscle**

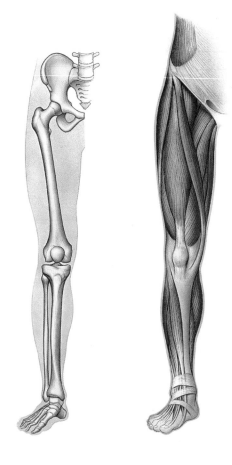

The leg contains large, strong bones (left) and powerful muscles (right).

Leif Eriksson

Leif Eriksson (*leef AIR ihk suhn*) (A.D. 980?–1025?) was a Norse explorer. He was the son of Erik the Red. He led what was probably the first European trip to the North American mainland. His life is told in long stories called sagas.

Leif Eriksson was born in Iceland. In 985, his family sailed to Greenland, where his father, Erik the Red, built the first settlement.

About 1002, Leif sailed west from Greenland. Sagas tell of Leif and his men landing in a place they named Vinland. No one really knows where Vinland was, because Eriksson made no maps. Some experts think it may have been what is now the island of Newfoundland in Canada. Others believe it was closer to what is now Cape Cod, Massachusetts.

Other articles to read: **Erik the Red**

Leif Eriksson discovering North America

Lemon

Lemons are small fruits. They belong to a group called citrus fruits, which also include limes and oranges. Lemons are oval and have a yellow rind, or peel. Most lemons taste sour, so people rarely eat fresh lemons.

Lemons are used to flavor soft drinks, desserts, and many other foods. Cooks use lemon juice and oil from the lemon rind to flavor meat and fish. Lemon oil is also used as a scent.

Lemon trees grow up to 25 feet (7.6 meters) tall. They have thorns, pointed leaves, and sweet-smelling white blossoms. The trees often have flowers and fruit at the same time.

Lemon trees can be damaged by freezing weather. Growers use heaters, big fans, or water sprays to help protect the trees from cold.

Lemon

Lemur

Lemurs (*LEE muhrz*) are long-tailed animals with fluffy fur. Lemurs are mammals, animals that feed their young with the mother's milk. They belong to the group of mammals called primates, which also includes monkeys, apes, and humans.

Lemurs live only in Madagascar and Comoros. Both countries are islands off the coast of Africa. The smallest lemurs—lesser mouse lemurs—look like furry mice. Ring-tailed lemurs are gray on top and white underneath. They look like monkeys with a pointed nose. Their tails have rings of black and white fur. Ruffed lemurs are usually a mixture of black and white with a fluffy white ruff, or collar.

Lemurs have few enemies on the islands where they live. Still, many kinds are in danger of dying out, because people have cut down the forests where they make their homes.

Ring-tailed lemur

Lenin, V. I.

V. I. Lenin (*LEHN ihn*) (1870–1924) was the founder of the Communist Party in Russia. He led the October Revolution of 1917, in which the Communists seized power in Russia. He then ruled the country until his death in 1924.

Lenin was born on April 22, 1870, in Simbirsk (now Ulyanovsk), Russia. His real name was Vladimir Ilyich Ulyanov. He changed his name to *Lenin* in 1901. He earned a law degree from St. Petersburg University in 1891.

Lenin studied the political ideas of Karl Marx, the founder of revolutionary Communism. In 1898, Marxists formed the Russian Social Democratic Labor Party. In 1903, the party split into two groups, the *Bolsheviks* (members of the majority) and the *Mensheviks* (members of the minority). Lenin was the leader of the Bolsheviks, later called Communists.

World War I (1914–1918) brought economic hardship and political unrest to Russia. In early 1917, the Russian people overthrew the *czar* (emperor) and set up an elected government. That autumn, the Bolsheviks, led by Lenin, seized power and established a Communist government. Lenin immediately withdrew Russia from World War I.

The new government soon took over Russia's industries and forced the peasants to give the government most of their farm products. Lenin became the nation's dictator and ruled by terror. People who opposed the Communists were imprisoned or murdered.

From 1918 to 1920, a civil war in Russia was fought between the Communists and the anti-Communists. The Communists won. In 1922, Lenin and his followers transformed Russia into the first Communist state, the Union of Soviet Socialist Republics. Lenin died on Jan. 21, 1924.

Other articles to read: **Communism; Russia; Union of Soviet Socialist Republics (U.S.S.R.)**

V. I. Lenin

Lens

A lens is a piece of curved glass, plastic, or some other see-through material. Lenses may be used to make objects look bigger or smaller. Lenses may also be used to make what we see look sharp and clear. There are two main kinds of lenses, convex and concave. Convex lenses are curved out, and concave lenses are curved in. Lenses are an important part of binoculars, cameras, microscopes, telescopes, and many other devices.

The lens is also an important part of the human eye. Our lenses help our eyes make sharp pictures of objects that are near or far. When people have blurry eyesight, they wear eyeglasses with glass or plastic lenses to correct the problem. Sometimes they wear contact lenses on the eyes.

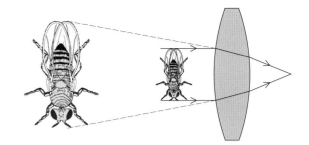

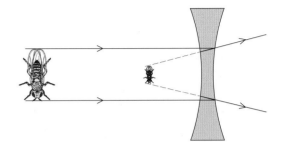

A double convex lens curves out on both sides. It makes things look larger. A double concave lens curves in on both sides. It makes things look smaller.

Leonardo da Vinci

Leonardo da Vinci (*lee uh NAHR doh duh VIHN chee*) (1452–1519) was one of the greatest painters in history. He was gifted in many other ways as well. Leonardo was one of the most important people in the Renaissance (*REHN uh sahns*). The Renaissance was a time when the importance of arts, sciences, and many kinds of learning grew very rapidly.

Leonardo was probably born outside the village of Vinci, near Florence, Italy. His name, *da Vinci,* means *from Vinci.* He studied with Andrea del Verrocchio, a leading painter and sculptor in Florence, and then worked for him.

Leonardo had his own studio in Florence for several years. Then he went to Milan to become an artist in a duke's court. While he was there, he also worked as an engineer. He designed forts, weapons, locks for Milan's canals, and stages for shows. He also painted his first important work, *Madonna of the Rocks* (about 1483).

Leonardo da Vinci

Mona Lisa **by Leonardo da Vinci**

He painted *The Last Supper,* a religious picture of Jesus and his apostles, around 1497.

In 1499, the French overthrew the duke. Leonardo returned to Florence. His work in Milan had gained people's respect. He was hired to do a large battle painting. While he worked on it, he painted the *Mona Lisa*, a picture of a young woman. The battle painting no longer exists, but the *Mona Lisa* is probably the most famous painting of a person ever created.

In Leonardo's later years, King Francis I of France invited Leonardo to become his royal painter, engineer, and architect. Leonardo spent his last three years in France.

In his work, Leonardo looked at things carefully and made many drawings. He studied the human body and the bodies of animals. He also studied plants, the stars and planets, and many other science subjects. Leonardo planned to write books on the subjects, but he never finished them. He kept notebooks full of drawings, ideas he had written down, and plans for inventions such as flying machines and a helicopter. His notebooks were published nearly 400 years after he died.

Leopard

Leopards (*LEHP uhrdz*) are large animals in the cat family. The leopard is the third largest cat in Asia and Africa. Only tigers and lions are larger. The biggest male leopards are almost 9 feet (2.7 meters) long from nose to tail.

Most leopards have light tan fur with black spots. Leopards that live in forests are darker. Black leopards are so dark that the spots are hard to see.

Leopards are fierce hunters. They kill and feed on such animals as monkeys, antelope, peacocks, snakes, and goats. They are good climbers and often carry the animals they kill up a tree. Females have two to four cubs at a time.

Leopards have been hunted for their beautiful fur. They are now disappearing in many places.

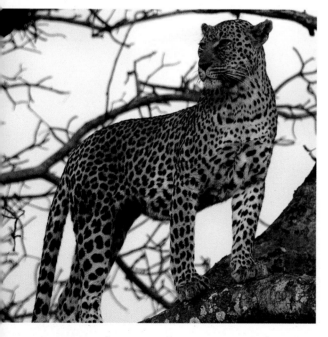

Leopard

Lesbian, gay, bisexual, and transgender (LGBT) rights movement

Lesbian, gay, bisexual, and transgender (LGBT) rights movement works to protect rights and win equality for people who are *homosexual* (sexually attracted to people of the same sex); *bisexual* (attracted to members of both sexes); or *transgender*. Female homosexuals are often called *lesbians*. Individuals who are called *transgender* are those whose identity or self-expression does not match the *gender* assigned to them at birth. Gender includes the beliefs, feelings, and behaviors that people associate with individuals based on whether they outwardly appear to be male or female.

The LGBT rights movement was often called the *gay rights movement* until the 1990's. Since then, activists in the United States have used the abbreviation LGBT to refer to the movement and its members. The term LGBT is now commonly used in a number of other countries as well. Another variation of this abbreviation, LGBTQ, is sometimes used. The q stands for either *q*ueer or *q*uestioning (identifying with neither gender).

The LGBT rights movement works to educate people about LGBT issues, to encourage gay individuals to publicly declare their sexual orientation, and to encourage transgender individuals to express themselves according to the gender identity they have chosen. A major goal of the LGBT rights movement is to change laws that restrict or ban same-sex sexual relations. Most supporters of the movement believe that same-sex couples should have the same rights as male-female couples, including the right to marry. LGBT rights groups also work to improve the ways in which gay and transgender people are shown in the mass media and to pass laws that protect homosexuals from unfair treatment.

Most historians trace the birth of the modern LGBT rights movement to a 1969 police raid on a New York City gay bar called the Stonewall Inn. Such raids were common then, but this raid met with strong resistance from the gay community. Bar patrons began a riot that lasted several days and caused gay communities throughout North America, Europe, and Australia to take action. After Stonewall, gay rights activists created new organizations and developed many political strategies still used today.

LGBT rights activists

Lesotho in brief

- **Capital:** Maseru.
- **Area:** 11,720 mi² (30,355 km²).
- **Population:** *Current estimate*—2,176,000; *2016 census*—2,007,201.
- **Official languages:** English and Sesotho.
- **Chief products:** *Agriculture*—beans, cattle, corn, goats, peas, potatoes, sheep, sorghum, wheat, wool.
- **Money:** *Basic unit*—loti. One hundred lisente equal one loti.
- **Form of government:** Constitutional monarchy.
- **Climate:** Mild, moist. Highlands have some freezing temperatures and snow in winter.

Flag

Lesotho (*lay SOO too*) is a mountainous country in Africa. It is surrounded by the Republic of South Africa. Lesotho is about 200 miles (320 kilometers) from the Indian Ocean. Maseru (*MAZ uh ROO*) is the capital and largest city.

Most of Lesotho's people are African people called Basotho or Basuto. They live in villages and raise crops on nearby land. The people own all the land together, and the chiefs decide where each family will farm. The Basotho also raise animals.

Lesotho is a beautiful country, but it is poor. Too much farming has worn out the soil. There are not enough jobs for everyone, so many men go to South Africa to work. Factories in Lesotho make clothing, processed food, and textiles. The country also mines diamonds.

In the late 1700's and early 1800's, wars between African peoples broke out. Some groups escaped into the area that is now Lesotho, where they were protected by a strong chief named Moshoeshoe. Both the British and Dutch settlers fought Moshoeshoe's people. Finally, Moshoeshoe asked Britain for help. The area came under Britain's control. It was called Basutoland. Basutoland became the independent kingdom of Lesotho in 1966.

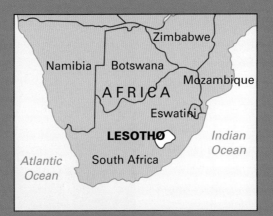

Lesotho and its neighbors

Lettuce

Lettuce is a leafy green vegetable. It usually grows close to the ground. It is used mainly in salads, and most people eat it raw. It is a very healthful food.

There are three main kinds of lettuce. Head lettuce is the most common. Its leaves curl around the center and form a ball shape. Leaf lettuce grows in thick, leafy clumps instead of heads. Gardeners grow more leaf lettuce than any other kind. Romaine lettuce grows long and upright. The leaves curl inward. Romaine contains more vitamins and minerals than any other kind of lettuce.

Most lettuce is planted right in the ground, but some lettuce is started in buildings called greenhouses. Plants in greenhouses get enough light and water and are protected from cold. Lettuce must be packed, cooled, and shipped right after harvesting because it spoils easily.

Kinds of lettuce

Boston lettuce

Iceberg lettuce

Romaine lettuce

Bibb lettuce

Leaf lettuce

Celtuce lettuce

Lewis, C. S.

C. S. Lewis (1898–1963) was a British author. He is known for his clever and amusing stories. Lewis wrote more than 30 books, including children's stories, science fiction, and books on religion. Most of his writings teach lessons about right and wrong.

Clive Staples Lewis was born in Belfast, Northern Ireland. As an adult, he taught literature, the study of writings, at both Oxford and Cambridge universities in England. Between 1950 and 1956, he wrote a popular series of children's books called *The Chronicles of Narnia*. His other books include *Out of the Silent Planet* (1938), about three scientists who travel to Mars.

C. S. Lewis

Lewis and Clark expedition

A Native American Shoshone woman named Sacagawea traveled with Lewis and Clark.

Lewis and Clark were explorers who led an important expedition. They traveled through what is now the Northwestern United States.

Meriwether Lewis (1774–1809) was a captain in the United States Army. President Thomas Jefferson asked him to plan the journey. Lewis asked William Clark (1770–1838), a former officer, to join him.

Lewis and Clark started out from St. Louis, Missouri, in May 1804. They traveled up the Missouri River, across the Rocky Mountains, and along the Columbia and other rivers to the Pacific Ocean. They returned in September 1806, after traveling about 8,000 miles (12,800 kilometers). They brought back maps and information about plants, animals, minerals, and Native Americans. The United States then claimed the land that is now Oregon, Washington, and Idaho.

Other articles to read: **Sacagawea**

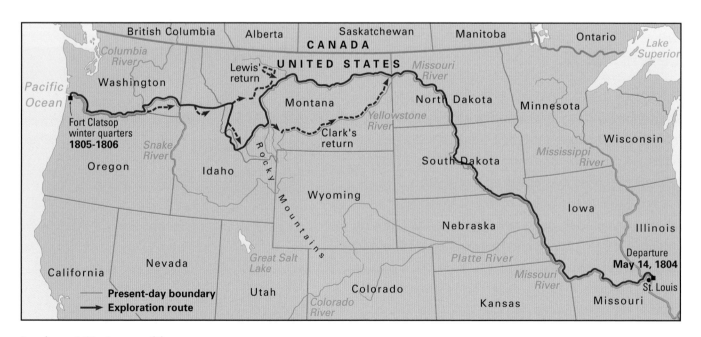

Lewis and Clark expedition

Liberia is a country in west Africa. It is bordered by Sierra Leone on the northwest, Guinea on the northeast, Côte d'Ivoire on the east, and the Atlantic Ocean on the west. Monrovia (*muhn ROH vee uh*) is the capital and largest city. Liberia has a rugged coastline. Away from the ocean, the land is higher, with low hills.

Most Liberians are Africans. Some of them are people whose families came from the United States more than 150 years ago. In the early 1800's, a group of people in the United States bought land along the coast. Some enslaved Africans in the United States had been freed. The group sent them to settle there. Other Liberians come from families who have always lived in Africa. They include Kpelle and Bassa people.

Many Liberians farm for a living. People in cities work in schools, stores, factories, and offices. Liberia has diamonds and gold, and some people work in mining.

Liberia's earliest people were from eastern Africa. Portuguese explorers began to trade with people along the coast in the 1400's.

In 1847, Liberia became independent. It was a poor country. Most of the power belonged to the people whose families had come from the United States. War broke out in 1989 between various groups. In 1996, the people agreed to stop fighting and try to start a new government. Elections were held in 1997. But various groups continued to fight the government. In 2003, such groups controlled most of the country. Soldiers from other countries came to help restore peace. In 2005, elections were held.

Liberia in brief

■ **Capital:** Monrovia.

■ **Area:** 43,000 mi² (111,369 km²). *Greatest distances*—east-west, 230 mi (370 km); north-south, 210 mi (338 km). *Coastline*—315 mi (507 km).

■ **Population:** *Current estimate*—5,324,000.

■ **Official language:** English.

■ **Chief products:** *Agriculture*—bananas, cacao, cassava, coffee, corn, palm oil, rice, rubber. *Mining*—diamonds, gold.

■ **Money:** *Basic unit*—Liberian dollar. One hundred cents equal one dollar.

■ **Form of government:** Republic.

■ **Climate:** Hot and humid, with heavy rainfall, especially along the coast.

Flag

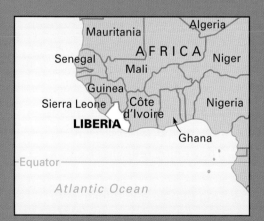

Liberia and its neighbors

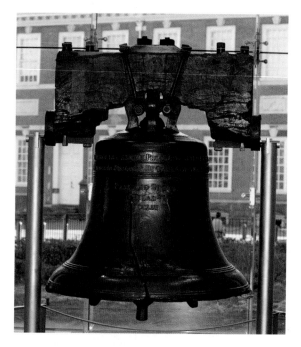

Liberty Bell in Philadelphia

Liberty, Statue of. See Statue of Liberty.

Liberty Bell

The Liberty Bell is a symbol (*SIHM buhl*) of independence in the United States. It was brought from England to Philadelphia in 1753. It rang to mark special events and to call people together. One event was on July 8, 1776, to announce the adoption of the Declaration of Independence. The Declaration of Independence was signed on July 4, 1776. In 1841, the bell cracked.

Until 1976, the Liberty Bell was kept in Independence Hall in Philadelphia. It now hangs nearby, in the Liberty Bell Pavilion, but the bell is no longer rung. However, it is struck like a gong on important days and the sound is broadcast so that everyone can hear it.

Students reading in a library

Library

A library is a collection of many kinds of information. A library has books, magazines, newspapers, videos, films, computer programs, and recordings. In a library, people can learn about history, science, art, and government. They can also go to the library to listen to a story, watch a film, see works of art, or listen to music. There are special libraries in universities and law offices, in hospitals, and in schools.

Public libraries

Public libraries serve all the people in a community, town, or city, including children. The children's librarian tries to make the children's part of the library a friendly place with colorful posters and interesting exhibits and displays. Tables, chairs, and shelves are set up in a special way for children. Children's librarians plan programs for many interests and age levels. They enjoy reading stories to children at story hours.

Librarians also help young people and adults learn about different jobs or careers. Sometimes librarians meet with groups to talk about books. People of all ages can find information and learn about community activities in a public library.

Public libraries also serve people with special needs and interests. Sometimes libraries buy books in different languages, or books on tape for people who can't see well. Sometimes they show the work of artists who live in the area. Sometimes they have neighborhood or visiting poets read their works. Many public libraries have classes to help people learn English or how to read.

Some cities have branch libraries. Then everyone in the city has a small library nearby. Some cities have bookmobiles. These are vans that stop at various places around the city to lend books. The books from public libraries usually cost nothing to borrow.

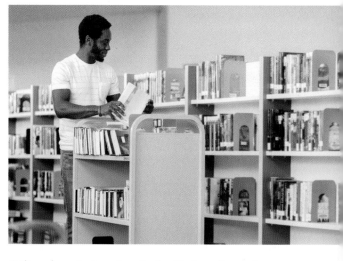

A librarian shelves books by their call number.

School libraries

Many schools have libraries. School libraries have materials that help children do their schoolwork or find out more about their special interests. Some school libraries have interesting objects to examine, such as

Students use computers at a library to find information.

Bookmobile

A children's librarian reads stories to children at story hour.

birds' nests, musical instruments, maps, and games. Some have computers and videos.

A school library helps teachers, too. For example, if a second-grade class is studying Mexico, the teacher can borrow photographs of Mexican life and compact discs (CD's) of Mexican music from the school library. Students may work together in small groups in the library, watching videos or discussing questions. Sometimes older students help younger students in the school library by reading aloud to them or helping them learn to write.

Challenges and problems

Librarians must take good care of books and find ways to handle them when they get old. Over time, paper crumbles. Librarians know how to repair old books. Sometimes they copy them onto film to save important information from the past.

One problem that libraries sometimes face is censorship. Censorship means that certain books or other materials are not allowed in the library. Some people object to books about religion, sex, or government, or books that have bad language. Other people think that all types of books should be in libraries. Librarians must listen to everyone and then decide what books to buy for the library.

Another problem that libraries have is theft, or stealing. Each year, books are stolen from the library. Libraries use different ways to check books that are going out. Sometimes a guard makes sure that people have checked out a book before they leave the library with it.

Some libraries have a system that rings an alarm if a person tries to leave the library with material that was not checked out.

Libraries have money problems, too. They must ask for money from the government and from other groups. They must figure out how much money they have and how much they can spend. Librarians must decide what books are best to buy and what services people need most.

Using the library

Most libraries have two sections of books and other materials. Books in the reference section, such as dictionaries and encyclopedias, must be used in the library. People cannot take reference books home. Most other books can be checked out and taken home if you have a library card. It is easy to get a library card. The librarian will help you fill out a form to get one.

Librarians give every item in the library a special number called a call number. Call numbers help you find books and other materials. They tell you where the item is in the library. You can get the call number from the library computer. You can look for books by author, title, or subject on the computer.

Or you can just walk around and look at the books on the shelves. Often, you find interesting books to read just by taking books off the shelves or by looking at the book jackets and book posters on the library walls. You can also ask the librarian to suggest a book about something that interests you, such as horses, mysteries, or jokes.

History of libraries

Libraries have been around as long as writing itself—about 5,500 years. At first, books were made of such materials as clay, bones, metal, wax, wood, plants, silk, and leather. Writings on

The children's section of a library often has books and furniture for younger readers.

Map library

Main Reading Room of the Library of Congress in Washington, D.C.

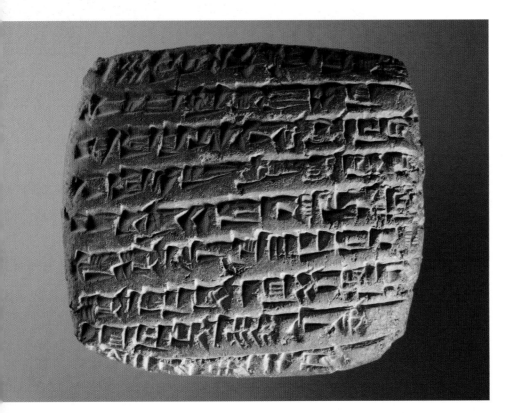

Clay tablet from Mesopotamia

clay tablets were found in Mesopotamia, a long-ago society that once was where Turkey and Iraq are today.

Libraries in ancient Egypt, Greece, and Rome had books written on paper that was made from a plant called papyrus. Then the paper was rolled up into tubes called scrolls. The most famous library of ancient times was the Alexandrian Library in Egypt. That library had more than 400,000 scrolls, including scrolls of writings from the Bible.

Most early libraries in colonial America belonged to ministers. Most of the books in these early libraries were about religion, medicine, and animals. Later, people could pay to belong to a library. Free libraries became popular in the 1830's. In the 1880's Andrew Carnegie, a Scottish-born American, gave millions of dollars to build more than 2,500 public libraries throughout the world.

Other articles to read:
Book; Literature for children; Magazine; Newspaper; Printing

Libya is a country in northern Africa, on the coast of the Mediterranean Sea. It is bordered by Egypt and Sudan on the east, Chad and Niger on the south, and Algeria and Tunisia on the west. Tripoli (*TRIHP uh lee*) is Libya's capital and largest city.

Most of Libya's people are a mixture of Arab and Berber peoples. The Berbers lived in the area long before the Arabs arrived. Almost all Libyans follow the religion of Islam.

The Sahara, a huge desert, covers most of Libya. A few people live in desert oases, areas where there is water. However, most Libyans live near the Mediterranean coast.

Only a small amount of land is good for farming, so Libya must buy most of its food. The country is rich in oil. Most of Libya's money comes from selling oil to other countries.

People have lived in what is now Libya for thousands of years. Arabs spread the Islamic religion to the area in the 600's. In the 1500's, most of Libya became part of the Ottoman Empire, which was based in what is now Turkey. In the early and middle 1900's, Italy and the United Kingdom controlled parts of Libya. The United Kingdom and France took control from Italy during World War II (1939–1945), with the help of Muslim forces from Libya.

Libya became an independent kingdom in 1951. In 1959, oil was discovered. Libya became wealthy, but few people shared the wealth. In September 1969, a group of military officers led by Colonel Mu'ammar Muhammad al-Qadhafi took over the country's government. Qadhafi ruled as a dictator until October 2011, when he was killed during an armed rebellion against his rule. In July 2012, Libyans elected a new national assembly and began to form a new government.

Libya in brief

- **Capital:** Tripoli.
- **Area:** 679,362 mi² (1,759,540 km²). *Greatest distances*—north-south, 930 mi (1,497 km); east-west, 1,050 mi (1,690 km). *Coastline*—1,047 mi (1,685 km).
- **Population:** *Current estimate*—7,107,000.
- **Official language:** Arabic.
- **Chief products:** *Agriculture*—almonds, chickens, dates, olives, sheep, tomatoes. *Manufacturing*—cement, petroleum products, processed foods. *Mining*—natural gas, petroleum.
- **Money:** *Basic unit*—Libyan dinar. One thousand dirhams equal one dinar.
- **Form of government:** Transitional council.
- **Climate:** Mild along the coast, with light rainfall. Extremely hot in the desert, with cool nights and almost no rain.

Flag

Libya and its neighbors

Liechtenstein in brief

- **Capital:** Vaduz.

- **Area:** 62 mi² (160 km²). *Greatest length*—17.4 mi (28 km). *Greatest width*—7 mi (11 km).

- **Population:** *Current estimate*—39,000; *2015 census*—37,622.

- **Official language:** German.

- **Chief products:** *Agriculture*—barley, corn, dairy cattle, grapes, potatoes, wheat. *Manufacturing*—ceramics, dental products, food products, machinery, metal products, pharmaceuticals, precision instruments.

- **Money:** *Basic unit*—Swiss franc. One hundred centimes equal one franc.

- **Form of government:** Constitutional monarchy.

- **Climate:** Mild.

Flag

Liechtenstein (*LIHK tuhn STYN*) is one of the world's smallest countries. It lies in central Europe. Liechtenstein is bordered by Switzerland and Austria. Vaduz (*VAH doots*) is the capital city.

The people of Liechtenstein come from a German group that settled in the area more than 1,500 years ago. They have many close ties with Switzerland.

The Rhine River flows along the western border of Liechtenstein. A narrow strip of farmland lies next to the river. Mountains cover most of the country's eastern and southern sections.

Until about 50 years ago, most people in Liechtenstein were farmers. Now the country has many industries. Ceramics, machinery, medicines, and metal products are some important products. Also, collectors around the world buy the country's beautiful postage stamps. Many farmers in Liechtenstein raise such crops as grapes and wheat. Other farmers raise cattle.

Liechtenstein was once two small states. A prince from Vienna, Austria, named Johann-Adam Liechtenstein became the ruler of one of the states in 1699 and of the other in 1712. His family has ruled Liechtenstein ever since.

Liechtenstein has been independent since 1719, except for a short time in the early 1800's. In 1924, the country agreed to join Switzerland in some of its services. The people use Swiss money, and Switzerland runs Liechtenstein's postal system and telephone service. Switzerland also handles some of Liechtenstein's trade agreements with other countries.

Liechtenstein and its neighbors

Life

Life is a special quality or condition shared by all living things. Such things as stones, houses, and cars do not have life, and are not living things.

There are more than 10 million kinds of living things. Some, like bacteria, are too small to see. Others, like blue whales and redwood trees, are huge. Living things are found in many places, but they are all alike in some ways.

What living things do

Living things can reproduce. They can make more of their own kind of living thing. Some living things, such as bacteria, reproduce by dividing in two. Most plants and animals reproduce by combining material from a male and a female.

Living things grow. Many plants grow by taking in chemicals from the air and water. Animals grow by eating plants or other animals.

Living things must use energy to live. They break down the chemicals in food to get some of the energy. Green plants also get energy from the sun.

Most living things move. In some living things, such as plants, much of the movement is inside. Animals may move in ways that are easier to see.

Living things can sense changes around themselves and react in some way. Often, they move. For example, a turtle pulls into its shell, and a plant grows toward the sun.

Living things grow.

Living things reproduce.

Living things sense changes.

Living things use energy.

Living things can change to survive (keep on living). Over many years, they may become able to eat new foods or live in hotter, colder, wetter, or dryer places.

What living things are made of

All living things are made up of tiny parts called cells (*SELZ*). The simplest living things have only one cell. Large living things, such as a dog, a tree, or a person, have many parts. So, they have billions of cells.

Each cell has a thin covering called a membrane (*MEHM brayn*). It separates the cell from other cells. Only certain substances can pass through it. Inside, most cells have a jellylike outer part and a center called a nucleus (*NOO klee uhs*). The nucleus is the control center. It tells the cell what to do.

Large living things have several different kinds of cells. Cells that work in the same way form tissues (*TISH ooz*), such as muscle. Several kinds of tissue form the body's organs, such as the heart, liver, and brain.

How life began

The religions of many people have stories of how living things came to be. In the Christian religion, the Bible tells how God created Earth and all living things.

Scientists have theories (*THEE uhr eez*), or ideas, about how life began. Long ago, some scientists thought that tiny cells floated to Earth from outer space. Most scientists today think life was created from chemicals here on Earth. Scientists are doing experiments to learn how that could have happened.

Other articles to read: **Adaptation; Biology; Cell; Creationism; Death; Evolution; Life cycle; Reproduction; Reproduction, Human**

Most living things move.

Eggs

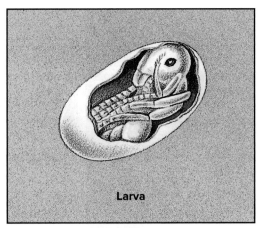
Larva

Pupa

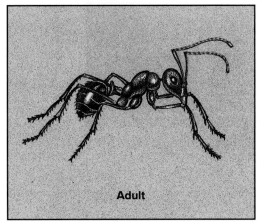
Adult

Life cycle of ants

Life cycle

A life cycle is a set of steps, or stages, that living things go through as they grow, change, and produce other living things. The life cycle starts at a certain point, such as when a queen bee lays eggs. It includes all the steps until a new bee becomes a queen and lays eggs.

In mammals, such as dogs, the life cycle is simple. The new animal develops in the mother's body. It is born and it grows. When it is grown, it reproduces. It becomes the parent of a new animal like itself.

Other articles to read: **Reproduction; Reproduction, Human**

Lift. See Elevator.

Light

Light is a kind of energy that makes it possible for us to see. Some things, such as the sun and lights in a room, give off light. We see all other things because light bounces off them and travels to us.

How light is made

Some light, such as sunlight, comes from nature. Other light comes from things people make, such as lamps. But all light comes from atoms (*AT uhmz*), tiny particles of matter that make up everything in the universe. Atoms sometimes gain extra energy and give it off as light. Sunlight comes from atoms that give off energy inside the sun.

One way to make atoms give off light is to heat them. A light bulb glows because electricity heats a wire inside it. The heated atoms gain extra energy and give it off as light.

A few things give off light without being heated very much. Some materials glow in the dark. Some insects and other living things glow.

The nature of light

Light acts as a wave. It has high and low places, like waves on a pond. Light waves can be long or short. Light also acts like tiny particles that travel in a straight line.

Sunlight is white light. It is made up of many colors. When passed through a piece of glass with a special shape, called a prism (*PRIHZ uhm*), it breaks into all the colors we can see, from deep violet, blue, and green through yellow, orange, and red.

The violet waves are the shortest waves we can see, and red waves are the longest. Waves too short to be seen are called ultraviolet rays. They cause sunburn and suntan. Waves too long to be seen are called infrared rays. They cause the warming we feel in sunlight.

How light behaves

When light hits an object, it may bounce off, or

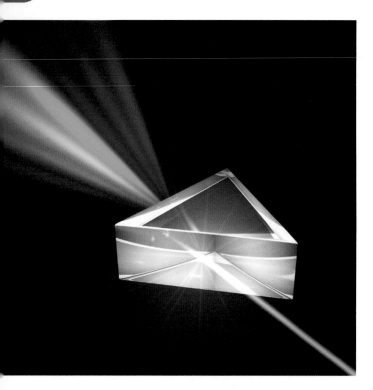

A prism breaks light that passes through it into colors.

A firefly makes its own light. Organs in its body contain chemicals that make it glow without giving off heat.

reflect (*rih FLEHKT*). If it hits a surface straight, it reflects straight back. But if it hits at an angle, it bounces in another direction.

When light passes through something, it may bend and change its direction.

When light hits an object, the object may soak up some colors and reflect others. The reflected colors are what we see.

Measuring light

Scientists measure the wavelength, brightness, and speed of light. The speed of light in empty space is always the same. In space, light travels at 186,282 miles (299,792 kilometers) per second.

Other articles to read: **Color; Edison, Thomas Alva; Electricity; Prism; Rainbow; Sun**

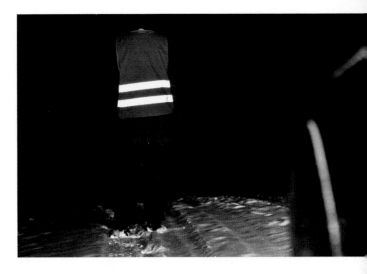

Light bounces off reflective strips on a road worker's vest. This helps drivers see the worker at night.

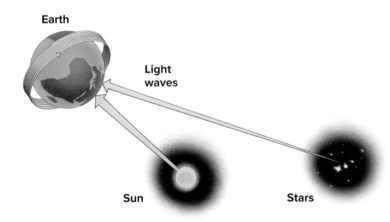

Light waves reach Earth from the sun in about eight minutes. Light waves from other stars take years to reach us.

Light-year

A light-year is the distance that light travels in one year. The light-year is used by scientists called astronomers (*uh STRON uh muhrz*). They use the light-year to describe the huge distances between stars, galaxies, and other objects in space.

Light travels very fast. It travels 186,282 miles (299,792 kilometers) each second. Therefore, one light-year equals about 5.88 trillion miles (9.46 trillion kilometers). A jet moving at a speed of 500 miles (800 kilometers) per hour would need to fly for 1.34 million years to travel one light-year.

Objects in space are usually very far from each other. Even the star nearest to Earth— other than the sun—is 4.3 light-years away. The Andromeda Galaxy, the large galaxy nearest to our own, is about 2.5 million light-years away.

Other articles to read: **Light**

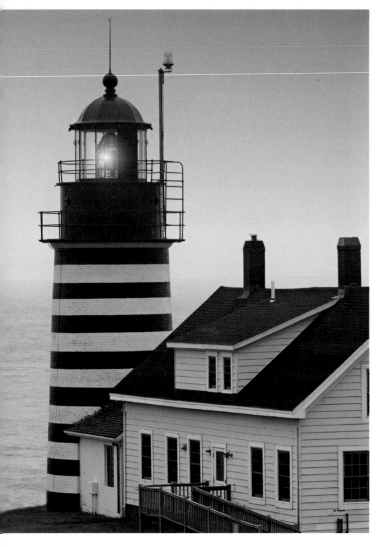

West Quoddy Lighthouse in Lubec, Maine, is painted with stripes so that, during the day, sailors can tell which lighthouse it is.

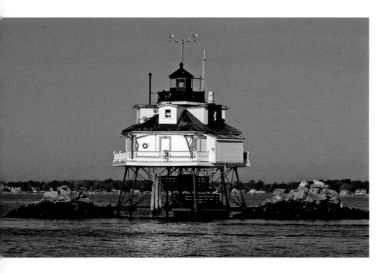

Thomas Point Shoal Lighthouse in Annapolis, Maryland, sits on a platform.

Lighthouse

Lighthouses are towers with a very strong light. They tell sailors that land is near and warn them of dangerous rocks and reefs. They also help sailors figure out where their ship is.

People build lighthouses on land that sticks out into the ocean, and on rocks that jut out of the sea. Some lighthouses stand in the sea itself. They are built on rocks beneath the water.

Every lighthouse gives off a different pattern of light. Some have a steady light. Others have patterns of long or short flashes. The patterns of light tell the sailors which lighthouse they are seeing. Then they know exactly where they are.

In daytime, sailors can recognize the lighthouse. Lighthouses that look alike are painted with different patterns, such as checks or stripes.

The lamps in a lighthouse shine through lenses. The lenses make the light stronger, so that it can be seen for many miles. Many lighthouses also use foghorns or bells to signal ships in bad weather, when the light is hard to see.

Lighthouses were probably first used by the people of ancient Egypt. At first, they built fires on hilltops. Later, they built towers. The ancient Romans built lighthouses in many places. The first lighthouse in North America was Boston Lighthouse. It was built in 1716.

Today, most lighthouses are automatic. They do not need people to run them. But in the United States, some people still work in lighthouses.

Lightning

Lightning is a giant electric spark. Most of the lightning people see is a spark between the sky and the ground. But lightning also travels within clouds and between clouds. Lightning makes the air in its path so hot that it rushes outward. The air makes a cracking sound that we hear as thunder.

Everything in the world is made up of tiny particles called *atoms* (*AT uhmz*). Sometimes the atoms in clouds become charged, or filled, with electricity. When charged atoms move toward one another, they create a spark.

The spark travels down from the cloud. When it gets close to the ground, an electric current rushes upward from a tall tree or building to meet it. That electric current makes the lightning that people see. A flash of lightning often has several quick strokes. This makes the lightning seem to flicker.

There are several kinds of lightning, such as forks, streaks, ribbons, chains, and floating balls. Heat lightning, which lights up the sky, is not a different kind of lightning. It is just too far away for people to see the flash or hear the thunder. Sometimes the lightning is hidden by clouds.

Lightning strikes Earth about 100 times each second. People can be hurt or killed by lightning. During thunderstorms, people are safest in a house or a large building. They should stay away from tall trees, water, high places, and metal things, such as bicycles.

How lightning forms

Atoms in a cloud become charged with electricity. There are two kinds of charges: positive (+) and negative (−).

Before a storm, a cloud's negative charges are pulled toward its positive charges.

During a storm, the charges separate. Negative charges from the cloud rush toward positive charges from objects on the ground. They make an electric current called lightning.

During a lightning storm, huge electric sparks jump between clouds or from the clouds to the ground.

Lily

Lilies

Lilies are flowering plants. They belong to a large, important family of plants. The lily family traditionally includes such plants as asparagus and aloe. A few other plants that do not have *lily* as part of their name are in the lily family. These include the sweet-smelling hyacinth. Some plants that do have *lily* in their names, such as the water lily, are not true lilies.

There are hundreds of kinds of lilies. They grow from scaly bulbs. Most lily plants have straight stems and bright-colored flowers. The flowers are trumpet-shaped and have six petals.

Lilies grow best in rich, sandy soil that is not too wet. They need to be protected from strong winds and bright sun.

Lincoln, Abraham

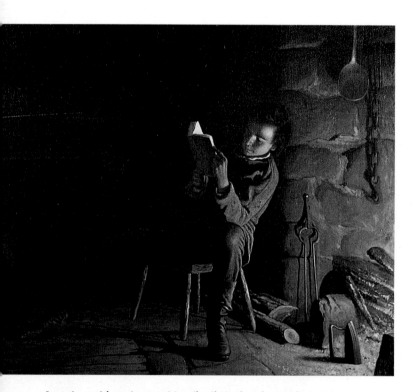

As a boy, Lincoln read by firelight in his family's log cabin. He had little schooling but loved books.

Abraham Lincoln (1809–1865) became the sixteenth president of the United States in 1861. He led the United States during the Civil War (1861–1865).

Lincoln was born in a log cabin near Hodgenville, Kentucky. He went to school for less than a year, but he learned to read, and he loved books. He started a store in New Salem, Illinois, but it failed. He studied law, became a lawyer, and moved to Springfield.

In 1858, Lincoln ran for Congress against Illinois Senator Stephen A. Douglas. He and Douglas debated, or argued, about slavery. In some states, people kept enslaved people. In others, slavery was against the law. Lincoln said that slavery was evil. He wanted to end slavery. Douglas said that people should vote on whether or not there should be slavery. Douglas won the election, but Lincoln became well known.

In 1860, Lincoln ran for president. He won easily, but several Southern States left the Union—the United States. The Civil War broke out early in 1861. On January 1, 1863, Lincoln said that enslaved people in states that had left the Union were free. In 1863, Lincoln also spoke at a battlefield in Gettysburg, Pennsylvania. His short speech, known as Lincoln's Gettysburg Address, became famous.

In 1864, Union troops were winning. Lincoln was elected again. On April 9, 1865, General Robert E. Lee surrendered. The Civil War ended soon afterward.

On April 14, only five days after Lee surrendered, Lincoln went to see a play. He was shot by John Wilkes Booth, a well-known actor. Lincoln died the following day. He was buried in Springfield, Illinois.

Abraham Lincoln as president

Lindbergh, Anne Morrow

Anne Morrow Lindbergh (1906–2001) was an American poet and writer. Her husband was the American aviator (*AY vee ay tuhr*), or pilot, Charles A. Lindbergh.

Anne Morrow was born in Englewood, New Jersey. Her father worked for the United States government. She became a pilot and made many long flights with her husband. She wrote two books about their trips together, *North to the Orient* (1935) and *Listen! The Wind* (1938). Her best-known books are *Gift from the Sea* (1955), about the meaning of a woman's life, and *The Unicorn and Other Poems, 1935–1955* (1956). Other books include *Hour of Gold, Hour of Lead* (1973) and *War Within and Without* (1980).

Other articles to read: **Lindbergh, Charles Augustus**

Anne Morrow Lindbergh

Charles Lindbergh

Lindbergh, Charles Augustus

Charles Augustus Lindbergh (1902–1974) was an American *aviator* (*AY vee ay tuhr*), or pilot. He made the first solo, or one-person, nonstop flight across the Atlantic Ocean.

Charles Lindbergh was born in Detroit, Michigan, and grew up in Minnesota. He studied engineering in college, but after two years, he left school to fly. In 1924, he joined the army and trained as a pilot.

A New York businessman had offered $25,000 to the first aviator to fly nonstop from New York to Paris. By 1927, no one had done it. Lindbergh helped design a plane, and a St. Louis businessman helped him pay for it. On May 20, 1927, Lindbergh took off from New York in his plane, *Spirit of St. Louis.* He landed at an airfield near Paris the next day. He had flown more than 3,600 miles (5,790 kilometers) in 33 ½ hours.

Lindbergh was honored with many awards. In 1929, he and Anne Morrow were married. In 1932, their first child was kidnapped and killed. The Lindberghs moved to Europe and lived there until 1939.

After they returned to the United States, Lindbergh did not believe the United States should enter World War II (1939–1945). He worked to keep the nation from fighting in it, and he resigned from the army. But in 1944, he went to the Pacific war area and flew fighter planes there.

After the war, Lindbergh traveled and lived on the island of Maui, Hawaii. He died there in 1974.

Other articles to read: **Lindbergh, Anne Morrow**

Lion

Lions are big, powerful animals. They are probably the most famous animals in the cat family. Lions are called the "king of beasts" because of their beauty and power.

Lions are very strong. Full-grown male lions are about 9 feet (3 meters) long from nose to tail. They have manes, or long thick hair that covers the head and neck. Females have no manes.

Most lions live on grassy plains in the middle and southern parts of Africa. Their color helps them hide. Their fur is brownish yellow, the same color as dry grass. A few lions live in the Gir Forest in India.

More than any other cats, lions like company. They live together in a group called a pride. Each pride has several grown males, several females, and their *cubs* (young). Their life is usually quiet. They spend most of the day sleeping or resting. Male cubs are chased away from the pride when they are about 2 years old. In time, some of them take over a pride of their own.

Females have their first cubs when they are 3 or 4 years old. The cubs are born blind and helpless. They live on their mother's milk for the first six weeks. Then they begin eating

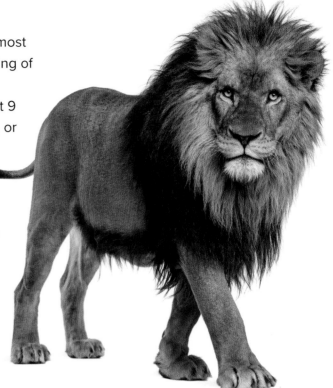

Male lion

Lioness chasing a zebra

meat. By the time they are about 2 years old, they hunt for themselves.

Lions hunt to live. They prefer large animals, such as antelope, buffalo, and zebras. Most of the animals they hunt run faster than the lions can. So lions surprise their prey. They creep up on it slowly. Then they rush at it, grab it, and pull it down. Sometimes several lions work together. They circle around an animal and chase it toward other lions that are hiding in the grass, waiting for it.

People are a lion's worst enemy. Some people kill lions to protect their farm animals. For hundreds of years, many people have also hunted lions as a sport.

In the Gir Forest of India, people have destroyed areas where lions live by cutting down trees. Africa has many wildlife parks where lions may not be hunted. Most people today would rather photograph lions than shoot them.

Liquid takes the shape of the thing that holds it.

Liquid

Liquids are one of the three forms that things can take. The other two forms are solids and gases. Water is a liquid, rock is a solid, and air is a gas.

All these things are made up of matter. The matter is made of tiny particles called molecules (*MAHL uh kyoolz*). The molecules in liquids can flow. They are not locked in place like the molecules in solids. So when liquids are poured into a container, they take the shape of the container.

When liquids are heated or cooled, they can change into gases or solids. For example, when water is heated, it changes into steam. The water molecules mix with the air—a gas. When water is frozen, it turns into ice—a solid.

Other articles to read: **Gas; Matter; Molecule; Solid**

Literature for children

Literature (*LIHT uhr uh chur*) for children includes all the stories, poems, and fact books that young readers enjoy. Some of these books are written just for children. Others may be books for grown-ups that children also like.

Pictures are a special part of children's books. And picture books are a special kind of children's book. The pictures, as much as the words, tell the story.

Kinds of children's literature

Even very young children enjoy poems. Nursery rhymes are short, simple poems. Some nursery rhymes are just for fun. Others teach the days of the week, the months of the year, the alphabet, or how to count.

People also write other kinds of poems just for children. Many of these poems are funny or even silly. Some poems are about make-believe people and things, and some are about the real world. Some are about feelings.

People of all ages enjoy old stories, such as folk tales, fairy tales, and myths. Parents told these stories to their children long before the tales were written down. Later, their children passed the stories on to children of their own.

Folk tales are stories about ordinary people. Fairy tales are about fairies, elves, and other make-believe people with special powers. The stories are told very simply. They have action and colorful characters, and some of them are funny.

Folk tales and fairy tales come from many countries. One famous collection is *Grimm's Fairy Tales*. The brothers Jakob and Wilhelm Grimm collected these fairy tales in Germany during the 1800's. Another famous collection is the *Arabian Nights*. It includes stories from Asia and North Africa, such as Aladdin and Sinbad the Sailor. Hans Christian Andersen was a Danish author and storyteller. He wrote many delightful stories in the style of folk tales.

Myths are ancient stories that try to explain why or how something happens, such as why the sun rises and sets. Myths also come from many lands.

"Mary, Mary, Quite Contrary" is a nursery rhyme that children have enjoyed for many years.

The Wonderful Wizard of Oz **by L. Frank Baum is a fantasy book. Fantasies include thrilling tales of imaginary lands. This illustration by W. W. Denslow shows the characters from the story.**

Toad, a good-hearted but foolish animal, slowly learns the error of his ways in *The Wind in the Willows* by Kenneth Grahame.

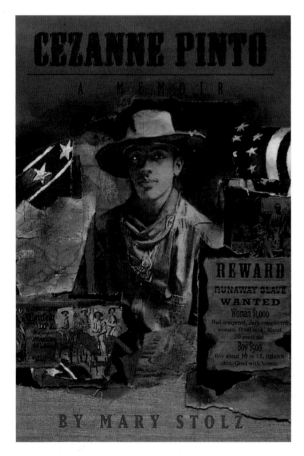

Stories like *Cezanne Pinto* by Mary Stolz, which tells of an enslaved African American boy who escapes to Canada and becomes a cowboy, are historical fiction.

Other old stories can be found in ballads and fables. Ballads are story-poems. They were often sung. Robin Hood is a hero from old ballads. Fables are short stories that teach a lesson about right and wrong. In many fables, the characters are animals that talk.

Fiction (*FIHK shuhn*) is one of the main kinds of writing for children. Fiction stories are not true. Writers make them up. Some of the stories are fantasies, or stories about things that could not really happen. Others are adventure stories and mystery stories. Some are about people in other countries and the way they live.

Historical fiction is about real times and events in history, but most of the characters are not real people. Science fiction is often about adventures that could take place in outer space, on other planets, or in the future.

Many stories are about people in everyday life. The stories show how people deal with their families and friends. The characters may have big problems, such as a death in the family.

Biographies (*by AHG ruh feez*) are another important kind of writing for children. Biographies are true stories about the lives of real people. The people may have made great discoveries, or been very brave, or created great art. Writers of biographies base their stories on facts.

Authors also write other types of nonfiction books—that is, books about facts and true events. Nonfiction books may be about art, history, science, or sports. Some books are about people in other cultures. Some are about challenges, such as moving to a new neighborhood.

History of children's literature

People have told stories to children since ancient times. However, the earliest known books written for children were teaching books. Among these early books was one written in England in the late A.D. 600's. It had lessons written as questions and answers between a teacher and student. This was a common way to write instruction books then, and it continued to be so for a long time. The book also contained riddles in verse.

In the 1600's, a teacher named Comenius made the first textbooks for children in which pictures played a part in teaching the lessons. He thought books for children should entertain them as well as teach.

From the 1500's to the 1800's, printers in England made a kind of book called a *chapbook*. These books cost very little and were sold by traveling peddlars. They often contained old tales and ballads. Chapbooks were not written just for children, but children enjoyed them. In the late 1600's, the first book of Mother Goose verses was published in France.

During the 1700's, two books became favorites with both adults and children. One was *Gulliver's Travels* by Jonathan Swift. The other was *Robinson Crusoe* by Daniel Defoe. The English publisher John Newbery published some of the first books written especially to entertain children rather than to teach lessons. These books included *A Little Pretty Pocket-Book*, which contained fables, games, rhymes, and songs especially for children.

In the 1800's, many people began to write books just for children. The 1800's are often called the golden age of children's literature. Some of these books are still favorites today. In England, Lewis Carroll wrote *Alice's Adventures in Wonderland* and *Through the Looking-Glass.* In the United States, Louisa May Alcott wrote *Little Women,* a story about an American family. Pictures began to be important in books. During the late 1800's and early 1900's, magazines for children also became popular.

More children's books were published in the 1900's than in all the hundreds of years before that. Authors also began to write some new types of children's books.

Picture books became favorites. *The Tale of Peter Rabbit,* by Beatrix Potter, was one of the first real picture books. The book was first published in 1901 with black-and-white drawings. It appeared with color illustrations in 1902. It is still a best-loved story.

In the mid-1900's, authors began to write books called *beginning readers.* These books have short sentences and chapters. Many of the books tell clever, funny stories and have wonderful pictures. In the late 1900's, board books with heavy cardboard pages became popular for infants and toddlers.

In the late 1900's and the 2000's, some books for children, and especially those for young adults, began to explore serious subjects. Authors wrote about such topics as homelessness,

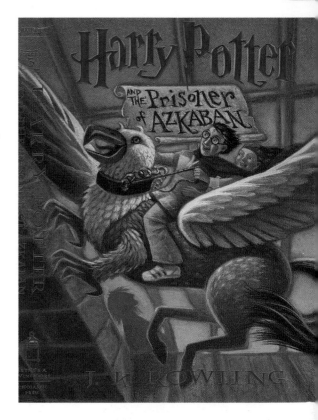

The popular "Harry Potter" series of books by J. K. Rowling tells the story of a boy who learns he is a wizard.

Pippi Longstocking by Astrid Lindgren is the story of a 9-year-old girl who has no parents but lives with her monkey, Mr. Nilsson, and her horse. She has many adventures.

Black Beauty by Anna Sewell tells the story of a horse that is hurt and treated badly by different owners but finds happiness in the end.

race relations, and wars. Graphic novels became increasingly popular during the early 2000's. A graphic novel combines pictures and text like a comic book, but it is much longer. Some graphic novels address serious subjects. Others describe adventures or are funny. Some of the books retell old stories in this new form.

Some important awards, or prizes, are given for children's books. In the United States, the Caldecott Medal is given each year to an artist for the best picture book. The Newbery Medal is given each year to a writer for the most outstanding book for children. In Canada, the Governor General's Literary Awards include a Young People's Literature Award for text and another for illustrated books. Many groups and many countries now give prizes to people who write and illustrate books for children.

Other articles to read: **Aesop's fables; Alcott, Louisa May; Arabian Nights; Arthur, King; Barrie, J. M.; Baum, L. Frank; Blume, Judy; Brooks, Gwendolyn; Bunyan, Paul; Caldecott Medal; Carroll, Lewis; Cleary, Beverly; Dahl, Roald; Dickens, Charles; Fable; Fairy tale; Grimm brothers; Hamilton, Virginia; Konigsburg, Elaine; Lewis, C. S.; Little Women; Longfellow, Henry Wadsworth; Milne, A. A.; Montgomery, Lucy Maud; Mother Goose; Mythology; Newbery, John; Newbery Medal; Peter Pan; Pied Piper of Hamelin; Poppins, Mary; Potter, Beatrix; Potter, Harry; Robin Hood; Robinson Crusoe; Rowling, J. K.; Sachar, Louis; Sendak, Maurice; Seuss, Dr.; Sewell, Anna; Silverstein, Shel; Snicket, Lemony; Steig, William; Stevenson, Robert Louis; Stine, R. L.; Swift, Jonathan; Travers, P. L; Twain, Mark; White, E. B.; Wilder, Laura Ingalls; Winnie-the-Pooh**

Lithuania (*lih thoo AY nee uh*) is a country in Europe. It lies on the shore of the Baltic Sea. It is bordered by Latvia, Belarus, Poland, and Russia. Vilnius is Lithuania's capital and largest city.

Much of Lithuania is made up of flat land. The country has about 3,000 small lakes and hundreds of rivers. Forests cover much of the land.

Most of the people of Lithuania come from Lithuanian families. They have their own way of life and their own language. Other groups in Lithuania include people from Russia, Poland, Belarus, and Ukraine. Most Lithuanians are Roman Catholics.

More than half of Lithuania's workers have jobs in hospitals, schools, stores, and other places that provide services for people. Factories in Lithuania make chemicals, electronics, machinery, and other products. Many farmers raise beef and dairy cattle. The most important farm crops include barley, potatoes, and wheat.

In the 1100's, Lithuanians joined into a single nation. In the 1300's, Lithuania and Poland were joined under the rule of one king. Russia took control of Lithuania in 1795. Lithuania was an independent country from 1918 to 1940. In 1940, the Soviet Union took control of Lithuania. When the Soviet Union broke up in 1991, Lithuania became an independent country again.

Lithuania in brief

- **Capital:** Vilnius.
- **Area:** 25,212 mi² (65,300 km²). *Greatest distances*—north-south, 175 mi (280 km); east-west, 235 mi (375 km).
- **Population:** *Current estimate*—2,731,000; *2020 official government estimate*—2,793,353.
- **Official language:** Lithuanian.
- **Chief products:** *Agriculture*—barley, beef and dairy cattle, chickens, hogs, potatoes, sugar beets, wheat. *Manufacturing*—appliances, chemicals, electronic products, machinery, processed foods, textiles, wood products.
- **Money:** *Basic unit*—euro. One hundred cents equal one euro. The euro replaced the Lithuanian litas in 2015.
- **Form of government:** Republic.
- **Climate:** Cold winters and mild summers, with medium rainfall.

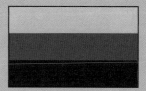

Flag

Lithuania and its neighbors

Little League Baseball

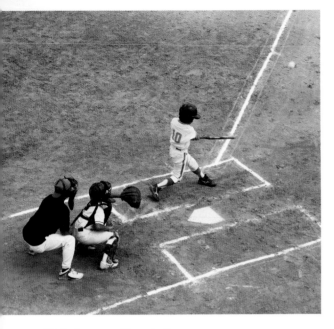

Little League Baseball game

Little League Baseball is an organization of baseball and softball programs for boys and girls. The boys and girls are from 5 to 18 years old. Both boys and girls may play in the baseball programs, but most of the players are boys. The softball programs are for girls only.

Each Little League team may have 12 to 15 players. Teams play at least 12 games each season to decide which is the best team. An all-star team, which includes the best players from each team, plays after the regular season.

Players who are 11 or 12 years old may participate in tournaments that determine 16 regional champions—8 from the United States and 1 each from the Asia-Pacific region, Canada, the Caribbean, Europe, Japan, Latin America, Mexico, and the Middle East-Africa region. The regional winners participate in the Little League World Series at South Williamsport, Pennsylvania.

The Little League program was developed in 1939 by Carl Stotz, a lumberyard clerk in Williamsport, Pennsylvania.

Little Women

Katharine Hepburn, Spring Byington, Jean Parker, and Joan Bennett (left to right) appear in a 1933 film version of *Little Women*.

Little Women, a novel by the American author Louisa May Alcott, has become one of the most popular works in American children's literature. The novel was published in two parts in 1868 and 1869.

Alcott set *Little Women* during the American Civil War (1861–1865). The novel tells about the March family, especially the four March sisters—Meg, Jo, Beth, and Amy. The March girls live in a small Massachusetts town with their mother, Marmee, while their father is away serving as a chaplain for the Union forces in the war. The central character is Jo March, a tomboy who wants to become a writer. The narrative follows the girls from their teen years into adulthood, describing their many adventures and their struggle to increase the family's small income.

Other articles to read: **Alcott, Louisa May**

Liver

The liver is the largest gland in the human body. A gland is an organ that produces chemicals. The liver is the body's main chemical factory. It also stores food.

The liver is reddish-brown. It is in the upper-right part of the abdomen (*AB duh muhn*), or belly, above the stomach and intestines. An adult's liver weighs about 3 pounds (1.4 kilograms).

The liver helps the body digest food. It makes bile, a liquid that helps break down fats. The liver also removes some digested food from the blood and stores it. Then, when the body needs the food, the liver puts it back into the blood. The liver also removes poisons and wastes from the blood and helps the body fight disease.

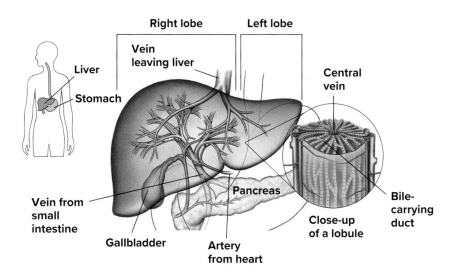

Right lobe Left lobe
Vein leaving liver
Liver
Stomach
Central vein
Pancreas
Vein from small intestine
Gallbladder
Artery from heart
Close-up of a lobule
Bile-carrying duct

The liver consists of two main sections—the right lobe and the left lobe—and two small lobes that lie behind the right lobe. Each lobe is made up of thousands of tiny units called lobules.

Lizard

Lizards are reptiles. They are closely related to snakes. The smallest lizards are less than an inch long. The largest lizards are the Komodo dragons of Indonesia. They grow up to 10 feet (3 meters) long.

Lizards are cold-blooded. The temperature of their bodies changes along with the temperature of their surroundings. So lizards are usually found in warm or hot places.

Most lizards live on the ground or in trees. Some climb trees with claws like a cat's. Some have toes like suction cups. These lizards can walk across ceilings and windows. Giant monitor lizards can swim. Flying dragons can spread out folds of skin and glide from tree to tree. However, they cannot really fly.

Chameleon

Gecko

Some lizards escape from enemies by shedding their tails. The enemy gets the wiggling tail, while the lizard gets away. It simply grows a new tail. Other lizards hiss and lash their tails to scare off enemies. Some change color to blend with their surroundings and hide from their enemies. A few, such as monitor lizards, are fierce fighters.

Most lizards eat insects and small animals. But marine, or ocean, iguanas feed on small water plants called algae. Most lizards lay eggs, but a few kinds give birth to live young.

Human beings are a danger to some lizards. Some people hunt lizards, gather their eggs for food, and sell their skins for leather. Many countries now have laws against hunting lizards.

Other articles to read: **Chameleon; Flying dragon; Gila monster**

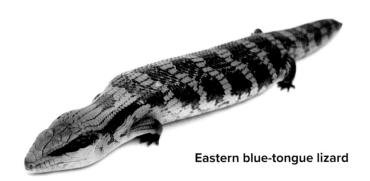

Eastern blue-tongue lizard

Chinese water dragon

Llama

Llama

Llamas (*LAH muhz*) are animals in the camel family. They and their relatives—alpacas, guanacos, and vicunas—live in South America. Llamas look like small camels without humps. They are about 4 feet (1.2 meters) high at the shoulder. They have long, thick hair that may be tan, white, gray, or black. Llamas can carry heavy loads. They are good at walking on mountain trails. However, if a llama's pack is too heavy, or if the llama feels it has worked hard enough, it lies down and will not move.

Native Americans use llamas to carry goods. They also get meat, wool, and leather from llamas. Some llamas are raised on farms in the United States and Canada.

Other articles to read: **Alpaca; Guanaco**

Lobster

Lobsters are animals that live on the ocean bottom. They are crustaceans (*kruhs TAY shuhnz*). Crustaceans have a hard shell, a body with sections, and jointed legs.

Lobsters' bodies have a head, a center section, and a tail. They also have five pairs of legs. American lobsters have heavy claws on the front pair of legs. They use these claws to kill other animals and tear their food apart. Lobsters eat clams, crabs, snails, small fish, and, sometimes, other lobsters.

The female lobster lays thousands of eggs at one time. They stick to her body until they hatch. As lobsters grow, they molt (*mohlt*), or shed their hard shell. They form a new, soft shell under the old one. Then they split the old shell and crawl out. They hide until the new shell hardens.

Many people think lobsters are delicious to eat. People catch them in the Atlantic and Pacific oceans.

Lobster

Loch Ness monster

The Loch Ness monster (*lahk NEHS MAHN stuhr*) is a large animal that some people believe lives in Loch Ness, a lake in northern Scotland. If there is such an animal, it prefers to stay away from people. However, hundreds of people claim to have seen the Loch Ness monster. The animal is said to have flippers, one or two humps, and a long, thin neck. Some people believe the animal may be related to a dinosaurlike reptile or to a modern sea animal.

The earliest known sighting of the Loch Ness monster dates back to the year 565. Since 1960, researchers have explored Loch Ness. So far, there is no proof that the Loch Ness monster is real.

Loch Ness monster

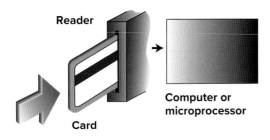

A type of electric lock

Lock

Locks are machines that prevent people from opening doors or other things. People use locks to protect themselves and the things they own.

Some kinds of locks are mechanical (*muh KAN uh kuhl*). That means they have moving parts that work without electricity.

Most mechanical locks have metal parts called tumblers. When the right key is put into the lock, it pushes the tumblers back. Then the key can turn part of the lock. As the part turns, it moves the bolt—the piece that keeps the lock shut. The bolt slides out of the way, and the lock opens.

Some kinds of locks are electric. One kind is opened with a special plastic card. The lock reads a code on the card. It sends the information to a computer. If the code on the card matches a code in the computer, the lock opens.

Another kind of electric lock opens with a combination of letters or numbers. People punch or dial the combination. If the combination matches one in a computer, the lock opens.

Some electric locks recognize people's fingerprints, eyes, voices, or other features. A scanner compares the feature, such as a fingerprint, with information in a computer. If they match, the lock opens.

Locomotive. See Railroad.

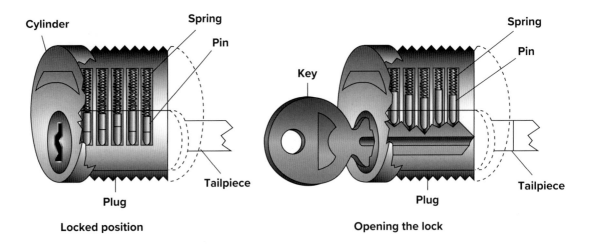

Pin-tumbler lock

Locust

Locusts are a kind of grasshopper. They migrate, or move, from place to place. Locusts live on every continent except Antarctica.

Most locusts are about 2 inches (5 centimeters) long. They have a large head, large eyes, and short antennae, or feelers. Locusts have long hind legs and four wings. They can make a sound by rubbing their hind legs on their front wings.

Locusts migrate only after many females lay their eggs close together. When the young hatch, they stay together. They meet other groups of young locusts and form a swarm. Some swarms have millions of locusts. Wherever they land, they eat and destroy plants. A swarm can make as much noise as an airplane. It can be so thick that it shuts out the sunlight.

Locusts have been known since ancient times. One swarm in 1889 was believed to cover 2,000 square miles (5,200 square kilometers) by the Red Sea, which lies between southwestern Asia and northeastern Africa.

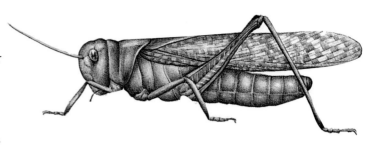

Locust

A swarm of locusts

Log cabin

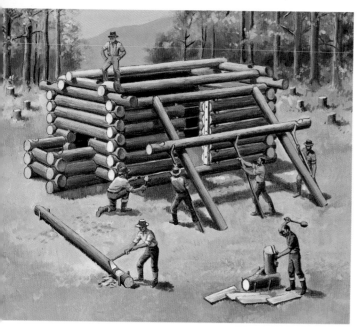

Pioneers built log cabins.

Log cabins were built by many early settlers in North America beginning in the 1600's. They could be built with very few tools.

The simplest cabins were made of round logs with curved notches, or cut-outs, near the ends. The first row of logs was laid on the ground. Then other rows were fitted on top of them. Each row of logs rested in the notches of the row underneath. The spaces between the logs were filled with stones or wood and sealed with mud.

People in Europe had built cabins for hundreds of years. Many different kinds of cabins were built in America. The settlers came from many different countries, and each group built cabins in its own style. Five American presidents—Andrew Jackson, James Polk, James Buchanan, Abraham Lincoln, and James Garfield—were born in log cabins.

Logging

Loading timber on a truck at a logging camp

Logging is the act of cutting down trees for lumber, or wood. Loggers are also called lumberjacks.

Before loggers go into the woods, a forester decides which trees they should cut. The forester is a scientist trained in taking care of forests. Foresters try to grow the kinds of trees that give the greatest amount of lumber.

Loggers called fallers cut down, or fell, the trees that the forester has marked for cutting. After a tree has been felled, workers called buckers cut up the tree trunks. This makes it easier to get the wood out of the forest.

Since the mid-1900's, large machines have done most of this work. For example, some machines can cut down a tree, remove its branches, cut it into logs, and gather the logs into bunches.

Taking the logs from the woods to the sawmill is the second step in logging. A sawmill is a place where logs are cut into lumber by machines. The loggers use tractors to skid, or drag, the logs to the landing—a central place in the woods. Then they use trucks to carry the logs from the landing to the sawmill.

At the sawmill, a moving chain carries the logs into the mill. In most mills, a log debarker removes the bark before the log reaches the first saw, called the headsaw. Large logs are moved onto a platform called a carriage, which carries them back and forth past the headsaw. Each time the carriage goes past the saw, the saw slices off a board. The boards are then trimmed and sorted by their quality, size, and kind of wood.

Machines at a sawmill cut tree trunks into boards.

Tower Bridge in London

London

London is the capital of the United Kingdom of Great Britain and Northern Ireland. It is one of the world's oldest and largest cities. People have lived in London for about 2,000 years.

The River Thames (*tehmz*) flows east through the middle of London. Central London has three main sections. Two of the sections, the City and the West End, are on the north side of the river. The third section, the South Bank, is on the south side.

The City is the oldest part of London, but most of the old buildings were torn down to make room for modern offices and bank buildings. The West End is the center of Britain's government, and the towers of the Houses of Parliament are a familiar sight along the Thames. The West End is also famous for its many theaters and shopping districts, especially around Piccadilly Circus, where six busy streets come together. The South Bank has many office buildings and a large, modern cultural center.

Each year, millions of people visit London's many museums, parks, and well-known places such as Buckingham Palace and the Tower of London. Buckingham Palace is the London home of the British royal family. Long ago, the Tower of London was a prison, but now it holds the royal jewels. Soldiers in fancy red uniforms guard the palace and the tower.

Other articles to read: **Big Ben; Buckingham Palace; London Bridge; Tower of London**

The Thames River and the London skyline

London Bridge

London Bridge is in London, England. It is one of the many bridges across the River Thames (*tehmz*) in London.

A new London Bridge was completed in 1973. It replaced the famous London Bridge that was built between 1823 and 1831. In 1967, workers took the old bridge apart. It was moved to Arizona and rebuilt in Lake Havasu City.

The first London Bridge was made of wood. It was built by the Romans and rebuilt several times. The first stone bridge was finished in 1209 and used until it was torn down in about 1832. It was the bridge in the nursery rhyme "London Bridge." The bridge had houses on both sides. Sometimes, when traitors were put to death, their heads were hung over the entrance.

Old London Bridge

Longfellow, Henry Wadsworth

Henry Wadsworth Longfellow (1807–1882) was the most famous American poet of the 1800's. Many of his poems are among the most familiar in American literature. Longfellow's best-known longer works include *Evangeline* and *The Song of Hiawatha.* Among his popular shorter poems are "The Village Blacksmith," "The Children's Hour," and "Paul Revere's Ride."

Longfellow was born on February 27, 1807, in Portland, in what is now Maine. His first book of poems, *Voices of the Night,* appeared in 1839. *Evangeline: A Tale of Acadie* (1847) made Longfellow the most popular poet of his time.

Longfellow lived for many years in Craigie House in Cambridge, Massachusetts. Today, the house and grounds make up the Longfellow National Historic Site.

Henry Wadsworth Longfellow

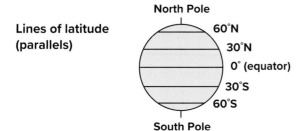

Lines of latitude
(parallels)

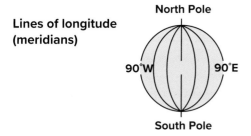

Lines of longitude
(meridians)

Longitude and latitude

Longitude and latitude are measurements used to locate any point on Earth. People who make maps use imaginary lines to divide Earth into sections. These lines are called meridians of longitude and parallels of latitude.

Meridians of longitude run north and south along the surface of Earth. Mapmakers think of Earth as a huge globe that is divided into 360 equal slices. Meridians of longitude divide the slices on the outside of the globe.

Parallels of latitude run east and west along Earth's surface. The equator is a parallel of latitude that circles the middle of Earth. The latitude of a point is measured by its distance from the equator.

Other articles to read: **Equator; Time**

Lopez, Nancy

Nancy Lopez (1957–   ) became one of the most popular players in the history of women's golf. She is the first person to win five tournaments in a row. She set the record in 1978. That year, Lopez, a Mexican American, also became the first Hispanic player to win a Ladies Professional Golf Association (LPGA) tournament.

Lopez was born in Torrance, California. When she was 12 years old, she won the New Mexico Women's Amateur title. After two years at Tulsa University in Tulsa, Oklahoma, she began playing professionally. In 1978, she won nine tournaments and was Rookie of the Year and Player of the Year. She has been one of the top 10 women golfers 13 times.

In 1987, Lopez became a member of the LPGA Hall of Fame.

Lorry. See Truck.

Nancy Lopez

Los Angeles

Los Angeles is a huge city in southern California. It is on the Pacific Ocean. It is the second largest city in the United States, after New York.

Los Angeles is one of the fastest-growing cities in terms of people. It is also very large in land area. It has spread by taking in nearby cities and towns.

Los Angeles—especially the Hollywood district—is famous for making movies and television shows. Other industries in Los Angeles produce such products as airplanes, spacecraft, and computers. The city's people also work in banks, restaurants, hotels, and other businesses.

Los Angeles has many museums and theaters. It also has fine beaches and is close to mountain vacation spots.

Los Angeles has some big problems, too. For example, earthquakes there have caused a lot of damage. A shortage of open land and a serious problem with pollution are other concerns.

Los Angeles, California

Louisiana

Louisiana

Louisiana

State flag

State seal

Louisiana is one of the Southern States of the United States. It lies on the Gulf of Mexico between Mississippi and Texas. Arkansas lies to the north.

Louisiana is called the *Pelican State* for the brown pelicans that live along the coast. It is also known as the *Bayou State*. Bayous (*BY ooz*) are streams of slow-moving water.

Baton Rouge is the capital and second largest city of Louisiana. It lies close to where the Mississippi River empties into the Gulf of Mexico. It is a major U.S. port.

New Orleans, Louisiana's largest city, is one of the world's busiest seaports. It is famous for a celebration called Mardi Gras, held every year.

Land. Most of Louisiana is a low plain with rich, dark soil. The Mississippi Delta has the richest soil. It is the large area where the Mississippi River meets the Gulf of Mexico.

Sometimes the Mississippi and other rivers around the state overflow and cause flooding. The people of Louisiana have built special walls called *levees* to keep the water back.

Louisiana has many lakes, swamps, and marshes. Marshes are areas of land that are covered with water most of the time. Forests of cypress and oak trees are found in many parts of Louisiana.

Resources and products. Louisiana's rich soil is good for growing such crops as corn, cotton, peaches, rice, sugar cane, soybeans, and sweet

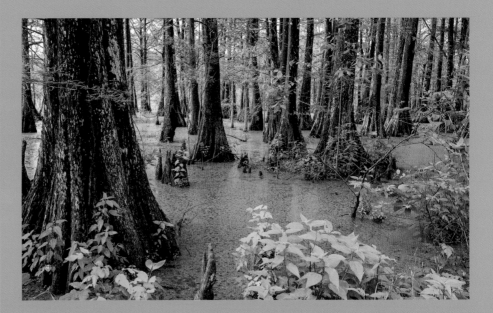

Trees covered in Spanish moss in a swamp in Louisiana

potatoes. Chickens and beef and dairy cattle are also important in Louisiana.

Mining is a major industry in Louisiana. Oil and natural gas are the state's chief mineral products. Some of the gas comes from underwater fields in the Gulf of Mexico.

Factories make many products. Chemicals, such as medicine and fertilizer, are the chief products. Ships, trucks, and airplanes are also built in Louisiana.

Other articles to read: **Gulf of Mexico; Jazz; La Salle, Sieur de; Louisiana Purchase; Mississippi River; New Orleans**

Important dates in Louisiana

Prehistory	Native Americans lived in Louisiana long before the first Europeans arrived. They belonged to about 30 groups, including the Atakapa, Caddo, Chitimacha, and Tunica.
1541	Hernando de Soto led a group of Spanish explorers into what is now Louisiana.
1682	French explorer René-Robert Cavelier, Sieur de La Salle, reached what is now Louisiana and claimed the area for France.
1699	The royal French colony of Louisiana was founded.
1718	The French governor of Louisiana, Jean Baptiste Le Moyne, Sieur de Bienville, founded New Orleans.
1803	The U.S. purchased Louisiana from France.
1812	Louisiana became the 18th state on April 30.
1861	Louisiana left the United States and joined a group of Southern States called the Confederacy. The Confederacy lost to the United States in the Civil War (1861-1865).
1862	United States troops captured New Orleans.
1868	Louisiana became a U.S. state again. It adopted a new constitution that made slavery illegal and gave Black people the right to vote.
Early 1900's	Jazz music probably began in New Orleans.
Early 1900's	People discovered deposits of oil and natural gas, two important sources of energy, in Louisiana.
1961	The Michoud Ordnance Plant (now Michoud Assembly Facility) in New Orleans started to produce Saturn rockets for space travel.
1975	A new state constitution went into effect.
1992	Hurricane Andrew struck Louisiana, killing 11 people and causing about $1 billion in damage.
2005	Hurricane Katrina struck the Gulf Coast, killing more than 1,000 people and causing tens of billions of dollars in damage.

Louisiana in brief

- **State capital:** Baton Rouge, since 1882 and from 1849 to 1862. Other capitals were New Orleans (1812–1830, 1831–1849, 1862–1882) and Donaldsonville (1830–1831).

- **Area:** 47,632 mi² (123,366 km²), including 4,433 mi² (11,481 km²) of inland water but excluding 1,951 mi² (5,054 km²) of coastal water.

- **Population:** 4,657,757.

- **Statehood:** April 30, 1812, the 18th state.

- **State abbreviations:** La. (traditional); LA (postal).

- **State motto:** *Union, Justice, and Confidence.*

- **State songs:** "Give Me Louisiana." Words and music by Doralice Fontane. "You Are My Sunshine." Words and music by Jimmy H. Davis and Charles Mitchell.

- **Largest cities in Louisiana:** New Orleans (343,829); Baton Rouge (229,493); Shreveport (199,311); Metairie (138,481); Lafayette (120,623); Lake Charles (71,993).

- **Governor:** 4-year term.

- **State senators:** 39; 4-year terms.

- **State representatives:** 105; 4-year terms.

**State bird
Brown pelican**

**State flower
Magnolia**

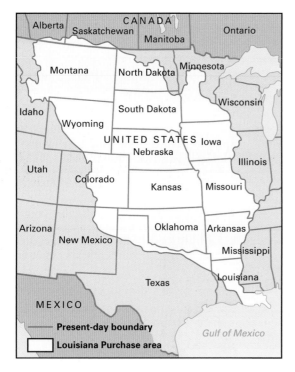

Louisiana Purchase

Louisiana Purchase

In the Louisiana Purchase, the United States bought a huge area of land from France in 1803 for about $15 million. This land, most of which was called the Louisiana Territory, extended from the Mississippi River to the Rocky Mountains. It nearly doubled the size of the United States.

For many years, Spain had owned the Louisiana Territory and the Floridas, which included Florida and land west to New Orleans. Americans stored many goods in New Orleans before they shipped them to other places to be sold. But beginning in 1798, Spain made it more difficult for Americans to store their goods. Then in 1800, France began to take control of the Floridas and the Louisiana Territory.

In 1803, U.S. President Thomas Jefferson sent messengers to France to try to buy the Floridas. The French offered to let the United States buy the Louisiana Territory and New Orleans. A treaty, or agreement, was signed in May 1803.

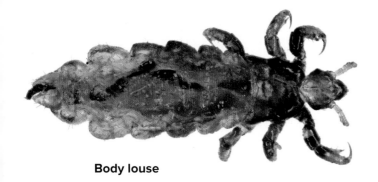

Body louse

Louse

A louse is a small insect with no wings. Lice are parasites. They live and feed on birds and animals, including people. Lice cause itching, and they can spread disease.

There are two main kinds of lice. Chewing lice are often found on birds. They do not live on people.

Sucking lice live on an animal's skin. Several kinds live on people. Head lice pass from one person to another when people share combs or hats. Body lice lay eggs in clothing or bedding.

The best way to keep from getting lice is to keep your body clean and wear clean clothes. Drug stores sell special shampoos and lotions to kill lice.

Lucas, George

George Lucas (1944–) is an American motion-picture producer, director, and writer. He wrote and directed *Star Wars* (1977), a space-travel adventure and one of the most popular movies ever made. He also produced *Raiders of the Lost Ark* (1981), which featured an action character called Indiana Jones.

George Walton Lucas, Jr., was born in Modesto, California. He won a national student film contest in 1967. He was one of the authors and the director of *American Graffiti* (1973), a story about teenagers.

Star Wars and two later films, *The Empire Strikes Back* (1980) and *Return of the Jedi* (1983), were successful in many countries. People liked the characters and the special effects. Three other films—*Star Wars Episode I: The Phantom Menace* (1999), *Star Wars Episode II: Attack of the Clones* (2002), and *Star Wars Episode III: Revenge of the Sith* (2005)—were about events that happened earlier than those in the first three films in the *Star Wars* series.

Lucas produced three more movies about Indiana Jones (in 1984, 1989, and 2008), *Willow* (1988), and *Red Tails* (2012).

Other articles to read: **Star Wars**

George Lucas

Lung

Lungs are important body parts, or organs. Lungs are the breathing organs of humans and other air-breathing animals. You have two lungs. They are inside your chest. When you breathe in and out, air goes in and out of your lungs. As blood flows through the lungs, it picks up oxygen from the air. The body needs oxygen to live. The blood also gets rid of a gas called carbon dioxide (*KAHR buhn dy AHK syd*) in the lungs. The body makes carbon dioxide as a waste material.

The lungs are like stretchy bags. They are filled with millions of tiny pockets of air called alveoli (*al VEE uh ly*).

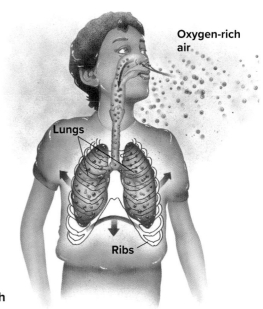

Oxygen-rich air

Lungs

Ribs

The lungs bring in fresh air and get rid of old air.

The lungs

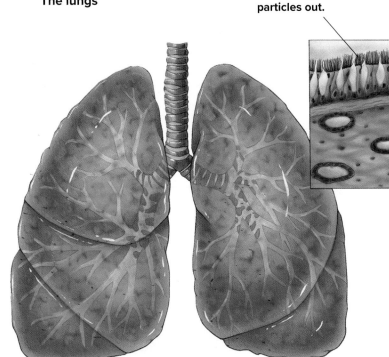

Cilia sweep harmful particles out.

Air enters the body through the mouth and nose. It passes through the back of the nose and mouth and through the voice box. It then enters a system of tubes that leads to the alveoli in the lungs. These tubes are a lot like a tree, which divides into branches and twigs.

In order to give oxygen to the blood and remove carbon dioxide, the lungs must bring in fresh air and get rid of old air. Fresh air is brought in when the muscles in the chest wall cause the lungs to increase in size. When the muscles relax, the lungs become smaller again. Air flows out into the surrounding air.

Blood that has no oxygen in it is pumped by the heart into the walls of the alveoli. These walls are so thin that oxygen and carbon dioxide move through them easily. Oxygen passes from the alveoli to the blood. The blood travels back to the heart. The oxygen-filled blood is then pumped back to the different parts of the body.

The lungs do other things for the body as well. They protect the body from harmful "invaders," such as bacteria, viruses, and dust, that are mixed with the air. A sticky fluid called mucus lines the lungs and traps most of these things. Tiny, hairlike structures push the mucus upward into the throat. There, the mucus and any invaders are coughed up or swallowed. The lungs also help clean the blood. The air from the lungs helps us talk and make other sounds.

Other articles to read: **Asthma; Pneumonia; Respiration**

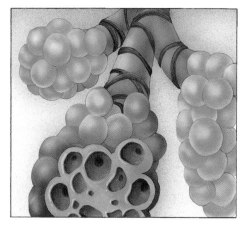

Old and fresh air change places in the alveoli.

Lung cancer

Lung cancer is a dangerous disease in which certain cells in the lungs multiply out of control. The cancer cells kill other, normal cells.

Smoking causes most cases of lung cancer. The more and longer a person smokes, the greater the person's risk of lung cancer.

Symptoms of lung cancer include a nagging cough, shortness of breath, coughing up blood, chest pain, or a hoarse voice. Many lung cancers have spread through the body by the time symptoms appear. Once lung cancer has spread, it is difficult to cure.

Doctors can sometimes cure patients whose cancer has not spread. They might operate and remove all or part of the lung. Doctors may also try to kill cancer cells using drug treatments, called *chemotherapy,* or *radiation* with powerful X rays.

Other articles to read: **Cancer**

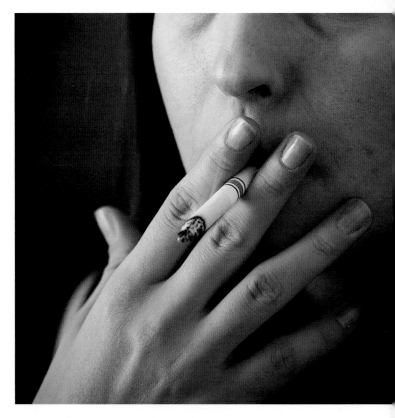

Smoking causes most lung cancers.

Luther, Martin

Martin Luther (1483–1546) was a religious leader who brought about many changes in the Christian Church. Those changes were called the Reformation. The Reformation led to the beginning of Protestant churches.

Martin Luther was born on November 10, 1483, in the German town of Eisleben. He became a priest and a teacher in Wittenberg.

At the time, the Roman Catholic Church told people they could pay money to help make up for their sins, or mistakes. Luther believed that this church practice was wrong. He wrote a list of ninety-five reasons why he thought so and nailed them to a church door in Wittenberg.

Martin Luther

Luther's list started a great argument in the church. Luther then questioned other things the church did. For example, he said that the pope and other church officials could make wrong judgments. He believed that God's teachings were in the Bible. These ideas were too different for the church to accept. In 1521, Luther was banned from the church, or kicked out.

Luther was asked to retract, or take back, his teachings, but he would not. That made him an outlaw. For a while, he was hidden by friends. Then he returned to Wittenberg. He wrote more papers explaining his beliefs. He also helped teach hundreds of pastors, or ministers, to bring his new ideas to the people.

By the time Luther died, a new church had formed. It was called the Lutheran Church. Luther was recognized as an important person for his powerful ideas about the Christian religion.

Luxembourg (*LUHK suhm BURG*) is one of Europe's oldest and smallest countries. It is bordered by Germany, France, and Belgium. The city of Luxembourg is the nation's capital and largest city.

The people of Luxembourg are like the people of Belgium, France, and Germany in some ways, but they value their own customs. They live better than many other Europeans. They use three languages: French, German, and Letzeburgesch. Letzeburgesch is a kind of German that many people use in everyday life.

Most of Luxembourg's people live in cities and towns. Most of the farms are in the southern part of the country. Farmers along the Moselle River grow grapes for wine.

Luxembourg has long produced steel. The country now has factories for making computers and other electronics. Companies also make such products as chemicals, plastics, and tires. Many people work in banking and in the businesses that help visitors to see Luxembourg.

Luxembourg was an independent, or free, state more than 1,000 years ago. From the 1400's to the 1800's, it was ruled by several countries, including the Netherlands. Luxembourg became independent from the Netherlands in 1890. Germany controlled Luxembourg during part of World War I (1914–1918) and World War II (1939–1945). Today, Luxembourg is a member of the European Union (EU), a group that works to encourage cooperation among European nations. Many European countries are EU members, and some important EU offices are in Luxembourg.

Luxembourg in brief

- **Capital:** Luxembourg.
- **Area:** 998 mi² (2,586 km²). *Greatest distances*—north-south, 55 mi (89 km); east-west, 35 mi (56 km).
- **Population:** *Current estimate*—647,000; *2020 official government estimate*—626,108.
- **Official languages:** French, German, Letzeburgesch.
- **Chief products:** *Agriculture*—barley, beef and dairy cattle, grapes, pigs, potatoes, rapeseed, wheat. *Manufacturing*—chemicals, computers, electronics, plastics, tires.
- **Money:** *Basic unit*—euro. One hundred cents equal one euro. The Luxembourg franc was taken out of circulation in 2002.
- **Form of government:** Constitutional monarchy.
- **Climate:** Mild and moist, with cold winters and cool summers.

Flag

Luxembourg and its neighbors

Acknowledgments

The publishers gratefully acknowledge the courtesy of the following artists, photographers, publishers, institutions, agencies, and corporations for the photography in this volume. Credits should be read from top to bottom, left to right on their respective pages. Unless otherwise stated, all maps and all illustrations are the exclusive property of World Book, Inc. Artwork for all country flags is credited to Shutterstock. State and province flags and seals were provided by the Flag Research Center unless otherwise credited.

Cover photo: © Rachen Art/Shutterstock

5	© Shutterstock
6-7	© Asayenko/Getty Images; © Shutterstock
8	© Shutterstock
10	© Shutterstock
12-13	© Shutterstock; © Shutterstock
15	© Shutterstock; © Shutterstock
16-17	© Shutterstock; NIAID; © Shutterstock
18	*Rouen Cathedral. Facade (Sunset)* (1892), oil on canvas by Claude Monet; Musée Marmottan Monet (Paris)
20-21	© Shutterstock; © Shutterstock
22	© Shutterstock
24-25	© Shutterstock; © Shutterstock
28	© Shutterstock
30-31	Public Domain; © Shutterstock
33	© Shutterstock
34	Anna & Michal (licensed under CC BY 2.0)
36	© Shutterstock; © Shutterstock
38-39	German Federal Archives (licensed under CC BY-SA 3.0 DE); CDC
40-41	© Shutterstock; © Shutterstock; Wellcome Images (licensed under CC BY 4.0))
42	© Shutterstock
44	© Shutterstock
46-47	© Shutterstock; © Shutterstock; © Shutterstock; © Shutterstock; © Shutterstock; © Shutterstock; © Shutterstock
48-49	© Shutterstock; © Shutterstock; NASA; © Shutterstock
50-51	© Shutterstock; © Shutterstock
52-53	© Karjean Levine, Getty Images; © Shutterstock
55	Library of Congress
57	© Shutterstock; © Shutterstock; © Shutterstock
58	© Shutterstock
60	© Shutterstock
62	© Shutterstock
64-65	© Shutterstock; © Shutterstock
66	Lance Corporal Samantha L. Jones, USMC
68-69	© Shutterstock; © Shutterstock
70-71	© Shutterstock; © Shutterstock
73	© Shutterstock
74	© Shutterstock
76	© Shutterstock
78-79	© Shutterstock; © Shutterstock; © Shutterstock; © Shutterstock
81	© Shutterstock; White House Collection
82-83	© Kris Connor, Getty Images; © Marka/Alamy Images; © Shutterstock
84	© Shutterstock; © Shutterstock
86-87	NPS; © Shutterstock
89	© Shutterstock
90-91	© Shutterstock; © Walter McBride, WireImage/Getty Images; Library of Congress
92-93	Public Domain; © Bill O'Leary, The Washington Post/Getty Images; White House Collection; NPS
94-95	© Shutterstock; NASA; © Shutterstock
96-97	Public Domain; © Shutterstock
98-99	© Universal History Archive/Getty Images; © Shutterstock
100-101	© Shutterstock; White House Collection; White House Collection
102-103	National Archives; © Stephen Dunn, Allsport/Getty Images; Public Domain; © MPI/Getty Images
104	© Shutterstock
106-107	© Nathaniel S. Butler, NBAE/Getty Images; Public Domain; © Shutterstock

108-109   © Shutterstock; © Bettmann/Getty Images

110   © Shutterstock; © Shutterstock

112-113   NASA; NASA; © Shutterstock; © Shutterstock

114-115   © Shutterstock; © Bettmann/Getty Images; © Shutterstock; © Shutterstock

116-117   © Shutterstock; © Shutterstock

119   © Shutterstock

121   Public Domain

122-123   White House Collection; White House Collection; © Harry Benson, Express/Getty Images

124   © Shutterstock

126   © Shutterstock

128-129   © Shutterstock; Library of Congress; Library of Congress

130-131   © Shutterstock; © Shutterstock; © Shutterstock

132-133   Louvre Museum; © Bettmann/Getty Images; Library of Congress

134-135   White House Collection; Library of Congress

137   © Shutterstock; © Shutterstock

138-139   © Shutterstock; © Shutterstock; University of North Carolina at Chapel Hill

140-141   © iStockphoto; © Shutterstock

142-143   © Shutterstock; © Shutterstock; © Simon and Schuster

144-145   © Shutterstock; © Bettmann/Getty Images; National Archives

146   © Shutterstock

149   © Shutterstock; U.S. Air Force

152-153   © Shutterstock; © Shutterstock; © Shutterstock; © Shutterstock

154-155   Public Domain; © Shutterstock

156-157   © Shutterstock; © Shutterstock

158-159   U.S. Air Force; © Shutterstock; © Shutterstock

161   Public Domain

162-163   NASA/Goddard Space Flight Center/Tom Zagwodzki; NASA

164-165   CMRF Crumlin (licensed under CC BY 2.0); Metaveld BV (licensed under CC BY-SA 3.0); © Museum of Holography, Chicago, IL; U.S. Navy; © Shutterstock; © Shutterstock; U.S. Army

166   © Shutterstock

168-169   White House Collection; Public Domain; © Shutterstock

170   © Shutterstock

172-173   © Shutterstock; © Shutterstock

174   © Shutterstock

176-177   © Shutterstock; Library of Congress

178-179   © Fine Art Images/Heritage Images/Getty Images; © Shutterstock; © Shutterstock

180-181   Public Domain; © Stock Montage/Getty Images

182-183   *Mona Lisa* (1503-1506), oil on poplar wood by Leonardo da Vinci; Louvre Museum (Paris); © Shutterstock; © Shutterstock

185   © John Chillingworth, Picture Post/Hulton Archive/Getty Images

186   Public Domain

188-189   © Shutterstock; © Shutterstock; © Shutterstock; © Shutterstock

190-191   © Shutterstock; © Shutterstock; © Shutterstock; © Kevin E. Schmidt, Quad-City Times/ZUMA Wire/Alamy Images

192   © Shutterstock; © Shutterstock

195   © Shutterstock; © Shutterstock; © Shutterstock

196   © Shutterstock; © Shutterstock

198-199   © Shutterstock; © Shutterstock; © Shutterstock

200-201   © Shutterstock; © Shutterstock; © Shutterstock

202-203   © Shutterstock; Library of Congress; Library of Congress; © New York Times/Hulton Archive/Getty Images

204-205   Library of Congress; © Shutterstock; © Shutterstock

206-207   © Shutterstock; © Shutterstock

208   Elizabeth Miles

210   Pat Traub

212-213   © Shutterstock; © RKO Radio Pictures; © Shutterstock

214-215   © Shutterstock; © Shutterstock; © Shutterstock; © Shutterstock; © Shutterstock

217   © Shutterstock

218-219   © Shutterstock; Jakethrelkeld (licensed under CC BY-SA 3.0); © Shutterstock

220-221   © Shutterstock; *View of London Bridge* (1632), oil on panel by Claude de Jongh; Yale Center for British Art; Public Domain

222-223   © Leonard Kamsler, Popperfoto/Getty Images; © Shutterstock

224   © Shutterstock

226-227   © Shutterstock; © Shutterstock

229   © Shutterstock

230   *Martin Luther* (1529), oil on panel by Lucas Cranach the Elder; Public Domain